SAN FRANCISCO'S
REIGN OF TERROR

By John Myers Myers

SAN FRANCISCO'S
reign of terror

JOHN MYERS MYERS

DOUBLEDAY & COMPANY, INC.
Garden City, New York
1966

To My Excellent Friend,
Geoffrey Chaucer,
The lad who first told me
that murder can't be forever hid.

Library of Congress Catalog Card Number 66-12822
Copyright © 1966 by John Myers Myers
All Rights Reserved. Printed in the United States of America
First Edition

ACKNOWLEDGMENTS

SPECIAL THANKS ARE due the following institutions and the fine people who work in them:

The Bancroft Library, University of California at Berkeley, for supplying a wealth of material and guidance, under the aegis of John Barr Tompkins.

Alan D. Covey, for putting the facilities of the library of Arizona State University, Tempe, at the disposal of a free lance, and Gerald Nelson for implementing library exchange service.

The Huntington Library, San Marino, California, for permission to quote from the Papers of the San Francisco Committee of Vigilance of 1856, and Miss Haydée Noya for directing my attention to other pertinent material.

Mrs. Autumn L. Leonard, of the Pennsylvania Historical and Museum Commission, Harrisburg, for turning up indispensable items.

Many thanks on the score of counsel, information and supplied material are also due these: Gilbert A. Cam of the New York Public Library; Mrs. Helen S. Giffen of the Society of California Pioneers, San Francisco; John Daly of the Department of Records, Philadelphia; Allan R. Ottley of the California State Library, Sacramento; William J. Van Schreeven of the Virginia State Library, Richmond; Dr. Jeannette P. Nichols of the History Department of the University of Pennsylvania, Philadelphia; Mrs. Mary M. Moses of the San Francisco Public Library; R. N. Williams, 2nd, of the Historical Society of Pennsylvania, Philadelphia; Joseph Miller of the Arizona Department of Library and Archives, Phoenix; Marcus A. McCorison of the American Antiquarian Society, Worcester, Massachusetts; Kenneth W. Rapp of the Archives Bureau of the United States Military Academy, West Point, New York; Ari Hoogenboom of the History Department of Pennsylvania State University, University Park, Pennsylvania; Andrew Wallace of the Arizona Pioneers' Historical Society, Tucson; James de T. Abajian of the California Historical Society, San Francisco; Harry B. Reiff of the Free Library of Philadelphia; Mrs. J. K. Shiskin, Museum of New Mexico, Sante Fe; plus a helpful gentleman, whose signature I couldn't for the life of me unravel, in charge of the Provincial Archives at Victoria, British Columbia.

ILLUSTRATIONS

CONTENTS

PART I

THE ANNALS
OF A FREE CITIZEN

PENNSYLVANIA'S GIFT TO CALIFORNIA

AMERICA'S GREATEST MAN hunt had as goal the stretching of Judge Edward McGowan's neck. By good chance his honor deserved a lot of attention, if not of that kind. Better yet, he lived to tell of the chase and of his hounders. Steered by a twisted genius, these sought not only to blast a man of straight mark in his life time, but to put the fix on him beyond the grave. This is his unmatched Columbian story; and theirs.

Back in 1936, when Europe festered with Fascist as well as Red gang rule, Sinclair Lewis wrote a novel called *It Can't Happen Here*. What he meant was that it could—"it" being the rise to power in the United States of a clique willing and able to ring the Liberty Bell backwards. There was one thing wrong with the author's urgent warning, though. This country had already had political rabies, albeit but locally.

None of the founders of Europe's police states had been so much as born when the San Francisco Committee of Vigilance of 1856 patented the whole bag of totalitarian tricks. There were public struttings and secret courts, the unleashing of dog soldiers with un-limited powers of search and seizure; and a mob schooled by a bought press to rough any who wouldn't cheer viciousness. There was even the picture of an eye—posted to let the serfs know that their masters were ever on watch—which George Orwell thought he had coined when lashing at statism in *1984*. As that was published in 1949, Orwell was even farther behind the times than Lewis.

What would have stunned both these now dead champions of freedom is what has since been said of those who rubbed it out in a great American city. The historic Vigilantes have fared better than the Round Table knights, romancers having allowed these human weaknesses. With California's scholars as faithful to the same story as katydids, the paladins of San Francisco have looked down from pedestals without their like in the land.

A good example is one made for them by Hubert Howe Bancroft, by some said to have been the greatest of Western historians: "The purity of purpose, the holy and unselfish considerations which urged forward these men of vigilance were as much superior to what is called patriotism as is Christ superior to Belial."

Still there's at least one other thing to say. On no authority but their own—and with nobody but themselves profiting by it—this corps of archangels killed, imprisoned, exiled, robbed, and tortured fellow American citizens.

Those they put the blocks to have been held up to scorn, by Bancroft and a long succession of echoes, for being members of the Law and Order Party. Of the fellowship of Belial, and not Christ, as it would seem, these clamored for the return of authority to elected, in place of self-chosen officers. Where not damned as villains, they have been held fogies who couldn't tell a holy crime wave from the standard sort.

As to what was gained by junking the American Constitution, locusts couldn't chime any better than have California's chroniclers. A preview of the millennium followed the burning of the Bill of Rights; and not just for a weekend. Rescued from felons and fools, San Francisco enjoyed upright government, with all attendant blessings, for decades to come.

In a world of unlimited chances, it all could have happened as sworn to. The findings of better than a century cannot be dismissed, besides, just because the cheese doesn't smell right.

Yet there is one crack, in the structure built over the years by so many agreeing hands, too big for the ivy to cover up. Side by side with the claimed happy ending stand San Francisco's stupendous criminal annals for the era the Vigilantes made. These, and not a guessed golden age, of which no trace can be found in the record, tell the truth of the outcome; and all pleas to the contrary are as hollow as John Falstaff's legs.

When a conclusion proves false, all the factors on which it was based become suspect; and it's time to wonder what's been left out that should have been fed the computer. In the case of the 1856 Vigilance Committee, the robot's been shorted on data, though not through ignorance. Set aside as of no value has been a large body of writings by those who saw the Vigilantes in action—but didn't like the view.

The events which account for the outlawing of informed testimony form the meat of this narrative. Chief among the uncalled witnesses was the said Edward McGowan, known as Ned to the hordes of friends and enemies he was alike skilled in making. To show why he was denied a hearing, re a drama in which he played one of the leads throughout, it is necessary to rip open a long locked door. A skeleton big enough to be Paul Bunyan's is one occupant; the true character of Ned McGowan the other.

The word "true" belongs, because a string of chroniclers fixed him up with a character he never had outside their pages. John S. Hittell and brother Theodore gave McGowan tar coatings in their respective histories of San Francisco and California at large. According to the reminiscences of Horace Bell, Ned had a corps of assassins, ready to knock off anybody in San Francisco at a nod from the master. Philosopher Josiah Royce decided that his run for his life was essentially amusing. Taking his cues from all of these, Bancroft served Ned up in *Popular Tribunals,* as a genius of evil cross bred with clown.

Bancroft also equipped McGowan with a pre-California criminal career, of which his alleged West Coast felonies could be seen as logical offshoots. In Pennsylvania, as *Popular Tribunals* explained, Ned had begun as a "shoulder striker," or bully-boy, slum politician; and though clever enough to take on a certain amount of polish, he had changed his spots only to gain bigger and blacker ones.

When Bancroft was through smearing acid, Ned was finished as a witness against his enemies. Yet it is but fair to point out that the celebrated historian did not know the man he furnished with a winding sheet of infamy.

One who had been close to McGowan offered a different report. If Colonel Thomas P. Ochiltree is now known to few, he had in his day all the cake of recognition that he could have desired. When Grant was President, the White House was a second home to him. He spoke abroad for such financial empires as that of John W. Mackay. Famed as a raconteur in French, in addition to English, he was as much in demand in the capitals of Western Europe as in New York and Washington. In the parlance of a time when society was organized on an international basis, and as stocked with lions as pre-Hemingway Africa, "he knew everybody."

Yet following the publication of *History of California* in 1888, he took exception to Bancroft's snarking. On the strength of a friendship which had ripened when blood flowed, as well as when wine did, Ochiltree wrote a signed article for *The New York World*. In it the colonel said of Ned, "In all my long and diversified experience, he is, I think, the most remarkable character I have ever encountered."

But books by ranking historians have many readers, as compared with the few fans of bygone newspaper articles. A man rated as unique by a connoisseur wound up without even the consolation prize of standing as a bad man, to judge by the writings of twentieth-century authors. Not one of the numerous books devoted to characters of California's pioneer era have given more than passing notice to the liveliest and most varied of the lot.

For trivets are no righter than Ochiltree was about Ned. The exploits of none other compare with his as to scope and variety. Nor did any of them match his mental achievements.

Ned was one of the real wits of his, or any, American era. He wrote a book which is still as fresh and full of wallop as when he wove it of perils faced down and a rare man's heart beats. He left the best, if still largely untapped body of early California source material. And, oh yes, he was the finest poet to hold forth anywhere west of the Appalachians before the nineteenth century's last quarter.

A bird of many tones, he could carol like a white throat, jeer like a blue jay, reflect like a vireo, squawk like a crow and—as he proved once—mourn like a dove. Witness the following, besides, he could be as jauntily cheerful as a chewink. When reading the first line, it should be borne in mind that for McGowan, as for Pope, "oi" was an exact rhyme for "i."

> In sparkling wine our glasses join
> They make the nectared drink divine
> Since mirth and laughter rule the hour,
> While roses plucked from friendship's bower
> Around our moistened temples twine
> And add fresh fragrance to the wine.

The small body of his work so far at hand shows that Ned had the faculty of thinking in terms of verse, aside from such times as when he was bent on writing poems in any formal sense. When a quip, personal dig or snicker at the passing scene occurred to McGowan, it was as likely to do so in metre as out of it. For a sample, he thus dealt with an exchange between an ardent French Vigilante and an annoyed San Franciscanette:

> "Mad'moiselle, I love you well,
> I fain would kiss your toe."
> "Ah! oui, Monsieur, my *cheeks* are near;
> You need not stoop so low."

Ned was also a skilled parodist. As he several times revealed in rhyme, he had a grudge against the man defeating fashions of the crinoline age. Yet on one occasion, with the help of a puddle left by a passing shower, he found a chink in this feminine armor. He borrowed Gray's *Elegy Written in a Country Churchyard* to celebrate this victory, in a work he called *Horrible!,* because he hadn't been able to resist the sacrilege of so using a revered poem:

The rustling silk—the knell of parted gold—
With waving ease floats by me like a sea,
When rising, lo, from many a lovely fold,
Much grace appears to sunshine and to me.

From out the ample hoops, invulnerable shade,
Where heave twelve yards in many a graceful heap,
Each in its place, and as if half afraid—
Feet like to mice from out their lair do peep.

The next line is straight McGowan. "The eye terrene" recognizes that it's only the earthly glim that's cheated by the vast dresses of the day. Without so much as mentioning the treat enjoyed by the all-embracing glance of Heaven, Ned both rings it in and raises the cry of "special privilege."

Full many a part, hid from the eye terrene,
The deep recess of crinoline doth bear;
Full many a charm is born to walk unseen
And waste its graces on the darkened air.

Let no grim prudery, with useless toil,
Hide all these charms in over anxious care;
Nor cynics hear with a disdainful smile
Of the dear, bewitching leg ends of the fair.

Yet because of the aforementioned puddle, a hoop had to be hiked high enough to answer a strolling male's prayer. To this McGowan testified in the final stanza of his take-off:

Who, not to dumb torpidity a prey,
At once a pleasing vision e'er resigned;
Passed a trim ancle on a muddy way
Nor cast one longing, lingering look behind?

Pennsylvania scholars have as yet taken no more interest in Ned's poetry than have California ones. When both tribes get on the ball there will, with luck, be more McGowan available. Unearthed so far, though, is enough to suit the ends of this chronicle. Its purpose is not to discuss, at any great length, a fine literary talent. This narrative is concerned only with lining out the story of a far-ranging adventurer, and with showing what he was really like, as opposed to what was written of him at the promptings of his foes.

The fact that Ned was an accomplished poet is the defense's first established point. "Shoulder-striker," Bancroft's glass eye!

Edward McGowan, bard as well as broth of a boy, was born in Philadelphia's Southwark District on March 12, 1813. He was christened a Catholic, though that's only worth mentioning, because it was one of the things his enemies held against him. Religion was no game for a man without a strain of orthodoxy, so he let it alone.

To say of a man named McGowan that he was of Irish descent is akin to guessing that a cat had feline ancestors. Yet it must be said, to give an idea of what Ned looked like. He belonged to that Irish physical type, which is at once very fair and with black locks. That's a good word here, because he was half a long hair. Either blue or gray, his eyes were deep set. Above them climbed a high forehead, and below was the usual set of other features, bold and firm in his case. When grown, he was about five-nine, with a best weight of some 145 pounds. A fraction of it was due to his sweeping mustache.

For the same reason that Ned's literary worth will be but incidentally dealt with here, there will be no shinnying up his family tree. This tale has a huge cast, counting stockholders who can't be shut out. The names of non-players—names that Ned himself never used in his reminiscences—are flowers of spring stuff.

Of his family he named only a brother named John McGowan, eight years older, and eventually in California as an officer in the Marine Revenue Service. Of Ned's boyhood he said only that he belonged to an outfit called the Youth's Library Company. That's also the only notice he took of his education, but he got a fine one somehow. It was supplemented by at least one trip to Europe. For he once spoke of having seen *Macbeth* on both sides of the Atlantic, as well as both sides of the American continent; and he knew things about Paris that he didn't pick up by staying home and reading Victorian travelogues.

How far he was from being a Victorian himself can be gauged by an anecdote in which he placed primdom's queen in rare conjunction with *le mot Berkeley*—for which Ned substituted a dash without loss of effect. In telling of his stampede to British Columbia he wrote:

"Here we were brought to bay by a revenue cutter, which was lying off the middle of the stream to head off boats going up river without paying a tax . . . I met an old Californian named Parker, a prisoner on board the cutter. He refused to pay the tax, as he supposed it was a little perquisite of the officers for themselves, and . . . asked what they did with the money. He was told that it was collected as 'pin money' for Her Gracious Majesty the Queen. 'Oh,—the Queen!' said Parker. They immediately put him under hatches as a prisoner. To an inquiry of mine, as to what were the charges against him, the officer told me what he had said, and then in an earnest manner added, 'You can't do that, you know.' "

A California newspaper item or so makes it clear that Ned was a man of choice chat. But as his hearers had bar glasses in their hands instead of notebooks, that's gone gossamer. Yet some idea of how his talk ran can be gathered from tags he jotted down himself. Here are a pair culled from two levels of his thinking:

"Before you commit suicide take an emetic. What you mistake for despair may be only a couple of pig's feet. Try it on . . . It is easier to pretend to be what you are not than to hide what you really are; he that can accomplish both has little to acquire in hypocrisy."

McGowan on his part was as candid as a plate-glass window. Whatever he thought, he wrote, and as brashly when he himself was the subject as when any one else was. It should be said, too, that he had a well-rounded and unblushing sense of humor. A joke was a joke to Ned, and he put things on his own record that paler souls would pay to have erased.

Everything about him was hearty. He was a doge who'd wed

the sea of drink with a ring he never regretted or betrayed. He prized the swank of gay clothes. He loved friends with an open heartiness and was alike wholesome in giving enemies of his best. Not certainly identified, there was one woman who fetched bottom in his spirit. Otherwise he liked the Atalanta type—fast but not too swift for overtaking by a man with the know-how.

To all seeming, in short, he was the storybook poet incarnate: a dashing cove but with enough solidity of character to assure use of his talent in between escapades to make him the toast of the day's Bohemia.

Yes, but he didn't want to be a poet, and never thought of himself as a writer in any professional sense. The ambition of this social hot rock was to be a pillar of society in general and a statesman in particular.

There have been other authors who have had as little regard for their true abilities as he. Jonathan Swift, to name but one, thought of his gift as merely a means of catching the eye of peers who could boost him politically. Swift would much rather have been a third-string royal counselor than the author of *Gulliver's Travels*—which he never would have written, if he had been allowed to prance around as a bishop with state papers under his arm.

As magnificent genius could have been thus disdainful of what others would give kingdoms to own, it cannot be taken as amazing that McGowan regarded his smaller model as nothing better than a game he could play well, when he felt like it.

In common with Swift, as has been indicated, McGowan's passion was politics. In his day the printer and the publisher were apt to be one and the same; so it was probably with a view to easing into his chosen field via journalism that Ned learned printing in the Chestnut Street plant of one Adam Waldie.

Yet he also learned accounting; for one of the contradictions of a man of no early interest in writing books was that he knew how to keep them. It was through this ability that he first got his foot on the escalator he thought would take him to Washington, as it can hardly be doubted. Certainly, as he later noted, he was running with a crowd, of whom several made the grade:

"In my native city I enjoyed intimate social and personal relations with Governor David R. Porter, Hon. Richard Vaux, Hon. James Campbell, U. S. Postmaster General, Hons. T. B. Florence and Henry M. Phillips, now members of Congress from Philadelphia . . . and a host of others." Ned was also favorably known to George M. Dallas and James Buchanan, the Philadelphians who became Vice-President and President of the United States respectively.

In view of that fact, it need hardly be said that McGowan was a Democrat. This, like Catholicism, was held against him by the Vigilantes. Unlike religion, though, politics was something that Ned took seriously. The philosophy of Democracy, as set forth by Thomas Jefferson, was a faith from which he never wavered, even when the Civil War pulled the house down.

But to get back to the bottom of that escalator that was to take him to Washington. Equipped, as an accountant, to keep track of a large community's outlays, McGowan got on when he was twenty-five:

"In the year 1838 I was elected Clerk of the District of Moyamensing, in Philadelphia County, living at the time of my election in the District of Southwark where I was born. I immediately moved into the District to which I had been elected and was re-elected five years consecutively to the same position. During the time I held this office I was secretary to the Watering Committee of the District, and was also one year Clerk to the County Board, composed of the Senators and members representing Philadelphia in the State Legislature."

Somehow nothing in America seems such a symbol of unassuming responsibility as a town clerk. It was a fine gambit for a would-be society bulwark; and about the time he made it, he did the other right thing by marrying and begetting his share of Moyamensing's new generation.

He never named his partner in this venture, who played no part in his central story. Although he didn't cease to support her, they were seemingly separate long before he left for California. As this was one personal matter about which he didn't choose to be newsy, there's but one more thing to be said. As Catholics, they didn't seek divorce, even when the continent stretched between them.

Yet before they split up, for whatever reason, she bore him a child he saw fit to notice in his memoirs. This was James A. McGowan, who was for a while Ned's companion in Mexico, as well as the American West.

The parent of three other lads, Ned presented to the world of the late 1830s and early 1840s a façade of flawless dignity. A beaver of civic affairs, a paterfamilias, a member of a society that worked at being correct, a man able to hold his own in what was then America's cultural center—it seemed impossible that Ned could be pried out of the mountain of respectability in which he was imbedded.

Running against his preferred grain, though, were two contrary elements in his makeup. One of them he mentioned himself; he was "mercurial." When he was crowded without warning, in other words, the cork could leave the champagne in favor of the ceiling.

The other trait he didn't note, and perhaps didn't understand. Of the two orders of adventurers, he belonged in the accident prone pigeonhole.

The professional leaders of exciting lives seek out danger for the pleasure of testing their hardihood. In this class were the filibusters, William Walker and Parker French, both of whom Ned was to know well. The natural adventurers, though, have the knack of stepping on land mines while following everyday paths that others tread unharmed.

McGowan was of this second category. If California was where the world really blew up in his face, he found hidden high explosives in Pennsylvania first.

2

BOTTLED GOLD AT CONNELLY'S

IN SOME MYSTERIOUS fashion Ned managed to stay out of destiny's clutches until he was thirty. By then he looked more glued to his chosen groove than ever.

In 1842 the voters of Moyamensing showed their satisfaction with his services, by voting to send their clerk to Harrisburg, to represent them in the Assembly, or lower house of Pennsylvania's legislature. How well McGowan stood with Democratic leaders can be seen from a note, written on his behalf at this time by a United States Senator. The man addressed was a State justice, to whom Ned wished to make himself known, when he reached the Commonwealth's capitol.

Washington City, Dec, 8th, 1842
My Dear Sir:

Permit me to introduce to you my friend, Edward McGowan, a Representative in the State Legislature from the County of Philadelphia. He informs me he is related to you and is anxious to make your acquaintance. I need scarcely solicit your kind attention to him—for this I know will be conferred upon him. Any kindness which you may shew him, will be gratefully acknowledged by your friend.

Very respectfully,
James Buchanan

Hon. Thomas Burnside.

In January of 1843 McGowan took his seat in an assembly dominated by Whigs. The journal of the session shows that he got the crumbs usually tossed to a freshman member of a minority party. In recognition of his professional work in both lines, he was assigned to the standing committees for printing and accounting. Both appointments looked as harmless as unimportant; but the one to the Committee on Printing was Black Friday bad luck.

Up to that time the Assembly's printing had been farmed out to whoever had enough pull to snag any given bit. The session of 1843 voted to change this by creating the office of State Printer—authorized to publish journals and bills according to a standard set of specifications and at a standard set of rates.

If McGowan didn't propose the measure, he was suspected of it by a Harrisburg printer who had before had the inside track, when it came to raking in contracts. With his gravy snatched, this chap threw himself into a scramble for the State Printer post. As there were many hats in the ring, the balloting went on for weeks. Nor did John B. Bratton's temper soften, when he began to lose support instead of gaining. As editor of the *State Capitol Gazette,* he was not without a means of expressing himself; and McGowan was one of those he turned his grouch against.

Ned, meanwhile, had been going great political guns. "He was mainly instrumental," to quote one of his obits, "in the repeal of the law for imprisonment in debt" in Pennsylvania. He sponsored a measure which made for industrial progress by increasing the flow of currency out of state banks. All that he proposed was well thought out, and he made no pitch designed to help a group or an individual at the expense of taxpayers as a whole.

He had come to Harrisburg to show his wares, and he was doing it. He was making exactly the sort of record to mark him as Congressional timber, when— But to get the full impact of what happened early in April, and how he reacted, Ned should be noticed as the author of this dulcet lyric:

> The spirit of Music passeth away
>   And is gone, alas, for ever;
> But the spirit of Beauty's golden ray
>   From earth departeth never.

The spirit of Music the soul enchants,
  But is lost in the listening air,
But the spirit of Beauty for which it pants
  Remaineth in all things fair.

The waves make sweet music upon the shore,
  And thunder rides loud on the storm;
But the marble and canvas forever more
  Imprison the lovely form.

Yes! Beauty is seen to be everywhere,
  In flower and tree and sky;
But Music will die on the summer air,
  And be breathed away in a sigh.

McGowan's political career made a noisier exit. But Bancroft wrote of its flitting in *Popular Tribunals;* and his account will be given first, so that it can be compared with the facts published in the journal of Pennsylvania's 1843 House of Representatives.

After bringing Ned to Harrisburg, Bancroft declared that, "he soon plunged into the arena of debate with a violent speech, abounding in the grossest personalities, against the governor of the state. The *State Capitol Gazette*, in an article reviewing this speech, excoriated the young Demosthenic bully mercilessly; and the next morning, McGowan seeing the editor, Mr. Brannan, seated at a desk in the hall of the assembly, deliberately walked up and stabbed him."

This is the lie direct and the lie circumstantial told by a man who knew very well where to look for a true report, had he but wished to offer one. Assuming a fracas on the floor of a state legislature—and there was one—the journal of said body was bound to take note of such a break with parliamentary procedure. Volume 1 of the journal of Pennsylvania's Assembly of 1843 tells of the special committee appointed to investigate the matter; Volume 2 gives the testimony of all the witnesses called, and publishes the committee's finding.

The statement that Ned dirty-named the Governor of Pennsylvania can be disposed of before opening Volume 2. Incumbent was David R. Porter, not only a Democrat but McGowan's provedly good friend.

As hinted above, it was actually Ned himself who was slammed with words, though in print rather than on the floor of the House. John B. Bratton—"Brannan" to Hubert Howe Bancroft—used his paper to mudcoat McGowan and two other Democratic legislators. For the issue of April 7, the Whig editor had written:

"You shall both have office in the Custom House if you vote for the Tyler candidate for State Printer, as J. Porter Brawley said to M'Gowan and Bacon. 'Agreed,' was the response—and they did vote for him sure enough. In our next we shall hold up to the public gaze every man who has been bribed."

Probably Brawley and Bacon were considered co-sponsors with Ned of the bill he had in all likelihood launched, as a member of the Committee on Printing. But in addition to scoring them off, Bratton's squib had the uses of withheld blackmail. If other Democrats didn't rally to the editor's support, they could expect to be pilloried, too, in other words.

With a view to seeing how his victims were taking the treatment, Bratton undertook to stroll into the House while it was in session. Against all rules, this was clearly done with the foreknowledge of Whig leaders, set to raise on the floor the charge of bribery leveled against their opponents. For although the date of the *Gazette's* poisoned issue was April 7, it was not distributed until the morning of the eighth. Giving his readers just time enough to scan his work, the author crossed the floor and planted his feet by the fireplace on the left of the Speaker's stand. Far from being seated or off guard, in brief, he posted himself where he could see every member of the Assembly.

Ned, this while, had read the item about him, and responded in a manner described by a witness named Henry Pettebone: "During the forenoon session of today, between 10 and 11 o'clock . . . the Sergeant-at-Arms came around and threw upon the desk the State Capitol Gazette . . . While reading, I noticed Mr. M'Gowan walking to and fro in the aisle between the desks; he appeared to be very highly excited; I heard Mr. M'Gowan say, 'the scoundrel' very indignantly; at the time I could not tell what induced him to make the remark; but after a while I came to the paragraph about Mr. M'Gowan and Mr. Bacon."

As Pettebone went on to say, Bratton showed up while Ned was in mid-sizzle. Others reported that McGowan promptly braced the editor, though not knife in hand. All that he held was the newspaper he flourished, while asking if Bratton had written certain dirty lines in it.

When the editor owned up, he got reader reaction. To use the delicate phrase of J. Porter Brawley, McGowan "blew spittle." Ned spat in Bratton's eye, that is, and kicked him, as a come-on for a counterattack.

What followed can only be traced via the combined testimony of startled bystanders, aided by the cooler eye of a man looking down from the balcony. This William Lewis noted that after the punching and wrestling observed by others, "Mr. M'Gowan then drew back about three paces beyond the Reporter's desk, and was bending his left knee."

Ned was sagging and almost out, for he had been given a sock on the forehead with something other than a knuckle. Having examined the mark it left, Richard L. Lloyd said that it had the look of having been made "with a blunt instrument." Actually it was the butt of a jackknife, clutched in one of the fists swung by Bratton.

Knowing that he'd been fouled, McGowan picked up a Windsor chair and drew claret from the editor by scoring a hit on his forehead. In response Bratton then used the point of his knife to back Ned off.

Hendrick B. Wright, Speaker of the House, described this part of the action, "Then Mr. M'Gowan retreated four or five steps back in the open space, Mr. Bratton followed him up with his arms raised in a threatening gesture, and made a pass toward him, but my impression is that he did not hit him."

Wright was wrong there. Lloyd reported that McGowan had received a scratch "the size of a pin" high up on one cheek.

That was when the bear really came out of his cave. From some nesting place Ned snatched a dirk, commonly carried in his day by City of Brotherly Lovers who didn't prefer pistols. It can be judged that he wasn't then brooding on the spirit of Beauty. The spirit of Music must have stayed with him, though, for he went for Bratton *presto* and *molta con passione*.

Seeing McGowan with a bigger blade than his, Bratton wanted out. To carry on with Wright, "Both of them at that time passed the back of the Speaker's stand. Bratton first and M'Gowan directly afterwards. As Mr. Bratton passed to the right of the Speaker's stand, I heard some one say, 'He has got a knife.' Some two or three persons took hold of M'Gowan; who they were I do not recollect. Mr. Bratton still going on until he must have advanced out in the open space, ten or fifteen feet. While they were holding Mr. M'Gowan, I heard him say, 'Be sure I have got a knife, I do not deny it, and he,' looking towards Bratton, 'has got a knife, too.' "

By then the editor had thrown away a weapon which Whigs kept from being produced as evidence; but that he had had one is implicit in words of his quoted to the same effect by two witnesses. One of them, a man named Lewis Plitt, had this to say:

"I then went into the committee room, to see if Mr. Bratton was hurt. Somebody asked him whether he had had a knife. He said he did not know but thought he had, as 'I am in the habit of whittling with a knife, and I think I had it in my hand.' "

What became of it was explained by the aforementioned Richard Lloyd, who was not a partisan, but a passerby drawn by the uproar. "Two gentlemen were standing together one of whom had a knife in his hand; and the person who had it said 'this is Bratton's knife.' He was then asked, 'how do you know it was?' when he replied, 'I know it is, I saw him have it. . . . the gentleman that was with him said, 'then keep it, don't let it be seen.' "

Now Ned didn't have charity as his star, when he chased a man who nearly slashed his face open, but he didn't get to show how he could carve. The balcony bird agreed with Wright that Mc-Gowan was a poor second when stopped. One House employee who saw Ned's dirk, at the moment it was taken from him, reported that there was no blood on it. Another, who saw Bratton with his coat off, said he could find no hole in the editor's shirt.

That question was raised, because several Whig House members swore that they had seen McGowan drive his knife home in Bratton's back. They weren't any better liars than the Democrats of the Assembly, though, for none of those could remember seeing a dirk in Ned's hand at all.

But there were more Whigs than Democrats on the investigating committee, and they got to write the report. Probably never before sifted, the many pages of testimony were faithfully included in the journal of the 1843 session. These were not read to the House at large, though; the members heard only the committee's findings.

Medically the report was and is a classic. For though it showed that McGowan had struck so forcefully that his dirk got permanent curvature of the spine, it admitted the patent fact that Bratton had suffered no wound big enough for anybody to have found. The reason for this was that the point had come in contact with a shoulder blade, in Bratton's case a sort of subcutaneous armor, tough enough to give steel the laugh.

It was further put forward in the report that Bratton's knife, not having been produced in evidence, probably never existed. McGowan, then—and he was not allowed to testify on his own behalf—was charged with being the sole weapon wielder.

Barred from appearing on the floor, Ned wrote a letter which was read in the House on April 10. "I intended no serious injury to the individual who had thus wantonly assailed me," it ran in part; "and it was only after he had drawn a weapon and struck at me with it, that I resorted to the means I did; but as I have already stated my conduct was all the result of an overpowering indignant feeling, altogether beyond my control . . . Whilst I admit my error, I feel assured that the House regards as I do, that the provocation was great, and might have prompted others to some mode of resentment not strictly within the rules of the House. I desire it, however, to be understood by the members of this House, that it is not in a mean and craven spirit I ask their indulgence; I do not throw myself upon their mercy but upon their justice."

The Democrats would have given him this, but the Whigs wanted one less to contend with. On April 12 they got their way.

Seeing that he had but the choice between being thrown out and leaving first, McGowan resigned.

If his party couldn't again run a man whom the Whigs could have murdered at the polls, its leaders could do their best for a stalwart they knew had been jobbed. In that same year of 1843, Governor Porter—known to Bancroft as a target of Ned's four-letter oratory—made McGowan Superintendent of the State Magazine of Eastern Pennsylvania. He held the post through 1844, by which time Porter was replaced by a governor with a different list of patronage deservers.

That left Ned free to take his second step in the direction of unsought trouble. In an 1845 election the Commissioners of Moyamensing chose him as the district's first Superintendent of Police.

Although that would seem a fairly safe position, it was while holding it that McGowan first drew the hostile notice of malign characters—and one in particular—whom he was to meet again in San Francisco. Yet in 1845 California was hardly a gleam in Uncle Sam's eye, let alone Ned's. Still bent on stretching his Philadelphia roots, he began reading law under Recorder Richard Vaux, in whose court he functioned as an attaché.

Nor did he stay away from Harrisburg. According to a death notice in the San Francisco *Examiner,* he was at this time the agent, or lobbyist, for a couple of railroads with Pennsylvania charters. He had reached the point, besides, where he was able to tap influence on the highest levels, witness a letter written to him by the Vice-President of the United States in 1847:

My Dear Sir:

The case of your brother, Lieut. John McGowan has been carefully and anxiously laid by me before Mr. Secretary [Robert J.] Walker, from whom I have a strong assurance that he shall not be forgotten, on a vacancy occurring which will warrant his promotion. It gave me pleasure to be able to send to the Secretary a strong testimonial to your brother's merit, in a letter I received from Capt. Nones.

I am truly and respectfully yours,
G[eorge] M[ifflin] Dallas

Edward McGowan, Esq.

A year later the Vice-President's chum was truly, if not respectfully, heaved in the calaboose. But here again it's necessary to raise a fence between what happened, and what California historians put forward as facts.

To tune in on Bancroft, "Then followed the Chester County Bank Robbery and the flight of Captain McGowan. He was captured in the western part of the state disguised as a drover, with some of the stolen money in his possession, and after undergoing a form of trial escaped to California, arriving in 1849."

In charity to Bancroft it should be allowed that there's no use in being a skunk, if you can't shoot the juice at somebody once in a while. What he wrote and what the record said were two different things, and he knew it. You've got to know the original, in order to parody it as faithfully as he did.

To begin the unraveling, Ned was not a police captain, he was the force's superintendent, as has been said. He was not seized in western Pennsylvania, though somebody else was. He was not accused of complicity in the robbery, which in any case was not the crime of gun-point violence, or midnight stealth, conjured up by the phrase Bancroft used.

Preserved by the Philadelphia *Public Ledger* and the city's Department of Archives, are the case's truths. On December 23, 1847, Dr. William Darlington, president of the Bank of Chester, went to Philadelphia and there got from the master Bank of Pennsylvania bills made out in the name of his own dispensary. The amount was said to have been $51,130; but Darlington confessed that he neither counted them, before tucking the bills in a piece of hand luggage confusingly described as a "trunk," or secured a list of their serial numbers.

After stopping in the bar of the Broad Street Depot for a bit of Christmas cheer, this nonchalant money changer got on a railroad car, Chester bound. The trunk he slipped under his coach seat. He said he only took his eyes off it to chat with an acquaintance's small daughter; but when he'd finished chucking her under the chin, he found that the fifty-one grand had vamoosed. So also had the man clad in a long cloak who had chosen the opposite seat.

Although not caught for months, the fellow who had sped from a train which hadn't yet started was John, alias Tobacco Jack, Thompson. In cahoots with him were George, alias Slappy, Williams and John, alias Old Duke, Whitehouse. None of these was an ally of McGowan's, nor was that ever pretended by the prosecution.

What Ned was accused of was being an accessory after the fact, through trying to fence some of the stolen funds. This charge wasn't made until late in the summer of 1848.

Several months earlier, or in May of that year, two men were arrested in the western Pennsylvania town of Bedford on a count that has to be explained. In a day when each bank was authorized to issue currency in its own right, the bills could only be redeemed in specie at the named counting house. It followed that people were gladder of locally sponsored greenbacks than ones issued by distant firms. Westbound travelers in Pennsylvania, then, would try to unload any eastern bills that they might have, swapping them for western currency which owners in the sunrise half of the state were glad to get rid of.

This was what Abraham Pence and a man calling himself Robert Harper were doing in May of 1848. The one an Ohio horse breeder and the other an ex-storekeeper, they were making their way by wagon from Philadelphia to Pence's home state. Ordinarily no one would have noticed their eagerness to trade eastern money for western; but because the bills they were unloading were all Bank of Chester issues, a citizen trailed the pair to Bedford and there had them collared.

Now because Darlington hadn't bothered to ask for a list of serial numbers, there was no sure way of telling the $51,130 worth of stolen greenbacks from more than a quarter of a million of unfilched currency circulating in the Bank of Chester's name. Seeing no way to impound the cash found on Pence and "Harper," Bedford County authorities allowed them to use some of it for bail. The two then returned to Philadelphia, where further arrest soon awaited one of them.

Along with other local police officials, McGowan had been trying to locate the Chester Bank robbery loot. Finding that "Harper" was passing bills that could have been part of it, Ned's men booked him under his full name of Robert Harper Lackey and stuffed him in the Moyamensing pokey.

In durance as of July 21, he was weary of it by mid-August and sent for an attorney. Through him Lackey arranged to be sprung in return for naming the master fence of the Chester Bank boodle. Possibly because he was in the Moyamensing jail, and certainly because he wanted a story which would make the district attorney lick his chops, Lackey put the finger on the superintendent in charge of the very hoosegow he was in.

According to the state's-evidence song bird, he hadn't known that any of the Bank of Chester boodle was in circulation until he was braced by a Philadelphia horse dealer named Benjamin Pratt. From him Lackey learned that McGowan—pointed out to him but never introduced—was the man who would say when it was safe to begin passing out hot money and taking in cold.

There was much more of it, including an anonymous letter and tales of eavesdropping, under circumstances where it was proved that he could have seen or heard zero. On nothing better than such stuff, Ned was arraigned in Philadelphia. So was the Ohio horse breeder, Pence—whom Lackey included, in an apparent effort to sing his way out from under the Bedford County rap, too.

Lackey was not arraigned when McGowan and Pence were; he was present only in the capacity of accuser. Benjamin Pratt was indicted, along with the other two, for conspiring to fence the stolen notes of the Bank of Chester; but he was not arraigned, in as much as he was on his way out of the state. Just before he could cross the Ohio border, Pratt was arrested in Mercer, on September 20.

The trial commenced in Philadelphia's Quarter Sessions Court on September 28, Judge William Kelley presiding. Either the jurist had it personally in for Ned, or he was dreaming of headlines which would tell how he had sent up an erring constabulary head.

Before deciding to talk his way out of jail, Lackey had told a warden named Andrew Morrison that he'd never set eyes on the director of Moyamensing's police force. Among other things, Kelley outlawed this defense testimony, while allowing the prosecution to ring in such a clinker as an anonymous letter.

With the judge slavering for conviction, it wasn't strange that the jury went along. On October 5 Ned, Pratt, and Pence were pronounced guilty, though they were never sentenced. Defense attorneys were so strong in their criticism of the judge's conduct that Kelley agreed to have the case reviewed by all four justices of the Quarter Sessions Court.

He hit Ned below the belt one more time, however. Turning down $10,000 in the way of bail, the judge ordered McGowan to try on a cell in his own bastille. And there he stayed for six perhaps educational weeks.

It was conceivably while a jail bird that Ned learned the underworld argot that sometimes salted his verse. An interesting feature of this jargon, as spoken in nineteenth-century America, is that it had changed very little from the thieves' slang of Queen Anne's England. "The scragging post lay" meant hanging to those in the know, for something like two centuries; and McGowan so used it when philosophizing about the death of a Vigilante.

> We know he has perished, but why shed a tear?
> The generous bowl all our sorrows can cheer;
> The Strangler has gone whom we knew in his day
> Delighted in banishing and scragging post lay.

Ned's cell door opened on Saturday, November 18. On that day he was admitted to bail because of a decision reached by Judges King, Campbell, Parsons, and Kelley. Either that justice had been talked to by his colleagues, or he regretted his handling of the case in the first instance, for the *Public Ledger* of November 20 presented him as concurring in a reversal which was essentially a slap at himself.

"Judge King delivered the opinion of the court, expressing the unanimous opinion of the judges that there ought to be a new trial, on account of the rejection of the judge who tried the case of the testimony of Andrew Morrison. This evidence, it will be recollected, was offered for the purpose of contradicting Lackey, by showing that after his commitment to jail, he told Morrison, a keeper, that he did not know McGowan, but it being objected to by Mr. Reed, who prosecuted the case, the judge excluded it on the ground that it was against public policy to admit in evidence the conversations between prisoners and their keepers. In this the court, including Judge Kelley . . . thought there was an error under the decision of the Supreme Court in Mosler's case, and that the testimony, if admitted, would have changed the result."

With Lackey recognized as a perjurer instead of a witness, the prosecution threw in the sponge, where Ned was concerned. He was dropped from the picture, via a nolle prosequi, or announced admission that there was no case against him. Pence and Pratt were reindicted, though.

Whether Pratt was guilty is not a problem for this chronicle. The fact of importance here is that, while under indictment, he had tried to leave Pennsylvania for Ohio, and was near the border of that state when caught. Whether or not this horse dealer was "disguised as a drover"—to use the phrase which Bancroft applied to McGowan—he perhaps dressed like one. But there's more to be said than that Pratt, and not Ned, was arrested while a fugitive. Bancroft had scrutinized the testimony of the Chester Bank conspiracy trial carefully enough to know that a would-be runaway had been captured in western Pennsylvania, and deliberately transferred the onus to McGowan.

Suspended as police superintendent while in hock, Ned got out of the law's clutches just in time to run for his fourth term. On November 28, 1848, the *Public Ledger* published the nominations for officers of Moyamensing. Put up as Superintendent of Police were McGowan and one Terence W. Hughes.

Although the *Ledger* didn't get around to announcing the outcome, the San Francisco *Examiner* declared that Ned was the head of Moyamensing's constabulary up until he left for California late in the summer of 1849. So much for Bancroft's tale that McGowan fled Pennsylvania, because he had become too hot for that commonwealth to hold.

Yet if the Chester Bank tanglefoot hadn't cost Ned his police post, it had doubtless hurt him as a lobbyist for the corporations he is said to have spoken for on political fronts. He still clung to what must have been shrunken roots, though, even when the all-American topic had come to be the gold of California.

By the spring of 1849 thousands were making for the Pacific Coast overland, via the Isthmus of Panama, or all the way by sea. In McGowan's private annals, though, the season was marked by the pasting he gave Ned Buntline.

Edward Zane Carroll Judson, to use the great dime novelist's real, if seldom used, handle, had in 1848 founded a political dog pack called the American Party. It had its headquarters in New York, where its *Führer* deified himself and abused his foes in a sheet called *Ned Buntline's Own*.

On May 10, 1849, the American Party made cultural history. It brought about the Astor Place Riot, in which the supposedly unpoetic Bowery Boys fought, bled and braved cannon fire over which of two actors was best entitled to play the lead in *Macbeth*.

Prior to bringing that off, though, Buntline had taken part in the presidential campaign of 1848. Recognizing that his pack wasn't strong enough to bark for its own candidates, the American Party's prophet threw the weight of his pen behind the Whigs. For him that had meant lambasting individual Democrats. As a prominent one who was in jail, as of Election Day in 1848, McGowan was a natural target that *Ned Buntline's Own* hadn't overlooked.

Its editor stayed out of reach in Manhattan until after the Astor Place Riot had ended the lives of many more men than Macbeth had polished off in the tragedy of that name. Fearing a backsnap from the carnage he'd sponsored, New York's Ned boarded his private yacht and unsuspectingly made for the port where the Pennsylvania one dwelt.

The meeting, which took place on June 8, was described in a jab at Judson published by a turncoat former aid of the editor named Thomas V. Patterson. Billing himself as "the Pirate of the Hudson," Buntline swaggered from bar to bar, buying drinks for all who would look impressed. At length the Pirate reached a

Philadelphia taproom where a man asked him to repeat his name, announced next that he was going to whip him, did so and kicked him out. The fellow who thus treated the terror of the Hudson was identified as a "Mr. Mcgowan."

Paterson's pamphlet didn't give the site of the encounter; but Ned later identified it, when interviewed at Guy's Philadelphia house [he also had one in Baltimore], by a reporter for *Forey's Press*. "My hasty temper led me into another little difficulty in the bar room of this hotel. E. C. Judson, alias Ned Buntline, was editing a Knownothing paper in New York and came to Philadelphia in his own yacht. He had given me a horrid raking over in his paper, and I vowed to thrash him if I ever met him. You see, I had not only my wrongs to avenge, but he had covered with abuse my friends . . . We were presented to each other by name, and he put out his hand saying, 'There's an honest hand—shake it.' 'Before I do,' I answered, 'I must know whether you are Ned Buntline or not.' 'That is my nickname.' 'Then I'm afraid I'll have to lick you first,' said I, and I did beat him pretty severely, but not as hard as he deserved."

Kicking Buntline out of Guy's was McGowan's last known undertaking, before he started for California. He didn't at first listen to the urgings of a friend who had returned from the Coast during the summer of 1849, bubbling with tales of the wealth to be found there. This was a genial Kentuckian called Albert S. Hobbs; but his eloquence proved fruitless until Ned actually saw natural treasure on an unnamed day in September.

"As was my daily habit," he wrote when telling how he was hooked as a Forty-niner, "I sauntered into Col. Harry Connelly's wholesale wine store at the corner of Seventh and Chestnut streets. Harry had a room nicely fitted up in the back part of his store, where a select party of gentlemen bon vivants, living in Philadelphia and elsewhere, would assemble to drink fine wines and brandies. Among the habitues of the place was Capt. John Nagles, the father of Henry M. Nagles . . . Young Harry was a captain in the famous Stevenson regiment [a New York volunteer unit sent out to hold California during the Mexican War of 1846–48] and he had sent his father a vial containing gold dust, which Capt. John Nagles was exhibiting to Gov. David R. Porter, Senator Bayard, Sr., and many other distinguished gentlemen who were present. This was the first gold dust I had ever seen, and I caught the California fever."

3

THE PANLESS PROSPECTOR

AS EDITOR John B. Bratton had learned, when Ned thought of doing something, he wanted action right away. Albert Hobbs had left Philadelphia, but deciding to be his shipmate to Eldorado, McGowan hurried in pursuit. He left so abruptly that he asked friends to send letters of recommendation—addressed to the military authorities who directed a province which hadn't yet been organized as a United States territory—to California by mail. If he considered that any more gear was needed, for a raid on a distant frontier, he didn't mention it.

Joining Hobbs in New York, he did so too late to get cabin passage and had to settle for steerage. He was still traveling first class ashore, though, for he noted that while waiting for the ship to sail, he was "in the habit of dining at Gay's, supping at Mrs. Banks' and taking an 11 o'clock lunch at Barnum's."

Yet he found time for one stroke of business. In the course of his duties as a police superintendent, he had had dealings with George Wilkes, founder of the *National Police Gazette*. If lively and careless of corns, this was not a titillating rag in the vein of later such gazettes. Soon to head West himself, Wilkes took McGowan on as correspondent, to tell what it was like to make for the land of golden promise by way of the Isthmus of Panama.

Ned was so far from making the furtive break for California, ascribed by Bancroft, that he left for America's Pacific side as a by-line writer for a newspaper with national distribution. His first letter was run by the *Gazette* in its issue of October 13, under this assembly of headings: "Casting off—Settlement of Accounts—The Secret Brotherhood—A Burial—An Auction—Trial for Snoring—Conjugal Fight—Arrival at Chagres."

The letter itself began: "My Dear Sir,—At about half past three o'clock, the 15th of September, we left New York in the Empire City . . ." All went well with what McGowan styled, "our journey for the golden regions of California" until a man who had dined and drunk well got a whiff of his quarters in the belly of the ship. Retreating to the deck, Ned, as he put it, "cast my accounts." Then he rolled up in a traveler's shawl and slept in the open.

Another might have had to glum out the voyage as a starved fugitive from the stinking air of the steerage. Bacchus has a way of looking after his own, though. The next morning, not long after Ned had been roused by sailors detailed to swab the deck, the ship's purser mistook him for his seagoing brother, John McGowan. Addressing Ned as "Captain," Peter Wilkins declared that he could find a better place for an officer to sleep than the deck's planking.

Not one to back away from luck, McGowan didn't tell a man who had offered his name (by way of reminding the "Captain" that they had met before), that they weren't old acquaintances. Instead he joshed the purser about having the same handle as *Peter Wilkins*—Robert Paltock's once popular tale of a land of flying men—by asking if Youwarkee and her fellow spirits were aboard. To this Wilkins came back by saying that in his cabin were spirits that he thought would make pretty good stand-ins. As this proved so, Ned had good sailing the rest of the way to the Isthmus.

The trip across that neck gave Ned plenty to tell the *National Police Gazette's* readers. It took three days, in log canoes manned by Indians, to win to Chagres. There a thirty-six-year-old man, who had spent all his life in cities, learned at firsthand why mules have a reputation for being balky.

Flung several times between Chagres and the Pacific, McGowan felt badly shaken by the time he reached Panama City. Or he did until he had limped into a hotel and met a do-gooder with a bottle of *aguadiente*. After splitting most of it with Ned, the owner gave him a rub down with the rest. As a tonic for aches and pains, this proved so effective that McGowan spent his first night on the western sea at a fandango where he danced until sunup.

"Life on the Isthmus—Model Artists in the Chagres River— Panama Ladies at Their Bath—The Priests and the Nuns—Something Less than a Duel." So the *Gazette* headed the letter which made its issue of November 17. Dated October 5, this winds up, "I will write you again from the gold regions, should I arrive there safe."

Presumably that was done, but due to the *Gazette's* now defective files, the issue in which the supposed letter was published has not been found. In his reminiscences, though, Ned wrote of the trip from Panama to California—and included certain matters he perhaps would not have confided to the editor of a paper devoted to law enforcement.

Panama City was so crowded with gold rushers that it was ten days before McGowan could find a northbound steamer that would take him on. Steerage was the best he could manage this time, too. But by then the sense of sailing toward certain good fortune gave the halo of a lark to minor hardships met en route. Besides, life in the steamship *Panama's* slums wasn't too bad by the time Ned had finished adjusting things.

There were a few stuffed shirts among the cabin passengers who tried to put the steerage riffraff in their place. McGowan's answer was to find a chap whose talents can be judged by the fact that he was nicknamed Jeremy Diddler. With Ned for coach, Jeremy jimmied the doors of pantries meant to store food for the upper crust. The result was to raise the standard of steerage fare, while the cabin toffs wondered why their galley had run out of delicacies.

Yet if having fun on the *Panama,* McGowan shipped with two who were to seek his blood as Vigilantes. John Center, later the owner of the West's first circus, was a Scotchman described by Ned as "a wandering maestro of the bag pipes." Then there was George

R. Ward, later to show himself so gore-craving that McGowan gave his middle name as "Robespierre." While aboard the *Panama*, though, what Ned noticed was that Ward tried to make up for semi-dwarf stature by being as chesty as a blow fish.

But big or small, the steamer's passengers swarmed ashore in California on October 31. What they found was described in the *Annals of San Francisco*, published six years later.

"At the close of 1849, the population of the town numbered at least twenty, and probably nearer twenty-five thousand souls. A very small proportion were females—a still smaller one, children of either sex; while the vast majority were adult males in the very prime of manhood . . . There was no such thing as a *home* to be found. Both dwellings and places of business were either common canvas tents, or small rough board shanties, or frame buildings of one story. Only the great gambling saloons, the hotels, restaurants, and a few public buildings and stores had any pretensions to size, comfort or elegance."

With reference to this same period, the *Annals* took note of the streets, which were vile in dry weather and for muskrats only when it rained. "Indeed both horse, or mule and dray were sometimes literally swallowed up in the mud, while their owners narrowly escaped a similar fate. The town authorities caused numberless cart loads of brushwood and limbs of trees to be cut from the surrounding hills, and thrown into the streets; but these only answered a limited and temporary purpose . . . Nobody troubled himself to remove any rubbish from the way; but inmates of tents and boxes satisfied themselves with placing a few planks, tobacco boxes, bags of coffee, barrels of spoiled provisions, or any other available object, across and along the worst parts of the roads, to enable them to safely reach their own dwellings."

That's what Ned found; and it was lasting love at first sight. Bayard Taylor, who was then in San Francisco, gathering material for his survey of the era titled *Eldorado*, explains why men could overlook the bog-hole hell sketched in the *Annals*. What Taylor managed to catch and pass on was an exuberance based on the general feeling that past defeats mattered no more than present miseries. Here was rebirth in a land of such coming good chance that quagmires looked better there than rainbows in less favored airts.

McGowan looked back on the days of his first acquaintance with San Francisco with a nostalgia expressed in the San Francisco *Post* three decades later. "We sigh for the good old times of '49," he wrote, in a passage which didn't overlook the day's hardships. One of these was that chippies were so scarce—in a town which was all but without women of other leanings—that a man had to weigh out three ounces of gold to get so much as a buss.

Faring better than most as to quarters, nevertheless, Ned put up at the Parker House. Said by Taylor to have matched all but the best on the Atlantic Seaboard, it differed from the average one in leasing out its entire second floor to gamblers. Of this fraternity McGowan was for a brief time a pledge.

"Very few were following that particular business to which they had been bred," the *Annals* remarked in its survey of the 1849 scene. "Every immigrant on landing at San Francisco became a new man in his own estimation, and was prepared to undertake any thing or any piece of business whatever . . . The great recognized orders of society were tumbled topsy-turvy. Doctors and dentists became draymen . . . lawyers, brokers and clerks turned waiters or auctioneers."

So with others, so with Ned. A shipmate called Alfonso Brooks had brought a roulette wheel to California, which he asked McGowan to operate. Needing some sort of an income and not seeing any place in chaos where he could nail up a lawyer's shingle, Ned began spinning for all Parker House comers.

"I stepped behind the wheel, and gave it a whirl," he wrote of his first time up, "and it lodged in twenty-seven black. When I called out the number, I almost fainted at the sound of my own voice. I soon got used to it, however, and it turned me in a rich harvest."

Short though his trick as a gamester was, it kept him from presenting to bigwigs the letters of recommendation which Philadelphia friends had faithfully forwarded. Ned only performed as a croupier five or six days, but before they were up he had unforeseen observers.

"I remember once Governor Riley, Military governor of California was watching the game." Ned then decided to go it alone rather than to ask patronage of a man who had caught him off base. "I never presented the letters, for fear I might be recognized as 'the man at the wheel.'"

Albert Hobbs, the Kentuckian with whom McGowan had boarded the *Empire City* in New York, had meanwhile neither forgotten Ned nor parted company from him in any permanent sense. But he had celebrated his return to Cibola with a whingding —a habit of his which caused his death a couple of years later, when he tried to cure a hangover with morphine.

Sober, though, Albert had an eye for propriety, and was willing to put up money in its behalf. Shocked at finding a lawyer operating as a gambler, he gave Ned carrying funds, in the shape of $500 worth of dust, and said he'd back him in any dignified line of work.

In response to Hobbs' offer, McGowan moved to the patrons' side of the gambling line. "I cut off my beard and changed my slouch hat for a plug," he remembered, "and no one to this date, except a few intimate friends, knew that I had played a roulette wheel." He added that this overlooked phase of his life "would have been a nice little item for the mob press of San Francisco in 1856."

With a stake to give him freedom of movement, Ned began meeting men who were working to make California one with the rest of the United States politically. In 1849 the region was still more or less governed according to forms devised by Spanish rulers and kept by Mexican ones. Thus John W. Geary [later governor of both Kansas and Pennsylvania] was known as San Francisco's "First Alcalde," rather than its mayor.

Statehood for California was ten months in the offing, but so sure were its rambunctious citizens that they would get what they wanted, that they acted as though it had already been cinched. "I had been in the city but a few weeks," Ned noted, "when a dozen or two of us met and nominated J. W. Watson, afterwards Judge of Santa Clara County, and J. A. Patterson for members of the Legislature . . . We held the meeting opposite the plaza on Kearny street. There was a flight of steps running up the outside of the house, and we mounted the steps. It was raining hard and the mud was up to our knees . . . I held the lantern and Watson made a speech, and we nominated our men by acclamation, and they were elected to the first Legislature of California, called the Legislature of the Thousand Drinks."

So Ned was where he wanted to be—in politics. What he did for a living at this time is not clear, but when not working he was roving in a city custom built for his temperament. Under the spell of San Francisco's April, everybody was jolly. Even "the Puritan became a gamester," as McGowan put it, "and the young man taught to consider dancing a sin found his way to the masked balls." He went on to say that everybody at that time drank as heartily as they gambled, and cavorted in fancy costumes with the demireps who were alone available as partners.

On Christmas Eve the city's merriment was checked—or at least it was checked for such citizens as didn't profit by it—by the first of a series of great fires. But as the newspaperman that told who set the blazes hadn't arrived in 1849, conflagration number one was considered a common disaster.

It was a complete one for the owners of the Parker House; and it was probably because of suddenly finding himself without a roof that Ned caught the cold which laid him up for several weeks. Yet only a coffin could have kept him from answering a political call.

On January 8, 1850, a special San Francisco district election was held for the purpose of filling a vacancy in the not yet authorized California Senate. Of this event McGowan remarked, "I was taken out of the house, when sick, by some of my New York friends, to vote for Broderick."

That was Ned's first meeting with the man who was to become the storm center of California politics for the next nine years. Although born in Washington, David Colbreth Broderick had grown up in gangland New York. Unable to shine in politics there, he had packed up the hard-jawed ambition of a self-made man and sailed for coming country. When a state was made out of California, he meant to represent it in the U. S. Senate.

He didn't get there first. The Legislature of a Thousand Drinks elected as United States senators two men who had already cut the national mustard. These were John Charles Frémont, the explorer, and a former Congressman from Mississippi named William McKendree Gwin. But because of the practice of staggering senate terms, one had to be fobbed off with a two-year term; and a flipped coin had made Frémont the loser.

Actually serving only a year, because of having been illegally elected in 1849, John Charles would be rechosen or replaced by the Legislature in 1851. Broderick had therefore run for the California Senate, in order to be on deck at balloting time.

He had a right to think he could beat Frémont, a political maverick in a state-to-be where the main tugging was for control of the Democratic Party. Although there were other factions, especially in San Francisco, the real split down the middle came to be the fight between the pro-Broderick and pro-Gwin Democrats.

By training and instincts McGowan was closer to the urbane Dr. Gwin than to the rough hewn and humorless Broderick; but sides were chosen up in California by men who thought less of where they were than where they had come from. A Philadelphian, Ned joined the Democratic camp recruited chiefly, if by no means entirely, from former residents of the East's large cities. Again not wholly, but for the most part, Gwin drew the backing of Southern, Northern, and Middle Western Democrats hailing from non-industrial regions.

McGowan stayed close to a minor man of destiny until they found themselves on opposite side of the crevasse that whacked the country in two. To be sure they didn't share amusements. Broderick's ambition was of the grim stripe which wouldn't stand for any time off for fun. Although political foes didn't boggle at calling him a tipsy rake—sins assumed because he had owned a saloon in Manhattan—Ned knew and said otherwise:

"While in New York he read and studied all his leisure moments. He seldom drank or was seen in his bar room, and never visited houses of ill fame."

If not like that, McGowan had bounce enough to kick the ceiling, when he wanted to, and be hard at work the next day. "Time was money in those days," he wrote of 1850. And he added, "I had just as many law suits, acknowledging deeds and other legal papers as could be attended to from nine in the morning until five o'clock in the evening, at which time I dined."

Yet Ned had not immediately set up legal shop, after having been carried on a door to vote for Broderick early in January. As soon as he was on his feet again, he took San Francisco's Marshal, Malachi Fallon, up on an offer to act as his "attaché." Just what duties were covered by that term, McGowan didn't specify; but he must have seen service afloat as well as ashore. For lack of a regulation jail, corraled prisoners were jugged in *Euphemia*—a ship pictured in the *Annals of San Francisco* as standing off from the waterfront.

News of McGowan at this period is given via an entry in the diary of one Milo Hoadley, then an assistant of City Surveyor William M. Eddy. Of March 12, 1850, the which was Ned's thirty-seventh birthday, Hoadley wrote:

"Started A.M. for work on California street. Reached the head of Sacramento and driven in by rain. Loitered about—found Edward McGowan, shipmate and one of the Police—a good democrat and warm friend. Communicated to him the result of my surveys on the south beach and asked his advice with regard to informing the Council. Advised me to do so and agreed to arrange an interview with Col. Geary, the first Alcalde, who is also a Personal friend of his."

Having dug in on the ground floor, Ned was ready to climb, as soon as improved horizons made that possible. Step one was the first election of officers for San Francisco, held on April Fool's Day, 1850, on the corner of Clay and Kearny Streets. Furnishing a roof for the polls was the Bank Exchange Saloon.

One of the election's stagers, McGowan was able to give the

inside scoop. The Whigs had seemed the stronger party, but a couple of hours before an event scheduled for the afternoon, a gesture changed the picture. This was the dash to the scene of John Coffee Hays, whose exploits in the Mexican War had made him a national idol.

To quote Ned: "Col. Jack Hays rode a fine black charger over the plaza . . . The 'Texas Ranger,' was followed by the crowd and greeted with loud cheering as he gracefully mounted his spirited steed, which reared and plunged." Hays had been running for sheriff as an independent, but McGowan undertook to make him a Democratic candidate. "I saw at a glance that we would lose the whole of the county ticket, if we did not turn in and support Col. Hays for sheriff . . . All the voters wanted to see was the name of Col. Hays; they appeared to have little interest in any one else who was running for office." After stating that he'd arranged to have the Ranger's name printed at the top of his party's ballots, Ned finished by pointing out that, "In adopting this plan, we saved all the Democratic ticket but the County Judge, the District Attorney and County Treasurer."

But though the county judge was a Whig, McGowan joined him on the bench some three months later. And by that time he was besides a magistrate of lesser rank. Word of these successes was published in the *National Police Gazette* of July 13, the information being supplied by a correspondent who signed himself merely "W." The writer could afford to be thus offhand, as he was none other than the *Gazette's* publisher. George Wilkes had reached California early in 1850, to press the fortunes of his friend, Broderick, not to mention his own hopes of becoming a California Supreme Court justice.

From the tone of Wilkes' dispatch, it is clear that he expected his readers to know and care who Ned was. "Edward McGowan, from Philadelphia, who was elected about two weeks ago a Justice of the Peace to hold Justice Courts, has since been unanimously elected an Associate Judge of the Court of Quarter Sessions for the County of San Francisco. The last election was held agreeably to an act of the Assembly, by the Justices themselves, who held a convention for that purpose, when McGowan of Philadelphia, and a lawyer from New York State, by the name of Brown, were elected.

"The Court of Sessions for this county is composed of the following persons:

"Presiding Judge, Hon. R. N. Morrison, of New York City, formerly President of the Native American Association of that place. Senior Associate, Edward McGowan. Junior Associate, H. S. Brown. McGowan holds his Justice Court in the old Alcalde's building, formerly occupied by Judge Geary, on the main plaza, and although he has been two weeks in office, has entered upon his docket upwards of seventy civil suits, besides criminal actions. As the fees of the court are large, the office if properly attended, in two years will be a fortune. He also, as Associate of the Quarter Sessions, gets a large salary. So you will see that he has struck a vein of luck."

There was gold in California, then, and Ned had found it. Some of his take, as he reported, he sent to his wife in the form of regular monthly drafts. In view of later developments his choice of a banker is worth noting. McGowan's pick among San Francisco's money changers was an apple—not then turned rotten —calling himself James King of William.

4

THE SAN FRANCISCO
OF JUDGE McGOWAN

OF THE CASES brought before his court, Ned only left a full report of one. Aside from the picture it gives of McGowan in action on the bench, it deserves notice because of introducing a madam who several times breezed across his memoirs.

"After one of the big fires in San Francisco, Mrs. Irene Mc-Cready, desiring to change her locality and seek 'fresh fields and pastures new,' determined to go to the Territory of Oregon, and engaged passage for herself and several of her *ladies* on board a steamer bound for that country; also taking with her all of her gorgeous furniture, intending a surprise to the rural and steady population of that section of the Pacific Coast, and exhibit to them a taste of San Francisco's fashionable and demi-mondaine life."

A head wind sprang up, though, and such a fierce one that the ship was battered to the point of being in danger of scuttling. "During the gale," Ned then continued, "the sailors, naturally superstitious, attributed the storm and their bad luck to the frail passengers and the freight they were carrying. They did not, however, propose to cast them into the sea, as we read in the good book that the ancient biblical sailors did Jonah, as there were not, probably, whales enough in that latitude to gobble them all up."

After the steamer limped back to San Francisco for repairs, the line owners not only failed to return Mrs. McCready's passage money; they sent her a bill, taxing her for a share of the ship's repair costs. Unitemized, this assessment was tagged "general average."

Not protesting, she did express the wish to have the matter explained to her: a reasonable request to which the company responded by sending to her bagnio one of its promising young men. To this gosling, Mrs. McCready listened with grave interest, and paid the amount demanded. When he had gone, though, she made her way to Ned's court and asked him to issue a warrant for the line's call boy, whom she accused of having filched from her premises a diamond pin.

"Irene," Ned remembered telling her, "there must be some mistake; this is a respectable gentleman." But as she insisted on service from the court, McGowan directed his clerk to issue the warrant but not to record it. By so moving, he saved a man, of whose innocence he felt sure, from being celebrated in the press as a brothel looter.

The warrant gained good results for Irene, however. Knowing that he'd really make name and fame, if he protested a charge from such a source, the young line official hustled into court, with the company's lawyer for chaperon. After ascertaining the value placed on the brooch, the attorney paid the sum without arguing. When the notified madam sent her aide-de-camp to court, to collect what had been forked over, though, McGowan repeated that he thought a mistake had been made.

By way of reply, Mrs. McCready's courier said, "Judge, did you ever lose a diamond pin?" As the answer was, no, because he had never had one, Ned reported that he but stared back in silence. "That settled it," he wound up his recital; "Irene was only getting even on the 'general average' question. She was what might be termed 'bitter water.'"

When McGowan first became an associate county judge, as well as a justice of the peace, the courts were upstairs in a building whose ground floor was enlivened by a combination dance hall and gambling dive. The fancy dress balls held in the California Exchange, were, as Ned took occasion to note, "splendid affairs."

To go by an anecdote of his, they were also untrammeled ones:

"Chief Justice Murray and I attended one of the fancy balls, and after depositing our fire arms and overcoats with an officer in attendance to receive them, we entered the hall. In a few moments we were joined by a large, well formed, handsome woman named Rose Sheppard, gotten up in superb style . . . She had made a bet with one of her female companions of a bottle of wine that she would make the 'two judges' promenade with her . . . We halted for a moment, and she added, 'If you do not, I will slit both of your coats up the backs.' " Ned concluded by saying that he and his friend laughed and promenaded.

Because he wouldn't help Vigilantes to fatten their purses, Hugh C. Murray was roughly treated by Bancroft, among other California chroniclers. He seems, however, to have been a man of brilliant attainments. Only twenty-five at the time of the encounter with Rose Sheppard, he had been elected a judge of San Francisco's Superior Court. The following year he was appointed to the Supreme Court of California by Governor John McDougall, and in 1852 he earned the title given him by Ned by being elected Chief Justice of the state.

Commenting on this precocious success, McGowan wrote a death notice for Murray which can be read, too, as a glance back at his own fallen hopes of high advancement: "The dream of life, which to most of us, is the veriest illusion, was to him a splendid reality; for at an age when few have given evidence of any of those qualities that distinguish men from the mass of clay, out of which we are moulded, he displayed such eminent powers, as made him at once the ornament and delight of his noble profession, and won for him a reputation, that fixed upon him the eyes of the whole state, who delighted to enfold him with the robes of justice, which he wore so gracefully. Possessed of a mind of the very first order, the questions he adjudicated upon were distinguished by a clemency of expression, and a purity of reasoning such as carried conviction to the most ordinary mind."

But in 1850 the tuberculosis which was to drag Murray under while still young, hadn't begun to gnaw at his strength. He and

Ned spent many a night over the brandy and wine together; and with them was another of great capacities, who had sought California as an arena where they might shine early.

Because the man who became Senator James A. McDougall was also from Illinois, Murray had met him there, and was the one who had introduced him to McGowan. "This is a friend of mine, Jim, and I want you to know each other," was all Hugh made of the ceremony.

Some of the gaiety shared by the three rubbed off on a passage of Ned's which dealt, too, with a judge of different qualities than those he ascribed to Murray. While General Bennet Riley was still California's military governor, he had authorized a hackberry named William B. Almond to open a Court of First Instance in December of 1849. Still functioning under the government voted in by the Legislature of the Thousand Drinks, it had civil jurisdiction only. Yet just how civil the court was is open to question, for the *Annals* noted of Judge Almond that to while away the tedium of listening to arguments pro and con, he'd shuck boots and socks and pare the judicial corns.

Thus much for prelude. Of some unlisted night of 1850, Ned wrote that he, Murray, McDougall, and Almond "were having a jolly time of it one night at Tom Battell's drinking saloon, the Woodcock . . . The conversation turned on friendship. 'Oh,' said Almund [sic] 'what is friendship but a name, as Shakespeare says in his *Vicar of Wakefield.*' I replied, 'You old fool, Oliver Goldsmith wrote the *Vicar of Wakefield.*' Judge Almund and I got hot over it, as people who are tight sometimes do about small matters. McDougall and Murray were holding their sides with laughter. They understood the peculiarities of the learned Judge. I stood the drinks, and the Judge of the First Instance and I became good friends. He still thought Shakespeare wrote *The Vicar of Wakefield,* though."

Barren of snobbery and begrudging no man his due, McGowan had more to say of Almond than that. He confessed he had learned things from a man of rough and ready judgments, whose frontier training had taught him how to deal with matters and attitudes new to a man bred in the East.

Now the *Annals of San Francisco* also had praise for Judge Almond. Not before noticed, the authors were Frank Soule, John Nisbet or Nesbit, and a Dr. John Gihon. Whatever the bents of the last named, the first two came to be newspapermen in the service of the Vigilance Committee of 1856. The *Annals* can be taken, then, as a fair sample of Vigilante thinking re public matters; and what the book had to say about a semi-literate pettifogger can be stretched to cover the whole field of jurisprudence, as viewed by its authors.

"Judge Almond . . . organized his court in the old school house near the plaza; and the novel and summary manner in which he conducted his business and sometimes disposed of very important cases, was a source of as much merriment to some and mortification to others as anything then transpiring in town. His Honor . . . had a sovereign contempt for Buncombe speeches, legal technicalities, learned opinions and triumphantly cited precedents . . . His opinion once formed, and that sometimes occurred before the first witness was fully heard, his decision was made . . . Jury trials were then of rare occurrence, and the judge decided the cases that came before him; and there can be no reason to doubt that his decisions generally were far more just and equitable than those more recently given in courts claiming greater legal knowledge, where learned judges gravely occupy the bench."

Frank Soule, editor of the San Francisco *Chronicle*, seems to have been the chief compiler of the *Annals*. But whether he or one of his associates wrote the above passage, it nails to the mast a basic fact about Vigilantes. Essentially they had "a sovereign contempt" for the American judicial system. They scorned, that is as much as to say, the legal considerations which, by way of the Constitution, support the entire fabric of American civilization. Many of them, of course, were no more than rogues who wished to destroy the courts so that thievery could flourish unchallenged. But to take the Vigilante at his best, he was purse proud of his ignorance and suspicious of learning. He admired the snap judgments of a grackle like Almond, because he thought unaided horse sense equal to finding—and without stalling for thought—the right answers to problems over which the best minds of both hemispheres have been straining since before the rise of Greece.

It thus came about that San Francisco had no sooner achieved the dignity of a full-fledged judiciary than its courts were besieged by enemies. Where Ned could least have expected it trouble again bushwhacked him. By becoming a judge he didn't win to peace and respect but rather found himself in a cockpit where even the prisoners had to be armed when in court, to help keep the Yahoos at bay.

It took a while for the jumping cactus to crowd that close, though. At first the worst that happened was snarling among the city's merchants, hot over Ned's decisions re cases argued in his J.P. court. More often than not these involved disputes between sailors and shipowners as to whether seamen were entitled to be paid upon reaching California. Where not actually the agents of marine lines, San Francisco's commission men and wholesale auctioneers were in natural sympathy with the men whose craft served a ballooning seaport.

Court cases sprang from the decision of tars who had shipped from other home ports to stay in San Francisco, or some point in Eldorado at least. It was the plea of line owners that any one who left a ship's company before the end of a round trip should forfeit all pay as a deserter. But what McGowan fastened on was a clause in the articles of enlistment stating that a sailor was hired for a period of three years, "unless sooner dismissed by the captain."

Having studied maritime law in Philadelphia, Ned knew that Congress had had the rights of seamen as well as of ship-holders in mind, when drawing up a governing legal code. "Now," he argued, "if a captain had the right to discharge his crew, they had the same right in a 'home port,' [a status enjoyed by San Francisco, as many lines had opened offices there] after properly stowing the ship, to be released from the articles and paid off."

Although McGowan went on to say that in cases where it was

proved that sailors had shirked berthing duties, he would rule in favor of the owners, these and their allies remained unappeased. The growl along the water front ran to the effect that Ned was pro-tar and anti ship-holder.

Implicit in such snarls was that he was siding with poor men against prosperous ones. Venality could therefore not be laid to his account here, but that was the next hue.

This time his critics had something to go on, although Mc-Gowan didn't know anything about a deal which had been made. Closing it were County Judge Morrison and a pair of property vendors. Later to be a Vigilance Committee sagamore, one of them was Charles V. Gillespie. In tribute to this djinn's abilities, Ned once parodied a famous passage from Pope's *Essay on Criticism:*

> A little stealing is a dangerous part
> But stealing greatly is a noble art;
> It's mean to rob a hen roost of a hen
> But stealing millions makes us gentlemen.

Being without a court house, as of 1850, the newly organized County of San Francisco was in the market for one. To meet this demand, Gillespie and an unsung knave called on "old Rhadamanthus," as McGowan styled Morrison. In addition to being a logical man to discuss court house plans with, the judge was authorized to monitor the county's outlays of cash.

To quote Ned, "Gillespie and old Lafan owned 120 feet of land fronting on the plaza," or Portsmouth Square. The building on it McGowan described as a rat-infested wreck; and as he held forth there as justice of the peace, he wasn't just passing gossip.

In their conference with old Rhadamanthus, the owners agreed to sell their holding to the county at a price which would allow a comfortable margin of profit for all three. After the fact, Associate Justices Edward McGowan and Harvy S. Brown were invited to a dinner at which, as they were told, the topic would be the hoped-for court house. Present, too, were Lafan, described by Morrison as anxious to talk over the possibility of selling the county a site, and an attorney who was party to the swindle.

They dined, as Ned recalled, "at a French restaurant on Sacramento street . . . the very place to talk over a confidential affair or to meet a lady . . . We fell to, in right good earnest, and the turkey stuffed with truffles was delicious." McGowan likewise had kindly memories of "the iced champagne, and the good old $10 Port and Burgundy that Lafan had imported for his own private use . . . We all got gloriously drunk, and old Rhadamanthus became eloquent, he spoke in glowing terms of the beautiful edifice that was to be erected on this splendid site, a large slab of marble was to adorn the Temple of Justice, upon which were to be inscribed the names of the members of the first Court of Sessions of the County of San Francisco—the right and left bowers of the Court were to be in their proper places— another drink and a shout of applause from Lafan and a flap of the wings from the Court, and Rhadamanthus drew from his pockets $20,000 in 3% scrip."

McGowan was startled himself, and the shock to the junior justice was stunning. "Judge Brown rubbed his eyes as if to clear his vision, still doubting the truth of what he saw. He turned to us [Ned had been using the editorial 'we'] and said, 'What does all this mean, Mac?'" Although Morrison had announced that the scrip was "only a little perquisite of the Court," McGowan said that he hadn't felt up to answering his colleague. "We were either too far gone in our cups, or had not made up our mind how to act in the premises—but we remember, probably for the first time in our life, *we held our tongue.*"

The next day, though, having discussed the matter soberly and in private, the justices agreed to wig the Court. "Judge Brown and myself called upon Judge Morrison and informed him in positive terms that the $15,000 [at the dinner Rhadamanthus had slipped five grand to the lawyer, for services rendered] must be given back to Gillespie and Lafan."

That's when Ned and Brown learned that the deal had been wrapped up, with them inside the scandal. Very properly, there was a grand jury investigation, as soon as the stinging given the county became known. When the dust cleared, Justices McGowan and Brown were still on the bench, but as associates of Judge Alexander Campbell and not Morrison.

Yet because they didn't like the way Ned handled marine matters, many of the water front set were sorry that he hadn't been found out of line. As a matter of fact McGowan *did* operate on the far side of the law while a judge; but as it didn't touch their pocket books or business concerns, his enemies didn't think to have him impeached on that account.

Ned must have ranked as an arbiter of the code duello while in Pennsylvania, but the record is mum on the point. What it does say is that in San Francisco men prized his field of honor savvy.

The earliest of the duels in which he was on hand as "the friend" of one of the shooters, seems to have been one involving the famous filibuster, William Walker. In 1850 the newly started San Francisco *Herald* was edited by Walker and John Nugent, a Texas-gaited New Yorker who had come to California with Jack Coffee Hays. With both of these McGowan was personally on good terms; but when an old Philadelphia crony named Will Hicks Graham took exception to something printed in the *Herald,* Ned agreed to act as his second.

Having penned what the shooting was about, Walker was Graham's opponent. The arrangements made by McGowan and the other second called for Colt's revolvers at ten paces. But after each shot—always granted that both were still on their pins—the principals were scheduled to step one pace closer before firing anew.

Walker was the loser, but Ned testified to his show of the stuff of which filibusters are made. In the course of an exchange of three shots apiece, he was hit in one leg, and the foot of its mate; but until he fell, he neither gasped, flinched, nor gave any other sign that he'd been wounded.

If such encounters were illegal, those who took part in them were no more shorted of respect than were drinkers when Prohibition made its sorry try at slaying good cheer. And the same

could be said of those who held with a frontier amendment of
the dueling code.

More or less peculiar to San Francisco, this was the impromptu
duel, brought off without going to the inconvenience of leaving
town. In the eyes of many Golden Gaters, it formed a better way
of settling differences than pulling triggers by arrangement. They
felt that if a man was hot enough to want to shoot another, the
proper thing to do was to look him up, warn him, and start
slinging lead.

How normal these "street fights" or "affrays" were considered
is made plain by Ned, when telling of a time when Will Hicks
Graham didn't fare as well as he'd done with Walker. He had
more to be wrathful about than an objectionable newspaper item
this time, hence his hurry, in place of waiting to send a challenge.

A chap named George F. Lemon had introduced to Will a
woman that Graham married. Neither she nor Lemon, though,
had bothered to tell the bridegroom that they were having an
affair, but briefly interrupted by the wedding. Learning that he
was horned, Will set out to get George, a fact known to McGowan,
because the injured husband stopped by to tell the Judge of his
plans.

"The morning of the rencounter Graham brought a double-
barreled shotgun and placed it in my office and informed me
what he intended doing when Lemon came down the usual way
to his place of business. I said to him, 'Will, don't do that. Go out
and meet him on equal terms.' He left the gun and instead took a
Colt's revolver and met him on the south side of Merchant street
opposite the plaza."

Ready with a pistol of his own, and warned by the required
cry of "defend yourself," Lemon made out better than he deserved.
The shot he got off staggered Graham; and worse was to come for
him, as he had started what couldn't now be called off.

"Graham retreated backwards and tripped and fell on the steps
of the Union Hotel, when Lemon, while he was down . . . placed
the muzzle of the pistol in his mouth and fired, carrying away
several teeth." At this black point for Will, though, a rescuer

appeared in the person of Ned's Marine Revenue Service brother. Now on duty in Western waters and presumably on his way to see Ned, he undertook what wouldn't have occurred to His Honor of San Francisco's Quarter Sessions Court. "My brother, Capt. John McGowan, not being conversant with the customs of this kind of fights, interfered and took Lemon away, who still had another load in his pistol, and it no doubt saved Graham's life."

Yet if the San Francisco of Ned's day was robust, it was not overrun by desperados. The biggest joke sworn to and handed on by California's historians is the myth of a blood-flooded city, saved from going down in gore for the third time by the life preserver tossed by the Vigilantes.

If said chroniclers had ever looked over McGowan's memoirs— and to write of pioneer California without consulting Ned is akin to writing of early Greece without reading Herodotus—they'd never have tried to pass the queer so baldly. "Shades of Munchausen!" McGowan wrote, in commenting on John Hittell's avowal that San Francisco had had upwards of a thousand slaughtered citizens during the first few gold rush years. "A dead man in San Francisco every second morning for breakfast, and on Sunday one for breakfast and dinner. I wonder if there is room for one more inmate in the Insane Asylum."

Twenty years before Hittell published his so-called history Ned had published an item which told how the myth had sprung full grown from a typographical error. Nor had the bungled statement been anything better than an excited prosecutor's reach for dramatic effect, to begin with.

"Those 1300 murders and those 4000 orphans," Ned snorted in 1858. "The ridiculous story that was told in the House of Assembly last week . . . originated in this way about three years ago. H. H. Byrne, Esq., the District Attorney for San Francisco, in making a speech in a case of capital punishment, told the jury there had been 200 murders in that city in the past five years, with but few convictions and less executions. The next day it found its way into the newspapers with a mistake of 1000, making it 1200 instead of two hundred. This piece of information was ridiculed at the time."

Yet if homicides weren't a commonplace of salad day San Francisco, the city did have an extraordinary number of fires in that period. Following the one which had driven McGowan from the Parker House, there were five other block-jumping blazes. They were not all that changed the face of a town which had to be rebuilt time and again between 1849 and 1851. The classless city, where all were on an equal footing with opportunity, had given way to one broken down into the usual levels. To rephrase the *Annals,* doctors practiced medicine now and left dray work to those who found that their natural employment.

A novelty of San Francisco, though, was the nature of its merchant class. Elsewhere and earlier in America the pattern for mercantile advancement had been laid down by the maxims of Benjamin Franklin at his Poor Richard worst. Considered as reading matter, that is: they spoke for thrift, mickles pyramided into muckles by years of honest toil, unremitting attention to duty and other things that only a hard spirit would refuse a grunt of respect.

The merchants of San Francisco, though, had never read Richard's almanac; Haliburton's Sam Slick was more in their style. Yet they thought no less of themselves for having ambushed prosperity, in place of bagging it at the end of a long still hunt. In fact they felt themselves entitled to rule San Francisco, and Judge McGowan had been in office less than a year when they made their first try.

5

THE HIGH-STRUNG SCAPEGOATS

IN THE GOLDEN gate city's opening years its merchants needed as capital only gall, a cast-iron conscience and the means to get to California. That wasn't always costly, as some of San Francisco's counting house barons wested as stowaways.

But however they reached California, they could be sure of being followed by large stocks of goods, bought at the cost of a handshake and a signature. The prices paid in San Francisco were so huge, as gauged by all former American standards, that Eastern wholesalers would ship on consignment to anybody willing to act as an outlet in Eldorado's commercial capital.

Those who rushed to try their luck in a double or quits market were in general men who had already had schooling in living by their wits. Some that Ned had known in Philadelphia he described as sidewalk auctioneers and pitchmen. Some that George Wilkes had known in New York he noted as drifting rascals, "disgraced clerks," and commercial "desperados."

In California they didn't sell their goods but put them up for bidding by San Francisco's retailers and distributors to the rest of the state. But the commission merchants didn't let items go on the same terms by which they had obtained them.

When shipments for which they had paid nothing arrived, the fly lads of the water front auctioned them off to dealers heeled with bags of gold dust. As long as there was a demand for whatever they purveyed, they kept their credit rolling by paying off their Atlantic seaboard suppliers. If the market turned sour, the commission merchants brought it around by a method set forth in the *Annals of San Francisco.*

After telling of a fire which had razed more than half the city, the *Annals* philosophized: "The greatest misfortunes often bring a breath of consolation on their wings, so of this dreadful conflagration. The city had been crowded with goods. The enormous profits which the adventurers had realized, had induced many others to make large shipments. Thus a vast amount of goods filled the stores and storehouses, and the market was as a natural consequence dormant and ruinous. The fire came and furnished a market for a great portion of the stock, and although the returns made no very flattering balance in the ledger, still the enhanced value of what remained partially compensated for what had been lost. Consequently business soon revived."

Although that could hardly be more explicit, Frank Soule et al. didn't point fingers in the same direction their pens aimed. They blamed the blazes on robbers, although nothing could be more absurd. Thieves cannot flourish by destroying property; they can't fence off ashes or pawn cinders. The only profiteers of arson are those who illegally put the bite on insurance companies, or get out of paying creditors for consigned goods which can't be either sold or returned. Or else they are men who want to sweeten the market in the way spelled out by the *Annals.*

There was one newspaperman who did say who the fire bugs of San Francisco were, however. This was George Wilkes, later to win esteem as the ablest war correspondent to deal with the Civil War. He came to be recognized as the nation's most penetrating and accurate reporter, that is. Wilkes lived in San Francisco from 1850 to 1853, a period during which all but the first of the city-eating blazes took place. Having turned his trained observer's eye on the scene then local to him, he in due time published the following in the *National Police Gazette:*

"The warehouses of San Francisco were glutted to the roofs; but the precious commission merchants of San Francisco could not

make returns to their Atlantic shippers; and then came the terrible
conflagrations which gave them a clear balance sheet . . . 'Thieves,
thieves, incendiaries!' shouted the merchants. 'Hang them! Hang
them!' echoed the ignorant and the timid—they have set our city
on fire.' And they did seize and hang several poor devils . . .
though nobody benefited but the merchants of San Francisco."

That was written of the first, or 1851 Committee of Vigilance.
Before it grew bold enough to commit gang murder, though, the
group had as its chief project the heckling of the courts of San
Francisco, city and county.

The ring leaders had the purpose of hiding their skulduggery
behind a screen of virtue, thrown up by the trusty method of pretending outrage at the state of public affairs. They drew a following made up of the usual well meaning tagalongs that rogues can
always count on as abettors when they jostle the law openly.

In a manuscript memoir Judge Harvy Brown drew bead on both
these factors. "There were a great many of the Committee who
were conscientious men . . . believing they were right. But on the
other hand there were scoundrels and criminals among them, who
made themselves most officious for the purpose of cloaking themselves and turning the public attention from themselves—one of
them has since been sent to the state prison two or three times for
grand larceny."

Dr. Henry M. Gray defined the nature of the Vigilantes more
specifically than did Judge Brown. The author of a pamphlet
called *Judges and Criminals,* based on personal observations of the
1851 and '56 mobs, Gray said, "Both organizations were mainly
composed of merchants; a great many of whom were bankrupt and
had robbed their creditors."

The diversionary racket they raised took the form of charging
that the courts were too slow to keep up with the crime rate and
too soft in handing out punishments. Their solution was that the
American judicial system should be junked in San Francisco and
replaced by the kangaroo tribunals in vogue in unorganized mining camps.

Harvy Brown's answer to the first objection was that the newly authorized Quarter Sessions Court had had a long criminal calendar passed to it by the District Court; and the judges had to shovel their way out of that snow, before they could catch up with current felonies. Ned threw the second raspberry back at the critics by pointing out that in jury trials the judge does not make the final decision but accepts what is agreed upon by the twelve there to heft the evidence.

"It may be as well to state that the Grand and petit jurors at that time, were generally composed of members or sympathizers with the Committee and the petit juries had, in most cases, the awarding of the punishment. Yet the hue and cry of these . . . scoundrels was, in all cases of failure to convict, to attach blame to the court."

Not violent at the beginning, the hecklers acted like baseball fans, rooting for their side, which was the prosecution, and booing defense counsel and witnesses.

"During these times," Judge Brown recalled, "scenes occurred in court which would have disgraced a city of barbarians. For example a man would be tried for a felony, and members of the Vigilance Committee would crowd into the court room and cheer the District Attorney, attempting to overawe the court and juries."

Yet even when there were convictions, and the severest sentences allowed by California's penal code were meted out, the braying didn't stop. Clamorers who were looking only for excuses to take things into their own hands were satisfied with nothing.

At a fancy dress ball one Charles P. Duane had slapped a fellow merry maker down with his open hand; and a Vigilante-managed grand jury indicted him with assault to kill. The cry raised was for socking Duane with the maximum punishment of fourteen years. When Ned and his colleagues gave the lightest possible term, for the offense with which the prisoner was falsely charged, a show of weapons was all that kept the pack from storming the bar of justice and dealing with Duane in their own fashion.

"The mobbites who had crowded the court house, jumped on the benches and commenced hissing and showing other marks of disapprobation," McGowan reminisced. "They offered no further violence; if they had, many of them would have bitten the dust that day. David C. Broderick, Governor McDougall . . . and the prisoner himself had on a pair of Colt's revolvers, and many others were armed—two or three with double barrel shotguns under their cloaks, and Colonel Jack Hays, the High Sheriff, was in personal attendance on the court."

The episode which did set a murder-bent mob in motion was one involving mistaken identity. California's first genuine bad man, as opposed to the probably mythical Murietta, was James Stuart. He had well earned his reputation as a death-dealing bandit when, on February 19, 1851, two men entered the San Francisco premises of C. J. Jansen & Co. Finding Jansen alone in the store, they blackjacked him and walked off with about $2000.

The conclusion jumped to was that one of the pair was Stuart, so when a man sporting his earmarks was found in San Francisco, he was brought to the bed in which a hard rap on the noggin had laid Jansen. The merchant identified the prisoner as the one who had coldcocked him; and several who had met California's ace rogue identified the bird in hand as James Stuart. The prisoner himself, though, insisted that his name was Thomas Berdue, or Burdue, as some records give it.

As nobody would heed what was taken as a silly effort to escape punishment, Berdue and a supposed accomplice named Windred were indicted for assault and robbery. But proceedings against them had gone no further than a hearing in the court of Recorder Frank Tilford, when the water front gang intervened.

Step one was to distribute handbills accusing the courts of readiness to free a man who was in fact awaiting trial on a rap which he seemed to have no good chances of beating. "Are we to be robbed, assassinated in our own domiciles, and the laws let an aggressor perambulate the streets?" one broadside demanded. "If so, let each man be his own executioner. Fie upon your laws! They have no force."

"Now there might have been some excuse for this incendiary handbill," as Ned wrote, "had they known the two prisoners to be positively guilty, or had the courts refused to take action in the matter. The sequel will show that these men were innocent, and there is where the danger lies from an excited mob—call it a rising of the people, a Vigilance Committee, or by any other name you please."

The next move of the risen people was to organize—which they hadn't done in any formal sense up to that time. They hadn't even called themselves anything except "the people of San Francisco."

While action largely took the form of mass meetings, all comers of the city were indeed welcomed. Yet when organizing was agreed upon by the merchant leaders, they moved indoors and shut others out. As a member called G. W. Ryckman declared in his manuscript reminiscences, the body first called San Francisco Regulators, and then the San Francisco Committee of Vigilance of 1851, was "a good deal like a Free Mason's Lodge."

The group was initially aimless, because the man who was to give it direction wasn't originally a member. The for a while missing link was the most extraordinary visitant of pioneer San Francisco, other than Ned McGowan.

Something about William T. Coleman could be inferred from the fact that he was the son of Napoleon Bonaparte Coleman. William, indeed, had the Little Corporal's enthusiasm for power, and no small part of his organizing genius. Yet Coleman had been christened William Tell, which wreaks of irony, as in San Francisco he was not tyranny's crossbow defier but the ramrod of dictatorship.

This he does not seem to have intended. He appears rather to have been a perfect example of McGowan's apothegm, "Genius, like fire, is a good servant but a terribly bad master." Not being able to curb his genius for organization, Coleman wrought mightily in direct opposition to his own ambitions. In a sense—and Ned had the perception to realize it—Vigilantism was also a tragedy for its architect.

According to the memoir of a Vigilante associate named O. B. Crary, "Coleman came out here for the purpose of being elected United States Senator by the Democratic Party." A native of Kentucky, William Tell had planned to enter politics by way of the

law. Forced to quit his studies, though, he went into business, and
did so well at it that he never resumed his chosen course. He never
gave up on wishing to shine politically—in 1864 he ran for the
Senate, in a day when a Democrat couldn't have been elected
street sweeper—yet all his effective efforts undermined the very
party whose standard bearer he wished to become.

As a Southern Democrat, he was not a natural ally of the other
Vigilante leaders. Almost all from the East, these were Whigs in
1851; Know-Nothings and Republicans later. Nor did any of those
who wrote about him in their respective reminiscences like him.

Some of their hostility can be ascribed to the fact that he was a
bigger shark than the rest, and dealt too fast for them. Not many
merchants get to have an internationally known mineral named after them; but William Tell made it with colemanite, after he became the world's champion borax tycoon.

But he was obviously as erratic as gifted; and his colleagues
fastened on that fact, when brooding on a man whom they had
followed in spite of being baffled by him. "Coleman is today one
man, and another day an entirely different," as Isaac Bluxome,
secretary of both Committees, put it.

Charles V. "court house site" Gillespie was also confused by William Tell. After first writing that Coleman was too bold, too much
of a "go ahead" man, Charles went on to say that he "was a man
apt to get excited, not as cool as he ought to have been . . . In
a tight place he will want assistance, something to lean upon."

Coleman, to repeat, was not a charter member of the 1851 Committee, as loosely organized under the leadership of a Down Easter
named Sam Brannan. He did not know most of the Vigilantes, in
fact, having led a California career which hardly allowed for much
in the way of San Francisco associations.

Westing as a Forty-niner, he operated in Hangtown, as Placerville was first known, for the rest of that year and part of 1850.
According to information later supplied Ned, Coleman took it on
the lam from Eldorado County, in preference to telling how he had
come by a couple of barrels of salt pork. But in any case he wanted
to get into the big time as a commission merchant in San Fran-

cisco. Seeing that for that purpose, his best move was to make himself known to New York wholesalers, he went East. Nor had he long set up his grocery depot on Sansome Street, when the Vigilantes began arguing with each other as to how their organization should function.

How William Tell came to join was described by himself in a statement prepared for Bancroft. He was, he said, so far from being a member of the blue ribbon mob that he hadn't even given its frenzies a thought, until he passed the Regulators' frat house at the end of a certain day's work.

While thus strolling by, he heard wrangling which told him that the club members didn't know how to go about doing what they wanted to. Pained by such bumbling, he began to think of ways and means by which they might get somewhere.

The fascinating part of his statement is that he didn't care about the goal. But having a genius for working out courses of action, he soon saw a way of achieving what others were in a sweat about. Ergo, as he declared, he proceeded home, shed his stiff collar and went back to tell the Regulators how to become lynchers without seeming to be a mob at all.

What Coleman proposed was setting up a "people's court." This would monitor the operations of the regular courts, seeing to it that prisoners were tried promptly and got all the works that could be heaped on. When this was approved, William Tell laid out a plan for fast action. What he proposed was the appointment of a committee of twelve, authorized to call upon the Mayor and the Recorder, inviting them to cooperate in overseeing the trial of the supposed Stuart and his partner.

To offset action by an approving mob, that else would have stormed the jail, officials turned the fates of Berdue and Windred over to "the people's court." Endangering the prisoners was the disagreement between the California and kangaroo penal codes. Even if guilty the two men had not committed a capital crime. But the Committee announced that conviction in their court would be followed by hangings.

At last realizing his forfeited ambition to star as a lawyer,

Coleman himself was prosecutor. Yet even though he pressed his case where his own maneuvering had tilted the beam in his favor, he couldn't talk the jury into convicting. Witnesses who had known Stuart in various of the bandit's mining camp hangouts, had looked at the man said to be he, and shaken their heads. While agreeing that the face was a match for the desperado's, they declared that the prisoner lacked a full two inches of the real James Stuart's height.

The absence of sure identification, as well as other flaws in the prosecution's case, so impressed some of the jurors that three refused to say that Berdue and Windred were guilty. Informed of this, the mob raised a howl of, "Majority rules—hang them anyhow!"

At that time Coleman still had enough respect for the principles of law to throw the weight of his influence against an outrage he was later to endorse. So Berdue and his fellow were turned back to the proper authorities, and in the district court, the conviction which hadn't materialized in that of the "people" became a fact.

McGowan, to be sure, voiced the opinion that this wouldn't have happened, were it not for the squeeze put upon the jurors by "mobbites" and the newspapers which backed them. Conviction took place, nevertheless—but oh, the difference to the two most interested parties. Windred was sent to prison; Berdue was taken to answer another count against Stuart in Marysville—in place of being strung up.

Not much later San Francisco officers caught sight of a prowler they couldn't catch; but he looked so much like the fellow who had recently been shipped to Marysville, that a query was sent, to find whether Stuart was still in custody. It was then that officials at last began listening to the still imprisoned Berdue, who thus got off the mistaken identity hook, taking Windred with him.

The realization that they had tried hard to end the days of innocent men might have abashed some people. In the case of the Regulators the revelation didn't spill from their sails so much as a hatful of wind.

By the time Windred and Berdue were once more free citizens, the Regulators had become the San Francisco Committee of Vigilance of 1851. Not much later Coleman bulwarked the outfit with a mystery novel façade. A keen eye for ham is part of the equipment of any skilled usurper, and William Tell understood that by operating as a secret society his crew would impress the rabble and could stampede weak sisters out of the opposition and into support.

His simple but effective method was to substitute numbers for names in publications of the Committee. The handle of a known counter jumper might not inspire much awe; while the same man, by using a figure as a mask, could graft on timid imaginations the picture of a very sinister fellow.

Isaac Bluxome, Jr., to pour concrete, was able to use a signature which daunted men who wouldn't have been bothered by his known capacities as a warrior. Yet they were quailed out of countenance when he hid behind a number which could have stood for a battler of dread proportions. Certainly he seemed to have the assurance of power, when he affixed it to an edict dated July 5, 1851:

Resolved,

That we, the Vigilance Committee, do claim to ourselves the right to enter any person's or persons' premises where we have good reason to believe that we shall find evidence to substantiate and carry out the objects of this body; and furthermore deeming ourselves engaged in a good and just cause, we intend to maintain it.

By Order of the Committee of Vigilance
No. 67, Secretary.

By the time the Vigilantes had thus wiped their boots on the Bill of Rights, they had realized their ambition of hanging someone for the fun of it. Or possibly there was more to it than that. The determination to kill a man whose offense was so small suggests that some of the Committee's leaders had personal reasons for wishing him done away with.

At all events, here are the reported details. On June 10 a dimwit calling himself John Jenkins saw a merchant named Virgin leave his shop without bothering to lock up. Whereupon Jenkins—who should have stuck by his real name of Simpton—walked in to find what was liftable. His choice was what G. W. Ryckman called "a small hand safe."

As nobody bothered to state the amount it contained, nothing more than petty larceny may have been involved. No matter for that, a robber who had scorned the secrecy of darkness was seen, followed and turned over to the committee instead of the police.

The failure to convict Berdue of being Stuart had meanwhile had the effect of doing away with "the people's court"—whose proceedings could be watched by any who could crowd in. Jenkins was given the business in a privacy described in the *Annals of San Francisco*. The passage can be taken as authoritative, as Frank Soule was a member of the 1851 Committee of Vigilance.

"The prisoner was next taken to the rooms of the Vigilance Committee, in Battery street near the corner of Pine street. About ten o'clock the same night, a signal was given on the Bell of the Monumental Engine Company; and shortly after about eighty members of the committee hurried to the appointed place, and on giving the secret password were admitted. Meanwhile knots of people, some of whom knew and all suspected what was going on, gathered about the premises and impatiently waited the progress of events. For two long hours the committee were closely occupied in examining evidence; and soon they had no reason to doubt the prisoner's guilt—though this he denied to the last."

Perhaps he was justified in doing so, in view of the report of his arraignment left by one of his combination jurors and judges. With reference to Jenkins, an 1851 Committee member called James D. Farwell wrote, "I don't know that we allowed him counsel . . . but we produced witnesses and proved satisfactorily that he stole the safe."

What witnesses, and with what credentials? Nobody but the gang ever knew. The only known fact was that early in the morning of June 11, there was a noise noticed by the *Annals:* "At midnight the bell of the California Engine House was tolled, as sentence of death by hanging was passed upon the wretched man."

It was never pretended even by the Vigilantes that Jenkins had committed any crime of violence. Possibly strolling off with no more than small change—and in all likelihood doing no worse than that, in as much as his accusers never named the sum he had taken—he was rushed into the Beyond by men who couldn't wait for another dawn.

Their hurry was commended by Bancroft, who made a fine distinction between lynching, as wrongly practiced by dirty-shirt miners of the gold camps, and ah so correctly carried out by San Francisco's white-collar class. "It was one thing for a half drunken rabble to take the life of a fellow-man," this shitepoke of rank opined, "but quite another for staid, church-going men of business to do it."

Jenkins didn't get any real advantage out of having upper class, religious hangmen. The record states that he, a Church of Englander, was allowed the attendance of a parson. Nice. But in his memoir G. W. Ryckman, as head of the Vigilantes on that particular occasion, told how the staid, church goers broke into the room where last devotions were being held for a doomed man, and cut the minister's holy water off.

After recalling that the Reverend Dr. Mines had been called as wrangler for the soul of Jenkins, Ryckman said of this divine, "He made a very long prayer, and consumed a great deal of time, and we began to get impatient, thinking the Police might rally and attempt a rescue, and knowing that Broderick was out with all his strength and very much opposed to us. I went up to him and said, 'Mr. Mines, you have taken about three quarters of an hour, and I want you to bring this prayer business to a rapid close. I am going to hang this man in half an hour.'"

So the victim was soon hoisted, and as many as could do it showed their satisfaction by putting hand to rope. Drawn to the site by the uproar, Ned was the wry observer of a crime which he reported in the San Francisco *Post* more than a quarter of a century later.

"I was an eye witness to a scene on the plaza in 1851—the night that Jenkins was hung for stealing a small coin safe from Long

Wharf . . . After the man had been strangled to death and while the crowd was still holding on to the rope, one of them, a Dutchman, turned to one of the fellows and said, 'Vell, vot did he do?' "

The boast of the Vigilantes of 1851 was that they would cleanse the city of its innumerable murderers. In point of fact they failed to find a single one so much as accused of taking life in San Francisco.

In the first four and a half months of their purge, the best they could be credited with accomplishing was to murder one petty and not very bright thief. A month later they hoisted a man who had committed a capital crime—but not in their city. In a word, they caught and stretched the real James Stuart. But if he had been turned over to law officers in other parts of the state, Stuart would have been served the same way, especially in Marysville, where he had killed a sheriff.

Although a feckless crime, the lynching of Stuart was the Committee's high point. Its low was attained six weeks later.

On August 20 the Vigilantes seized, secretly tried, and condemned to death a pair named Samuel Whittaker and Robert McKenzie. Unlike Jenkins and Stuart, no details of any crime lodged to their accounts are now known. The most that can be said is what was reported of them in the *Annals*. In that volume they were "charged with the various torts of burglary, robbery and arson."

As has been pointed out, arson is a felony from which burglars and robbers cannot profit—unless, of course, they are paid for it by those who do find blazes worth while. And that someone didn't wish McKenzie and Whittaker to talk can fairly be inferred from the extreme lengths to which the Vigilantes went, in order to whisk the two away from the sound waves audible to the living.

They were put to shifts, because they had for some reason postponed the hanging until August 21. Taking the Vigilantes by surprise, Sheriff Hays raided their club house and jailed the kidnapped men, pending an investigation of the offenses of which they were said to have been guilty.

The first problem of the Committee was to get rid of the Law and Order volunteers, posted to protect Whittaker and McKenzie against attempted seizure. Evidently on duty at the time, Harvy Brown told how this was accomplished.

"About eight o'clock Jack Hayes [sic] the Sheriff came up there and said the guard was to be discharged; that he had seen the Vigilance Committee men, and they had assured him on their honor that Whittaker and McKenzie should not be molested . . . I told Colonel Hayes, 'They will deceive you, Sir!' . . . He insisted they were gentlemen and would keep faith with him."

The next move was reported by James D. Farwell. Telling of a Sabbath coup pulled by what Bancroft termed "staid, religious" fogies, Farwell said, "Our men were smuggled in [the jail] as pretext of attending the . . . services" held for the prisoners.

With an armed cadre inside, the Vigilantes were set to do what they'd promised Jack Coffee Hays they wouldn't. The manner in which their two wanted men were snatched and scragged with break-neck speed was described with gusto in the *Annals:*

"About half past two o'clock, on the afternoon of Sunday, the 24th of August, an armed party consisting of thirty-six members of the Vigilance Committee, forcibly broke into the jail, at a time when the Reverend Mr. Williams happened to be engaged at devotional exercizes with the prisoners, among whom were Whittaker and McKenzie. The slight defense of the jailers and guards was of no avail. The persons named were seized and hurried to and placed within a coach, that had been kept in readiness a few steps from the prison. The carriage instantly was driven off . . . and nearly at the same moment the ominous bell of the Monumental Engine Company rapidly and loudly tolled for the immediate assemblage of the committee and the knell itself of the doomed. The whole population leaped with excitement at the sound; and immense crowds from the remotest quarters hurried to Battery street. There blocks with the necessary tackle had been hastily fastened to two beams which projected over the windows of the great hall of the committee. Within seventeen minutes after the arrival of the prisoners, they were both dangling by the necks from these beams."

Among the watchers was Dr. Henry M. Gray. In *Judges and*

Criminals he sketched the temper of the executioners, and those they entertained, as follows:

"The curses, jeers and imprecations which were heard on every side, the loud laugh and the obscene joke which was cracked in the crowd below; with the evident glee and humor with which the members of the Committee carried out their bloody purpose, will long remain vivid in the minds of those who witnessed those occurrences of blood, those violations of law, those violent outbursts of popular passion."

With the strangling of McKenzie and Whittaker, the lynchings of the 1851 Committee ended. The victims totaled four. The Vigilantes would have bettered that record, but they were foiled several times, when attempting to grab prisoners, as they were convoyed from jail to court or vice versa. Sometimes their defeat was owing to large posses, while at others they were backed down by units of the National Guard.

They had been beaten, too, in a try to force Ned off the bench. On July 22 they had passed a resolution to have him investigated as "an accomplice in the robbery of the Chester County bank." As McGowan was able to wave clearance papers under the noses of any who cared to search his record, nothing came of that heckle.

Two months later the Vigilantes pulled in horns which had been blunted by the National Guard, on the one hand, and mollified by improved mercantile conditions, on the other. September of 1851 ushered in a period of steady prosperity—a period marked by no city-devastating fires, by the way—which lasted nearly three years.

What with this and that, the Committee announced on September 16 that it had broken the back of community sin and was turning the conduct of affairs back to the local authorities. But before the Vigilantes of 1851 are dismissed, their tally of achievements should be examined, to the extent that they can be.

Only the ringleaders, on this point silent, could tell how much they had accomplished on their individual behalves. What they had wrought in the way of reform could be held comic, if they hadn't murdered men, in the course of showing themselves up.

If they could be taken seriously, it could be said of them that they had proved that San Francisco was less in need of a scrubbing than any city in America's history. In seven months of searching, and with a large body of informers at their beck, the Vigilantes had been able to locate but three wrongdoers—Stuart was an outsider—dwelling in a largely masculine city of thirty-five thousand. Among the Golden Gaters proper they had found no manslayers; none guilty of felonious assault or armed robbery. When they had stamped out the lives of three men, and one of those the stealer of something about in the class with a piggy bank, they had left crime in such ruins that they could safely pull the Cincinnatus act and retire to lives of honest toil. Or some kind of toil.

The commission merchants went back to purveying "sour flour and soft pork," as their San Francisco critics said of them. Or they put on the market items such as those described in a newspaper later edited by Ned:

"A large quantity of damaged ginger, mixed with sawdust, has been put up in new cases, neatly labeled and sold for the genuine article—as also a large quantity of damaged saleratus—damaged oysters—damaged peaches, stinking butter in genuine firkins, marked with the favorite brand of Hope & Co., bogus yeast powders, with the mark of Preston U. Merrill on them—the peaches were bought at a low figure and put in new boxes made to imitate genuine Chile peaches, as they sell for a higher price; these . . . men have put his brand on their bogus stuff, as also on cream of tartar, which is very scarce and high priced now."

Such were some of the ways in which Vigilante art improved upon the bunglings of nature. If Coleman went in for any of these dodges, he did not long do so in person, after the 1851 Committee of Vigilance went underground in September. Early in 1852 he went East, and wasn't again in San Francisco for four years.

6

THE POLITICS OF A NEW STATE

ALTHOUGH CALIFORNIA DID not achieve statehood until September 9, 1850, the state's Democratic Party held a convention months earlier. There was a hassle over who should represent San Francisco, because factional lines had already been strongly drawn. In one corner was Broderick's team, whose main initial strength was composed of the "Boys" of New York and Philadelphia. Opposed was Gwin's largely Southern following, known to their rivals as the "Rosewater" crew or "the Chivalry."

With Ned in the middle of it, the first test of strength took place at San Francisco County's 1850 Democratic pow wow. While McGowan was fronting for a client in court, some of Gwin's men formed a list of state convention delegates which left him out.

"I felt slighted and waxed warm," Ned recalled. After drawing up a second slate, in which he was careful to include all the leaders of several fringe factions holding the balance of power, McGowan rode their coattails to where he wanted to be. Or as he said, with a bow to John Randolph of Roanoke, "We routed the Rosewater ticket, horse, foot and dragoons."

In California as a whole, though, Gwin remained on top. A man of his wing named John McDougall was elected to succeed Provisional Governor Peter Burnett in 1851. And even though Broderick proved a better kegler than Ned's friend, James Mc-

Dougall, he couldn't outbid the Chivalry for the prize he so
wanted.

As McDougall wished to be a U. S. Senator, too, and as both
knew that neither would have a chance, if they split the Northern
division of their party, James and David agreed to hold a bowling
match, the loser pledged to go down the line for the winner.
It was such a close match that it wasn't decided until Broderick
scored a strike in the final frame. Yet that wasn't good enough
to make him Frémont's successor in the Senate. The Chivalry
and allied Democrats banded to elect John B. Weller.

After losing out in 1851, Broderick couldn't again shoot for
the moon he wanted until 1855. The intervening years he spent
in efforts to build up his wing's strength, in readiness for that
tilt. As McGowan was one of his chief lieutenants—others being
George Wilkes and Frank Tilford—their stories were closely in-
terwoven during this period.

McGowan was particularly useful to Broderick as an advocate
of the "Boys" that David himself didn't have the polish to front for.
Ned, on the other hand, could speak the language of gentlemanly
officials, who were annoyed by the bluff approach of a man with
an alien background. An anecdote of McGowan's both lights up
this point and shows that he went his own way, when he found
that Broderick jibed when he should have luffed.

City Recorder, after Frank Tilford decided to try his luck in
Oregon, was George Baker. Pledged to dignity, he couldn't see
any excuse for the rambunctious ways of Broderick's New York
henchmen. Not a criminal class, but reared in a rough corner of
the world, they were often hauled before Baker for finding fights
in a bottle. And as a rule they were heavily fined until Ned was
asked to plead for them.

A great fact about McGowan was the faithfulness with which
he paid his debts to friend foe, or any one from whom he had
accepted a favor. In return for the lenience asked of Baker with
regard to the "Boys," Ned promised his faction's support at the
next election. By the time it neared, though, Frank Tilford had
returned from Oregon and wanted his old job back. Although

McGowan liked Tilford better, he felt Baker had earned his keep; and he thought others reasoned as he did, until Tilford turned up as the Democratic nominee in the city convention.

"Mr. Broderick had been quietly at work," Ned pointed out. "I was kicking up a fuss about Baker's defeat, and he said to me, 'How is it you're such a friend of Baker's?' I replied, 'You as much as anything else, have made me his friend, sending me to him to have your friends relieved from fines, etc.' He gave me one of his usual frowns, and that ended the conversation."

But Ned was sore at the double-cross. As a member of the convention which had nominated Tilford, he couldn't openly support Baker; but he told him to run as an independent, and have placards printed which read VOTE FOR JUDGE BAKER FOR RECORDER—A TERROR TO THE SHOULDER STRIKERS. The press picked up a slogan which charmed everybody but Broderick's crew, with the consequence that Baker landslid over both the Democratic and Whig candidates.

"Baker never betrayed me," McGowan stated, "as it would have been considered treason in me against the party. At the next election Mr. Broderick made no opposition to his being placed on the Democratic ticket."

As the bitterness marking city elections had much to do with the explosion of 1856, a review of the in-fighting between Democrats and two rival parties belongs in the story. While all three groups were guilty of rough stuff and overreaching, some of the feuding sprang from the clumsy wording of election laws in a town which hadn't yet found its political feet.

A new charter, scrambled together in 1851, called for the election of municipal officers at the time of its adoption in April. Yet it went on to specify that in succeeding years the city's authorities would be chosen on the same day as California's general elections, held in September. In the absence of clarification, there was doubt as to whether the men chosen in April were entitled to serve for eighteen months or only six. The Whigs, who swept the election, held that new municipal balloting wouldn't be in order until September of 1852. They therefore stayed away from the polls, set up in September of 1851 by the Democrats. As these won that time, naturally, San Francisco had two sets of officers, both convinced that their cause was just.

And the yarn got more snarled than that. When the Democrats brought suit to have the Whigs ousted, the petitioned court took note of the fact that the city code allowed all officers a year of tenure. The ruling therefore was that the Whigs could sit tight until April 1852, at which time the Democrats elected seven months earlier should take over.

Winning a reversal in the Supreme Court, the Democrats managed to install an administration before the close of 1851. But the Whigs, who had really been the victims of loose thinking on the part of the boll weevils who'd drawn up the election code, raised the cry of "fraud!" And fraud there was from that time on, with both parties vying for the championship. Fairness calls for saying, though that there were times when a struggle for supremacy rose above a reliance on deceit. There is nothing snide about rolling up a cannon, to keep unwanted voters away from the polls.

Still the favorite way to serve the right and confound wrongdoers was ballot-box stuffing. This could be done in various ways. Ballots could be added or subtracted, for the benefit of a given slate. Or a ballot box, with a proper balance of wise and foolish votes, could be substituted for the one actually in use at a polling point. Then there was at least one product of mechanical genius.

Something like a computer that's off its feed, this was a box which swallowed the votes cast and coughed up a different set. Promoting the use of this invention was one of the evils put on Ned's score card by the Vigilantes; but he pointed out that, however ingenious, the gadget was no go.

In commenting on it, he affirmed that insofar as he knew, its only tour of duty took place in the isolated county precinct of Half Moon Bay. On that occasion the "patent back action" box had worked up so much enthusiasm for the Democratic cause that it had spat out more ballots than there were voters in Half Moon Bay, or dogs to follow them to the polls.

After remarking that the device could not be used wherever

there were tally sheets against which to check the returns, Mc-
Gowan said, "I don't pretend to deny that I afterward knew that
this machine was in existence, but I do deny that I ever used it
or saw it used."

A change of pace from ballot-box fixing took the form of
strong-arm tactics. One party or the other would muster force
enough at a polling place to be able to turn away those suspected
of being of the wrong political faith. It was also done, in primary
elections, by contending wings of the Democrats. As Ned's memoirs
show, this happened in San Francisco's Seventh Ward in 1852.

"The opponents of Governor Bigler, backed by the Customs
House influence, took possession of this ward. I was attending to
my own election in the Fourth Ward. Dr. Mills . . . was on the
inside and saw that our friends could not get near the polls, and
sent word to that effect to his friends on the outside. Mr. Broderick
requested me to take a party and have the polling place cleared.
I drew a lot of $50 pieces out of the bank, and procured a party
. . . and soon cleared a passage, so that our friends could get a
chance to vote."

In the general election Ned lost out in 1852, for the Vigilantes
fielded a candidate for senior associate justice of San Francisco's
Court of Quarter Sessions who drew some Democratic support as
well as solid Whig backing. What happened to his J.P. magis-
tracy, or to his post as Secretary of the County Board of Health,
he didn't note. But if he lost those positions, he didn't long have
occasion to miss them.

Turning the tables on Gwin, Broderick had a man of his, one
John Bigler, elected to follow John McDougall as California's
Governor. When Bigler took over the capitol in 1852, he made
McGowan Treasurer of the State Marine Hospital; and after Moses
Flannagan resigned as State Commissioner of Immigration, Ned
was given that post also. As they should have, for both were
exacting jobs, these patronage awards paid their holder well.

In 1853 McGowan was also San Francisco County Chairman
of the Democratic Party. Yet he was so far from being the political

czar pictured by his enemies, that he often had to outguess, rather than order, the men more or less in league with him.

During his regime the Democrats held their convention in a hall on Commercial Street. "It was," he said of this meeting, "a pretty stormy one and hard to manage, as the 'boy' element and those on the 'see me' lay were prominent in it."

The Boys, on this occasion, tried to give Ned the run around with respect to a candidate they had promised to back. The man was named Haley, and to gain support for him, McGowan had tossed largesse into the kitties of political clubs maintained by shoulder strikers.

When balloting began, the arrangement was for white tickets to represent votes for Haley, and green ones for a rival candidate called Allen. Having smelled betrayal, though, Ned had thrown one more ingredient into the pot. At his request, theatrical manager Tom Maguire had printed and smuggled into the hall certain green tickets imprinted with the letters H-a-l-e-y.

There were eighty votes. Counting the green cards, as they were dropped into the box, Allen's backers chuckled, but prematurely. The official count revealed that forty-one people had voted for Haley. The Boys never knew who had put one over on them, but they were, as Ned philosophized, "beaten at their own game."

There were also physical hazards in being a San Francisco political chief. The first time Ned met a later to be dealt with man called James Casey, he was threatened with assault because of having wrought the defeat of a man Casey favored. Armed and unconcerned, McGowan waved a much younger chap aside and told him that if he wished a brawl, he could produce a fellow who would be glad to serve Casey what he liked. Ned didn't name the combatant he had in mind, but among his henchmen were two doughty ones who figure in this chronicle.

Of these one was Billy Mulligan, a Boy who had somehow served as a Texas Ranger under Hays in the Mexican War. A man of slight build he had buzz-saw qualities which men twice his size had learned to dodge, and that he would have gone into action at a word from McGowan was proved by a time he had done so without being urged.

"On the night of July 4, 1853, Jim Campbell tried to insult Mr. Broderick and myself at the Union Hotel." Having noted that Campbell was reckoned a hard customer, McGowan went on to say that at this juncture Billy Mulligan had blown in—dressed to the nines, in as much as he was bound for the firemen's ball. Finding what was afoot Billy took his coat and gloves off, caught the hands of a much larger man, butted him into polite silence, washed the blood off, donned his best bib again and marched to the party in good order.

Also in Ned's tail was the storied Joe Stokes. Not bred to pugnacity, this son of an Albany, New York, minister had wound up with rations of it for two.

According to McGowan, Joe's good nature and politeness led the Boys to cuff him around, until Stokes got tired of it and let daylight through a couple of tough carcasses. Thereafter, in Ned's words, "the boot was on the other foot." If there was any shoving, Joe did it; and he would do anything to oblige Ned, who had untangled Stokes from a manslaughter rap.

A glimpse of Joe in action can be caught by reviewing San Francisco's city election of 1854. To improve his chances of being chosen again, the incumbent Mayor Garrison brought artillery to bear on the First Ward's voting problems. When, at the mayor's suggestion, Democrats wheeled a loaded cannon up to the polls, it was Joe Stokes who stood at the fieldpiece's breech, holding a lighted fuse.

But if politics were rugged in San Francisco, nothing that took place there could match the Democratic State Convention of the same immemorial year. Of the electoral none such, staged by the Broderick and Gwin factions in 1854, Ned later vowed that even Tammany—when huge New York gangs were warring for control of that hall—had never roofed such a show. By the time he wrote that, he had watched Tammany factions go to it. As for California's Short and Long Hair Convention—so known because of the different coiffeurs of Northern and Southern Democrats—

McGowan could speak with authority, as he was one of the two chairmen who simultaneously presided over it.

After some shopping around, by other California legislatures, the one which convened in 1854 had voted to make Sacramento the state's permanent capital. Giving it a political housewarming, so to speak, State Democratic Chairman Broderick had picked the city as a convention site, and rented the Baptist church of a town which didn't then have accommodations of a more usual sort. Although Broderick himself naturally presided at the onset of the meeting which took place there, the rules called for installing a special convention chairman. As the wing that installed one of its men could go far toward directing procedures, it followed that all of long hair and short were alike determined to take this key trick.

"Each section met," Ned recalled, "without fraternizing or consulting what the plan of proceedings would be on the morrow; and every member and their friends were armed to the teeth, anticipating bloody work when they assembled to organize the conventions. The presidency of our wing of the party went a-begging . . . Judge Wells and Ben Lippincott both declined. Mr. Broderick, in his dilemma, fell back as usual on me. I informed him I would accept but that the chances were I would be killed, and in that event I wanted him to look after my family."

When tension was at its height, a follower of James McDougall named J. Reuben Maloney suffered an accident. His pistol went off, "shooting," as Ned wrote, "into the floor and wounding him in a tender spot."

Sacramento's Baptist church was never the same again. Thinking the expected war had begun, men who found windows nearer than the doors jumped out of them. As in the case of most stained-glass panes of the nineteenth century, these weren't equipped with sashes. Through them, therefore, leaped stampeded Boys and Rosewatermen.

After quiet of a sort had been restored, it didn't get much encouragement from Broderick. When James O'Meara, of Gwin's faction, nominated ex-Governor John McDougall as convention chairman, David ignored the motion, though recognizing that of a fellow who next proposed Ned. So the pot started boiling all over again, and when the steam thinned a little, Chairmen McGowan and McDougall were both seen advancing to the rostrum.

Nervous as he admittedly was about accepting this split honor, Ned subsequently learned that Broderick was on a much hotter spot. "My chances for life, if the 'ball did open,' were ten to one better than his, for General Estell and several others told me afterwards that Broderick was surrounded by a score of pistols, all ready, and that he [Estell], had one inside of his coat, cocked and with his hand on it, pointing at Mr. Broderick's stomach."

But as Ned explained, bullets were not all he feared on that July day in Sacramento. Somebody passed cocktails up to the rostrum, but as neither chairman knew the name or the intention of the mixer, they "both looked wistfully at the drinks but neither dared to touch them, for fear of being dosed." Yet finally McGowan's ever-ready thirst led him to pour part of each cocktail into the other. "It's a long time between drinks," he quoted, while handing a glass to his rival, "and if there has been any dosing of the liquor, we are both in for it."

Unable to unite, the divisions of what was also known as the Two-Headed Convention met in separate halls, where each nominated its own slate. Despite the schism, the Democrats elected the state's congressmen in 1854, but only because the two choices of the Broderick faction decided not to run. The weight of the party was thus fully put behind James W. Denver, for whom Colorado's metropolis is called, and a man whose name Bancroft gives as Philip T. Herbert. It is true that he signed communications "Phil." But he did that rather than to own that he had been christened Philemon, the last two syllables pronounced like the citrus fruit spelled the same way.

As to Denver, material supplied by McGowan to Oscar T. Shuck was to turn up in *The American Dictionary of Biography*. Phil Herbert was to become a co-adventurer and comrade in arms in many far-away places. In 1854, though, McGowan was more concerned with a product of Ned Buntline's bizarre genius.

The political party started by the man Ned had bounced from

the tap room of Guy's Philadelphia house, six years earlier, had branched out of New York and flourished for a time on a national scale. This the American Party had been able to do because for a few years, marked by the collapse of the Whigs, it offered the only out for those who didn't wish to be Democrats.

It was as missing of principles as Buntline himself; but its leaders covered that absence by taking the stand that their beliefs were too lofty for public discussion. Those who joined were supposed to take the wisdom of the founding spirits on faith; and when queried as to what it was all about, to seem wise by professing an ignorance that was real. From this practice sprang the habit of calling members of the American Party "Know-Nothings."

By 1854, the American Party had reached its peak and was giving way to Republicanism in the East; but while fading there, it took hold in California, where it hadn't before been active. It was especially strong in San Francisco, as Ned pointed out in a passage which shows how Buntline's disciples bore themselves:

"In 1854 the Knownothing party carried the city of San Francisco. A paid organizer for this secret order was sent to California from the East who inaugurated 'wigwams' in every county in the state. The 'dark lantern' party merged in it all of the Whig party and many Southern democrats and a few from non-slave holding states. They held their meetings in secret, and to be admitted to their lodges you had to be initiated and put in possession of their grips, signs and passwords. It was a kind of Freemasonry; they could distinguish each other by their signs; and when any brother was in distress or wanted help politically, he could bring members within call by bellowing at the top of his voice, "ki-eye, ki-eye! . . . I remember the first time I heard this ki-eye-ing call was in the Fourth Ward on the day of the election, and they came running to the scene faster and more numerous than rats from a burning slaughter house."

The Vigilantes were in general Know-Nothings, first because they could no longer be Whigs, and secondly because the secret ways of the American Party appealed to men who had enjoyed being referred to by numbers instead of names in 1851. But changing parties had not altered either the suspicion with which they viewed Democrats or the complacence with which they smiled upon their own crookedness.

Carrying on with his discussion of the wigwam braves, McGowan wrote, "The whole of the Knownothing ticket was elected by a large majority, except three or four Aldermen . . . And it carried through the Hon. Baillie Peyton for City Attorney—who was armed with a party of followers all the morning of the election, crying out 'fraud and ballot box stuffing,' and tried to take possession of several of the polling places where his party was in the minority and put in by force his men as watchers, and some of whom did not reside in the ward."

After the election of 1854, the claim of the Know-Nothings that all the polls were in tricky hands wasn't heard for a while; but the resourceful Broderick gave them a new cause for screaming. What he rammed through the Legislature was a bill moving San Francisco's election of 1855 from September back to May. The effect of this stroke was to shorten the terms of incumbent Know-Nothings by four months, while giving Democrats a chance to regain lost offices that much sooner.

Yet the man who swung that club couldn't make his second bid for the Senate stick. Illegally elected in 1849, and actually serving only five instead of six years, Senator Gwin had to pay for jumping the gun by putting his title on the line in 1855. If Broderick's reach for it turned out to be short, neither did Gwin find the legislative backing needed for re-election. Then as no third contender was able to break the stalemate, nobody was chosen; and for the next two years California was represented in the upper case of Congress by only Senator Weller.

Broderick's switchback of San Francisco's election worked out pretty well for his party there, though. The Democrats regained quite a few offices in a city where the Know-Nothings were beginning to lose heart, because of learning that their party was on its way to the junk yard nationally.

As the provinces hadn't yet got the message, the American Party had grown in strength throughout the state as a whole.

Aided by non-Broderick Democrats, the Know-Nothings scored a
Pacific side victory in a season which saw the wigwams folding in
the rest of the country.

Elected governor in 1855 was J. Neely Johnson. Along with
Ned's re-elected friend, Hugh Murray, a former Texas Ranger
named David Smith Terry was chosen as a justice of California's
Supreme Court.

As for McGowan, the election of a Know-Nothing meant the
end of the patronage he had enjoyed. Ironically, there was an effort
on the part of some of San Francisco's leading merchants to have
him kept on as Commissioner of Immigration. For if they hadn't
liked the way he had operated as a justice of the peace, they did
approve of the honest and efficient way in which he had handled
a post of importance to the business community.

A representative of William T. Coleman & Co. among them,
they petitioned Governor-elect Johnson to keep in office a man
who gave his reason for saying he would not have accepted, had
his well wishers been successful. "I am one," Ned declared, "who
believes that to the victor belongs the spoils."

Out as Treasurer of the State Marine Hospital at the same
time, McGowan was entirely off the public payroll. Nor, as 1855
yielded to the, for him, fateful year of 1856, was he an official of
any sort of California's Democratic Party.

7

A CITY AND SOME PRIVATE LIVES

WITHIN FIVE YEARS of Ned's landing there, San Francisco had changed from a disorganized encampment of 25,000 people to a well-ordered city with twice that population. Cart tracks, winding to dodge the worst sink holes had been replaced by regularly laid-out streets. Planked over where not paved with cobblestones, these were not seasonally dread seas of goulash.

The tents, shacks, and packing boxes which had served alike as residences and places of business had been supplanted by an array of structures comparable to those found in any city in the land. Any city too new to have developed slums, that is.

The town was "particularly improved," to quote the *Annals*, "by the erection of a large number of elegant and substantial fire-proof brick and stone buildings . . . Some of the more finely finished edifices have either the whole front or the lower story formed of Chinese granite; while the fronts of all the larger buildings, constructed of brick, are covered with a fine gray-colored mastic which gives them all the appearance of being made of stone . . . The later fire-proof buildings, like the earlier ones, are all provided with exterior window-shutters and doors of thick wrought-iron."

At night coal gas was burned, indoors and by the city's street lighting system. On tap for any purpose was an ample supply of pure and palatable water. This, together with an extensive chain of volunteer fire companies, kept the occasional fire that broke out from sweeping the community.

San Francisco had a horse-drawn public transportation system. To a limited extent, besides, it had a public communications system. Telegraphic wires connected San Francisco with Sacramento and some other towns, and from Telegraph Hill word of the nearing of inbound vessels was flashed to the city at the foot of that eminence.

Yet all things considered, the greatest change since the day of the Forty-niners was one noted by Ned in verse. Although he wrote the lines a little later, the condition he celebrated had come to stay by the end of 1854.

> What spreads itself upon the walk
> And makes the dandies stare and gawk,
> And forms a theme for public talk?
> > The hoop.

> What fills the car and omnibus
> And makes the passengers growl and cuss?
> What always makes a mighty fuss?
> > The hoop.

> What barks a fellow's shins and feet
> And shoves him out into the street;
> What, for a broom, cannot be beat?
> > The hoop.

> What knocks the children in the head
> And makes them be picked up for dead?
> Why 'tis as I before have said,
> > The hoop.

> What guards the women 'gainst the men,
> And forms a kind of little pen?
> What saves them, time and time again?
> > The hoop.

What flutters in the summer breeze
Like petticoats hung on the trees—
Goes through a crowd like knife through cheese?

                    The hoop.

In fine what is the greatest rage
Upon life's variegated stage
In this red petticoated age?

                    The hoop.

Complete with wives inside them, the hoops had rolled into a bachelor land, altering the Argonaut age past any power of man to restore it. The swagger town where everybody gambled, everybody sopped it up and everybody waltzed with tarts in public was one with the Erech of Gilgamesh and the Sparta of Menelaus.

Now only some did those things, and they formed not the core of society, as of old, but operated on its fringes. Looking down on them were not only the hoop wearers but mates of theirs who had reverted to puritanism with the passing of San Francisco's shaggy boyhood. In secret they might still do the things they officially frowned upon, especially when it came to keeping private whores. Yet in being covert about it, they felt that they were morally superior to those who had so little sense of grace as to be open as to actions decried from the pulpit.

For religion, as well as the hoop, was now entrenched in the city; and in churches stemming from the puritan tradition there was the usual chat about sins of the flesh—of which hanging a man for pleasure or profit was probably not one that was dwelt upon. The Vigilantes were all in the pews, though, because of a curious fact about wealth in America. Especially when villainously come by, it makes for some church as inevitably as the deer turns up at the salt lick.

Aware of this, Ned said it neatly in a poem he called *The Age of Gas*. In part (and naming Wall Street's pioneer wolf in line four), the verses ran:

Look at our Bourse, a sort of course, where worthless fancy
    stock is
Spurred to a rise by well feigned lies by Satan's nimble
    jockeys;
When these "make play" who's in the way, they care not jot
    nor tittle,
They'd rob and maul the Apostle Paul as soon as Jacob
    Little.

Turn from the street where tricksters meet, to one of
    Fashion's churches,
Where mild as milk, a man in silk, the hearts of sinners
    searches;
See how they doze, in well dressed rows—broad cloth and
    velvet collar—
In dreams they nod and mutter "God," but mean the Almighty
    dollar.

Now the religious bents—Protestant—of the Vigilantes were
doubly involved in their story and Ned's because of a not yet
mentioned fact about the Know-Nothings. Although that point
wasn't understood by the Bowery Boys whom Buntline had talked
into pulling the Astor Place Riot, the American Party was not only
anti-Catholic but anti-Irish. Buntline had borrowed these tenets
—about the only ones the Know-Nothings had—from the more
frankly named Native American Party.

Also organized in New York, and a few years before the plain
American Party, the Native Americans had viewed with alarm the
first great nineteenth-century wave of immigration. This was an
Irish comber, fish eaters on Friday down to the smallest, freckle
faced drop of it. Not being able to exclude these, the Native
Americans were for keeping them from being enfranchised; and
most especially from holding office. Their platform, indeed, consisted of a desire to keep the reins of government in the hands of
Protestants hailing from the British Isles.

As the big Northern cities had not then been hit by the im-

migration waves from other nations, the Irish were the only enemies singled out by the Know-Nothings, when they rose from the
cinders of the Native Americans. And in a day when America's
Protestant churches were militantly anti-Catholic, the Irish were
identified with a religion which most in the United States were
taught to regard with horror.

What the Vigilantes did in 1856 can only be understood via the
realization that they came by their hatred of Celts and the Papacy
through two passion-stirring channels. They talked it up in their
political wigwams themselves, and they had it thrown at them in
the name of God in their sacred lodges.

From the pulpit, too, the Vigilantes received Heaven's authority to despise those who led lives which differed in certain aspects
from their own. That was an important consideration in Ned's
case, for when billing him as a monster, his enemies drew upon
his private as well as his public life. Nor did they overlook sources
which included his stolen personal correspondence.

Because they had committed that act of indecency, it is possible
to learn some of the things laid to an urbane man's discredit by
prudish rascals. One of the letters preserved among the papers of
the San Francisco Committee of Vigilance of 1856 indicates that
there had been mutterings against Ned's way of life, as well as his
supposed political practices, as early as 1853.

Its writer was Judge Alexander Wells of San Jose. McGowan
once remarked of him that he was "a man of genius and a pleasing
orator." He was also a man of mirth and delight in good living.
After decrying Ned's failure to make a promised visit, Wells proceeded:

"And now, you rusty broken down hack-horse, spavined and
wind-galled politician—you infernal old schemer—you dreadful
and to be dreaded shoulder striker—you stuffer of ballot boxes—
you who reside at a French boarding-house of equivocal character
—you luxurious dog who lives on the fat of the land, and never
said gruel once—you ex-member of the judiciary department who
exercized admiralty jurisdiction—I say unto you 'roll your bones.'"

The dubious boardinghouse was kept by a Madame Dubrecourt,

of Pike Street. Ned also lived at the Union Hotel; and before Wilkes and Broderick quarreled over a judgeship which George wanted and David wished to bestow on somebody else, those two and McGowan had adjoining rooms in the home of Tom Maguire.

One of the worst things Ned did, to go by puritan standards, was to associate with show people; and not only male entrepreneurs but female performers. Among the letters pilfered from McGowan, and turned over to Bancroft, was one from the talented Matilda Heron. One of the great American actresses of the nineteenth century, she wrote some of the dramas in which she starred, as well as translating several French plays.

Of a well-to-do Philadelphia family, she had gone on the stage against the wishes of her guardian elder brother. Ned knew other Herons, of whom one is named in his reminiscences; and there is every reason to believe that he had been asked to look after her, when she arrived in San Francisco under circumstances described in the *Annals:*

"This young lady had left Philadelphia for San Francisco in company with Mr. George Lewis, her agent . . . who having died on the route, she accordingly landed unknowing and unknown. Several gentlemen, however, having heard of her coming . . . actively interested themselves in her behalf."

McGowan was undoubtedly one of these men, and as a friend of theatre-running Tom Maguire, he was just the chap to make satisfactory professional arrangements for a young woman who at that time was a comparative nobody of twenty-three. The enthusiasm she found in San Francisco gave her the confidence she needed in order to shine in larger spheres. Recognizing her Golden Gate days as the turning point of her career, she wrote Ned a letter which gave him his full meed of credit for an assist. Datelined Paris, March 3, 1855, it evidently followed a note in which she had mentioned an illness of some nature.

Edward McGowan, Esqu.

My dear friend,

. . . My eyes are still very weak, indeed, and pain me much, or I would write you a longer letter . . . But it will not require many words to assure you of all the grateful memories I entertain of you; I often close my eyes and think I see you, every night before the rise of the curtain, walking down the aisle of the parquet of the Metropolitan Theatre, a bill in your hand, and looking so cheerfully at everybody near you, as though you would say, 'Well, have you come to see my daughter play tonight?' Oh, those happy old times . . . Have you had any new pets since I left? I hope the artists who have followed me have not eclipsed me from your heart. It would give me pain to think so, for neither fate nor circumstances could change my thoughts of you.

I am studying very hard in the sweet hope to be, some day, worthy of the good name which San Francisco has already crowned me with; it will give me great pleasure to return to you all once more and show you the good use I have made of my time; and then, judge, we will have a good old chat about the old times. Will we not? Until then may God be with you, and believe me ever your grateful friend,

Matilda Heron

Using such terms as "Lothario," Bancroft presented this ingenuous letter as proof that McGowan had an affair with, of all things, a person of the stage. While Ned would doubtless have shacked up like a shot with an attractive actress, under conditions satisfactory to both, no such relationship is to be inferred from words which rather make it plain that he was acting as Miss Heron's guardian.

She didn't stay Miss Heron. In 1854 Matilda married Henry H. Byrne, District Attorney of San Francisco. For years a close friend of McGowan's this fellow turned on him in crisis, to win favor with the Vigilantes. But Matilda found out he wasn't a man to tie to long before Ned did. She broke with Byrne permanently at the end of four months, and shortly thereafter sailed for Europe.

About the time McGowan got the quoted letter from her, he was having a liaison with a French courtesan named Fanny Perrier. The story of this amour is one for Boccaccio. It is, besides, one that nobody but Ned would have been generous enough to share with coming generations, from whom he could easily have withheld its details.

After first having the premises redecorated to suit her tastes, McGowan installed his Parisienne in a cottage he owned on Pike Street. The "charming Fanny," as he called her, must have been all of that, for she next persuaded Ned to deed her the property.

What he didn't know, however, was that La Perrier was one of a string of courtesans in the keep of a German named Alfred Godeffroy. A financier of sorts, Alfred banked for women whose frailties included an inability to hold on to their considerable revenues. By advancing them money, when needed, Godeffroy first got control of their purse strings, and next of their persons.

So when McGowan turned his redone bungalow over to Fanny, she passed it to the pimp who owned her. Finding this thief on what had been his premises, Ned took a shot at him. It was not meant to kill, or McGowan would have fired his revolver, instead of one of the two derringers he always also carried. Snapped at too great a range for this type of weapon, it earned its target what Ned called "cast iron posterior notoriety." Godeffroy won this spur by making such speed in the same direction taken by the bullet that it flattened out, instead of burrowing, when it reached Alfred's other fanny.

But as Godeffroy still had the cottage, the rest of the joke was on Ned. Where most would have grouched, he saw that it was funny, and joined in the laugh raised by the city's non-puritan residents. As a faithful payer of all debts, though, McGowan did not overlook the one he owed Madame Perrier.

Learning that she was by way of housewarming a place that had once been his, he conferred with an aforementioned retainer named Stokes. This obliging lad agreed to plant Ned's contribution to the warming—a petard calculated to disturb rather than harm—where it would do the most good.

"It appears," as McGowan stuck his tongue in his cheek to write, "that Madame 'Fanny,' who occupied a bijou of a cottage on Pike Street, having had her place renovated and her old furniture removed, proposed to give her distinguished friends a good time . . . At the instigation of some rejected lover, or other, no doubt, one of the 'boys' by the name of Joe Stokes put some loose powder in a bag and placed it on the stoop of her house. To this powder was attached a slow match. Before it ignited, however, one of the French servants saw something burning on the porch and stooped to pick it up. The moment he touched it the powder burst and without doing the man further injury than a severe fright and scorching from the powder, blew him over the fence."

La Perrier never had the least doubt as to who had sparked the explosion. For on the strength of eyewitness accounts, Ned was able to report that she fluttered about, screaming, "Oh, *mon dieu, mon dieu! Le juge, le juge!*"

Because of the injury to a person, where only a blown-in door had been foreseen, there was a to do which led to the departure of both the charming Fanny and loyal Joe. Seemingly because he didn't wish her to be quizzed in court re the shuffled cottage deed, Godeffroy sent Madame Perrier back to Paris. And to keep Joe from being exposed to any legal backlash, Ned paid his way to Nicaragua, where William Walker was in need of filibuster reinforcements.

Judge McGowan escaped without any scratch that he could detect at the time. Yet he had scandalized the merchant climbers who viewed themselves as the city's elect. Proof that the episode had been stored up against him lies in a growl later vented by one of the Vigilante newspapers. This classed Ned with Guy Fawkes by pointing out his part in "the infamous Gunpowder Plot."

If the Pike Street cottage business shows McGowan as the footloose bachelor he in effect was while in San Francisco, he had not ceased to take an interest in his family. In 1853 James McDougall had gone to Washington as a House Representative of California. Before being replaced by James Denver or Phil Herbert two years later, McDougall had secured an appointment to the United States Military Academy for Ned's oldest son, James A. McGowan.

Ned also continued to send monthly drafts to his wife. As long as it was possible to do so he used the services of a man whose life is now due for examination.

Already noticed, McGowan's banker was a native of George-town, in the District of Columbia, named James King. As it chanced that in this then small community there dwelt several other James Kings, he had plucked from his family tree the dis-tinguishing fact that his father had a name that the sires of the others didn't. Hitching this to the stern of his given and family handles, he came up with the combination James King of William.

After he reached San Francisco in 1849, King of William was an independent banker for five years. Because of having invested too much money in a sluiceway Ned referred to as "the Tuolumne ditch," James had to shut up shop in 1854. He was then invited by Isaiah C. Woods, head of the express house called Adams & Company, to take charge of the banking branch of that firm. The reported arrangement was for Adams to take over King's accounts —McGowan had stuck with him, among others—and to pay him $1000 per month.

King stayed with Adams & Company until February of 1855. When the banking firm of Page, Bacon & Co. celebrated Washing-ton's Birthday by suspending service, Adams went into receivership under circumstances pictured by James O'Meara. Author of *Broderick and Gwin* and *The Vigilance Committee of 1856,* O'Meara was the man who had nominated Governor John McDougall as Ned's rival chairman of the Short and Long Hair Convention.

"Mr. King continued with Adams & Co., as manager of the bank, until the failure of the company. The bank had failed one afternoon. Up to noon that day King had received deposits. It was known to other banking houses in the city that the bank would be obliged to close as it did. The word got out and some withdrew their deposits, notwithstanding Mr. King's assurance that the bank was solvent and solid. Others took his word for it, allowed their deposits to remain, and lost all they had in the bank. There was some mysterious handling of the large amount of money known to be in the bank at the time of failure. The parties in charge re-fused to allow Mr. King any part in their transactions as to the disposition of this money—reported to be considerably more than $100,000 in gold coin. He then published a statement reflecting upon the persons in charge. This was responded to by a scathing statement in the Alta [*Alta California*] in which Mr. King was held up to public condemnation as a dishonest man guilty of faithlessness and fraud. The popular sentiment was that the charges were sustained."

What seems to have been true of James King was that he had been an honest and agreeable man, who cracked morally when he went bankrupt. Willing to make underhanded deals then, he turned misanthrope after the crooks he had covered up for didn't cut him in on boodle taking the form of money left with Adams & Company by the depositors King had hoodwinked.

After one more abortive attempt to stay a financier, King moved into a field where his soured disposition could find satisfaction by inflicting wounds on others. In October of 1855, that is to say, he became an editor who had nominated himself as the community fault finder.

Newspaper work was not new to James King of William; he had been trained in fact by the eminent Amos Kendall. What was novel about the San Francisco *Bulletin* was the purpose for which it was launched.

This was not supplied by Messrs. R. H. Sinton and A. A. Selover, the men who had agreed to finance the venture. In short order, as it turned out, King vilified Selover; and when the latter protested in another journal, "of William's" boy threatened to have it out with him on mortal terms. "Mr. Selover is said to carry a knife," he wrote. "We carry a pistol."

King's line was dirt slung in high-flown terms. According to a prominent San Francisco lawyer called Charles T. Botts, James of William made his rag a dirty one, because of the town's newspaper situation.

In a commentary on it published in 1855 by Alexander S. Taylor, this frontier bibliographer pointed out that there were then eight dailies in San Francisco, not counting two printed in German. Noting as much in a court address quoted by the *Herald*, Botts said of King, "He commenced a line of business already crowded to suffocation. It was necessary to call attention to the new paper; it must be startling; else it will not pay; he resolves to cater to the public appetite for slander."

But General James Madison Estell—the cove who had covered Broderick's navel with a pistola at the Short and Long Hair Convention—had something else to say. In a subsequently published speech, made while he was in California's House of Representatives, Estell affirmed that the *Bulletin's* director had been backed by a crew who had told him to go the limit; and that if anybody in consequence got rough with King, they'd string the fellow up. This, as the general added, was the true beginning of the 1856 Vigilance Committee.

As Estell didn't enlarge on his statement, it cannot now be said which was the hen and which the egg. The policy adopted by the publisher might have attracted the notice of a group who saw how they could use the *Bulletin*. On the other hand, as King had himself been a member of the 1851 Committee, the paper might have been the organ of a conspiracy from the outset.

Certainly King of William began reminding his readers of the first Vigilante uprising when his sheet was but a few weeks old. Historically the *Bulletin* did succeed in making the people of the city as a whole receptive to usurpation on the part of the Committee. Assuredly, too, there were hungry politicians among the leaders of the Vigilantes, who won to offices they wouldn't else have had, through their gang's machinations.

The American Party of San Francisco was desperate. Although carrying California in 1855, they knew their set was dead nationally; and they could foresee the collapse of the Know-Nothings in their own state which did soon take place. As the Republican Party hadn't then made itself felt on the Coast, they could see nothing to look forward to but a city dominated by Democrats, world without end. The only hope of a reversal was drastic action. Hailed by both Ned and O'Meara as a knowing man, General Estell said the Vigilantes took that action. All the facts that can now be marshaled indicate that he knew exactly what he was talking about.

The evident strategy was to work the general populace into such a state of mind over things as they were, that they would howl for a Vigilante take-over. By upping its tail and skunking prominent citizens, the *Bulletin* endeared itself to those who weren't well known. In short order it was being read everywhere by people eager to learn what villain in a silk hat James King was going to pillory next.

Study shows that the *Bulletin's* targets were not picked at random. Its favorite one was David C. Broderick. Remembering when he'd studied Cicero's orations in high school, King guessed that the "C." stood for Catiline. The editor was thus posing in a toga as a high-minded patriot, warning his fellow citizens of the traitor who was in some unexplained way planning San Francisco's destruction.

The courts got a regular going over, and the district attorney and the sheriff. As in the case of the 1851 Vigilantes, in short, the scheme was to discredit every regular law-enforcement agency. And in all cases where individuals were hammered at, they were Democrats.

While James King ran it, Ned was never a target for the *Bulletin,* though. McGowan was not then a holder of any patronage, nor was he a party office holder. The only time he made political news at this period was when he had to be restrained from poking the Governor of California in the proboscis.

A Know-Nothing, J. Neely Johnson had undertaken to charge his Democratic predecessor with putting patronage in venal hands. He was on safe ground when he used this old dodge to smear others. When he accused Judge McGowan of holding back fees collected as Commissioner of Immigration, though, Ned celebrated his forty-third birthday in Sacramento, into which he had stormed two days earlier.

According to that town's *Democratic State Journal,* McGowan established a one-man bridgehead in California's Capitol on March 10, 1856. It seems to have taken a corps of bouncers to get him out of the governor's office.

The rest of the fighting was done in California's Senate. The Know-Nothings in it wanted Ned prosecuted for trying to assault the state's chief executive. The Democrats, sure of their man, called for an investigating committee, to see whether or not McGowan had been provoked by a false accusation. He had. The records of the State Controller's office showed that, as Commissioner of Immigration, Ned had kicked in with the handsome sum of $53,786.40.

But in spite of his raid on Sacramento, McGowan had come to feel that his liveliest days were behind him. Moving in a circle where most were a decade or more younger, he had become an amiably regarded landmark. Some of his youthful associates called him Uncle Ned, and he liked that. He thought of himself as an old man; and according to the actuarial figures of the day, he was.

Getting little exercise, he had got out of trim by thirty-five pounds or more. He didn't care as he owed every ounce of it to the best restaurants and bars in town.

For the rest, he went to the theatre and contributed items to the newspapers, usually signed Caliban. As always, he read a great deal, although he certified in *The Age of Gas* that he found much of it the produce of doughheads. The reference to "steam" in the fifth line of the ensuing quotation, by the by, is owing to the fact that it was the form of power that then ran the presses:

The iron age has passed away, when knights with sword and
  cuirass
And spurs of gold the crowd controlled as if it were a
  mere ass.
Knights of the Quill we have though still, with multitudes
  of pages
And Common sense has less defence than serfs in former ages.

Ream upon ream, got up by steam, ridiculous and solemn,
Legions of books, like flocks of rooks, rush forth in solid
  column. . . .
We're bored until, sick of the swill, we wish—although
  'tis wicked,
The press combined had one behind, and ours the foot to
  kick it.

A century before the birth of the beatnik generation, Ned understood that such fellows wore beards, so they wouldn't be confused with their epicene consorts. When the fashion of slacks for women was still in its droopy infancy, he wrote with respect to the existentialists of his day:

> The blessed crew (thank God! they're few), are curiously
> appareled,
> The women folks wear manly cloaks, and garments double
> barreled.
> The other chaps, for hats wear *flaps,* and beards whose growth
> they humor
> Lest in the dark, some girl her spark, should take for
> Sister Bloomer.

Ned himself wore a plug hat, always white. His mustache was beginning to show traces of that shade, too, but he faced aging with the comfortable mind which only those who have made their fortunes can afford. Always carefully groomed, besides, he looked the part of the bon vivant and successful professional man that he was. Yet he didn't at all give the impression of being what he also was: a man with his paunch bulging over the starting line of a wondrous series of adventures.

PART II

THE SAGA
OF A FUGITIVE

8

THE SHOOTING OF JAMES KING

AMONG THE NON-Broderick Democrats of San Francisco was a peppery article from New York called James P. Casey. In view of the fact that he has been dog-faced by California historians who never met him, it is pertinent to see how he was viewed by a chronicler who *had* known him.

Of this cogwheel in Ned's story, James O'Meara wrote: "James P. Casey was a young man of bright, intelligent and rather prepossessing face, neat in his person, inclined to fine clothes, but not flashy or gaudy in his attire . . . He had served as Assistant County Treasurer for two years, handled a large aggregate of money in that capacity and his accounts squared to a cent when he handed over the books to his successor. He was twice Supervisor. His record in that office will compare favorably with that of any who have succeeded him. During his life time in San Francisco he was never accused of crime."

An honest appraiser, O'Meara did not try to whitewash Casey on all counts. "Ballot box stuffing was charged to his credit," the journalist wrote, "also fraudulent counting in elections. Doubtless there was a foundation for each charge. But there were members of the Executive Committee [the directing clique of the 1856 Vigilantes], who had been associated with him in these gross wrongs."

Reaching San Francisco in 1853, James P. had tried to make

book with Broderick on his own terms. When that didn't work, Casey had succeeded in building out of anti-Broderick Democrats a following which swung the balance of power in the city, as of 1854.

Rebuffed by the entrenched leaders of his own party, he decided to show them his value by making book with the opposition. That he succeeded is proved, among other things, by a statement of Ned's re the 1854 balloting:

"In the Sixth [ward] J. P. Casey was the Democratic inspector, and by some mysterious influence, they [the Know-Nothings], were satisfied and did not interfere with this ward, and this heretofore largely Democratic ward gave the American ticket nearly 600 majority."

Not a candidate for County Supervisor at the time, James P. was illegally voted a member of the board by grateful Know-Nothing incumbents. That went against the grain of some Democratic henchmen of his, though. They switched to Broderick; and when Casey strung with the American Party again the following year, five of them laid for a rejected chief who was not himself armed.

As O'Meara described this 1855 fracas, "One ball grazed his forehead on the right side, another the occiput just behind the left ear . . . Casey had been taken by surprise, but the slight creasing of the bullets, abrading the skin and stinging, instantly impelled him to rapid and desperate action. He rushed upon one of his assailants and wrested a knife from his grasp. With this he turned upon Cushing, plunged it in his body just below the lower ribs, and as Cushing was sinking to the ground, he turned the knife, and cut upwards with such power as to cleave the rib the blade struck against. One of the five had become so nerveless at the sight, that he dropped his pistol. Casey leaped and secured it. He shot at Bagley and the ball penetrated his breast. As he fell, Casey likewise secured his pistol. The two others were game but confused and shot wildly. The bullets went through Casey's coat and vest, riddling each in a dozen places, but never touched him."

From a fracas of which he knew nothing until news of it was

making saloon conversation, stemmed the troubles that were to plague Ned McGowan the rest of his life. Destiny worked with a slow fuse here, as it took eight months for the spark to reach the gunpowder.

When the affray took place in September of 1855, Ned was not an associate of Casey; and he might never have been, if John W. Bagley hadn't chose to resent being shot in the thorax. Recovered by November, Bagley challenged James P. to a formal duel and picked McGowan as his "friend."

Meanwhile Broderick had reviewed the electoral returns and decided to come to Casey, if not to Jesus. In other words, he had found that James P. had made the difference between beating the Know-Nothings and at best breaking even with them.

Broderick wanted Casey in his camp, and his chance came when James P. chose as friends a pair named Turner and Quin. Vi Turner—nobody ever said what "Vi" was short for, and perhaps he kept it dark—was one of the younger men of Broderick's inner circle; and that David told him to stop the duel between Casey and Bagley is implicit in a letter preserved among the Vigilance Committee papers.

Signed by Turner and Quin, this note asked Judge McGowan to confer with them for the purpose of settling the duel short of the firing line. Without saying what they were, the message said there were excellent reasons, and that all would be the gainers. As the only gains to the seconds could have been political, the desire to call the shooting off must have been one and the same with a wish to close Democratic ranks.

The duel wasn't fought, so Ned obviously used his good offices as requested. Undoubtedly the shaking of hands was celebrated by drinks all around; and thereafter he was on good terms with one he had previously regarded as a nuisance, if not a downright enemy.

Meanwhile there was a dirty plot to get even with Casey, of which the details weren't known until it was too late to do anything but groan. If Bagley had shown a willingness to meet James P. on even terms, others whom Casey had shot and knifed, after having been set upon in September, had pulled the lowest order of sneak play.

Like Casey, in having come from New York City, they sent to an associate, asking him to produce documents calculated to wreck James P. politically by showing that he had had a penitentiary background. The game would have been one for tumblebugs to back away from, had there been any facts to go on. But when telling the story—after he had lived in New York and had a chance to investigate—Ned branded the charges false.

"Casey and three or four of his former political associates had the bloodiest street fight ever seen in San Francisco; and it was the men he fought with that sent to their chum, Johnny Moore, of New York, a former Californian, and he forwarded the records to the court . . . The papers in question were handed to Frank Soule, then editing the old Chronicle . . . He refused to publish them and placed the document in the office safe to be handed back to the owner . . . James Nesbit—then of the Chronicle and afterwards one of the 'practiced pens' of the Bulletin—took the transcript and gave it to James King of William for publication."

That's one strand of the web in which Ned was to become tangled. Another involved James King and a gambler called Charles Cora.

In November of 1855, or about the time Bagley and Casey were drinking their differences away, Cora gave King a chance to tell what he was really up to by slaying U. S. Deputy Marshal William H. Richardson. It happened too late of a Saturday for the purposes of an afternoon paper, but on Monday, November 19, the *Bulletin* took note of an event then two days old:

"The excitement on Saturday night was immense, and strongly reminded us of the old Vigilance Committee times. We passed through those times and scenes when an incensed and outraged people, having no faith in the corrupt ministers of the law, took the administration of the public justice into their own hands and inflicted merited punishment on the heads of some of the murderers of those days.

"We think there is no necessity now for any such demonstration . . . The Courts we are satisfied will be all right, and we warn the sheriff and the gambler friends of this man Cora, that any attempt at rescuing him . . . will end with more fearful consequences than attended the expulsion of such men from Vicksburg."

That was a currently well-understood reference to wholesale lynching, though the provocation had no San Francisco parallel. What had happened at Vicksburg was that a band of belligerent gamblers, too numerous for a small town's peace officers to handle, had climbed up from dens along the Mississippi and tried to take over the commercial and residential community on the bluff. In quashing this move, and by way of discouraging a second effort, the Vicksburgers had hanged five.

King's assumption was, of course, that Cora was the guilty party. If he knew the true circumstances, he wouldn't have told them, but another journalist did.

As set forth by James O'Meara, the quarrel between Cora and Richardson was a purely personal matter. At a theatre Mrs. Richardson had undertaken to upstage the gambler's common law wife. Sucked into this cat fight, the men had ended by patching things up. Or they had until the peace officer began thinking things over while in his cups.

General Richardson, as O'Meara called him, was a "morose and at times very disagreeable man." The writer went on to point out that nobody wanted any part of the marshal when he was tight; and when he went looking for Cora, on the evening of November 17, he was so swacked that he asked encountered acquaintances if they had seen "Carter." O'Meara had himself met Richardson, the night of the fatal encounter, and had tried to get him to go home.

A mean drunk and an armed one, the marshal finally found the gambler outside a joint called the Blue Wing. Recognizing William's condition, Charles tried appeasement; but was at length pressed against a building by a man with clutched derringers. To quote O'Meara, "Cora had one of two things to do: either to kill Richardson or allow Richardson to kill him."

Shooting in self-defense, the gambler was nonetheless promptly and properly arrested. As homicide had taken place, he was held without bail, pending the next term of the Quarter Sessions Court.

The law had operated well and with speed. Nor would there have been any clamor as to the honesty of official intentions, if James King hadn't pretended to have smelled hanky-panky on the breaths of two Democratic office holders.

"Hang Billy Mulligan," was the caption of a *Bulletin* editorial, run on November 22. "That's the word! If . . . the Sheriff does not remove Billy Mulligan from his present post as Keeper of the County Jail, and Mulligan lets Cora escape, hang Billy Mulligan, and if necessary to get rid of the Sheriff, hang him—hang the Sheriff!"

When it was earliest feasible, Cora was tried on the charge of first degree murder placed to his account by a grand jury. The petit jury, according to O'Meara was by no means a packed affair: "Care had been taken to empanel only good, respectable citizens."

After weighing all the presented facts, though, they were split as to whether Cora was guilty as charged, or had acted in self-defense. On January 17, 1856, King reported as much, with an assist from Shakespeare:

"Hung be the heavens with black! The money of the gamblers and prostitutes [the latter a slam at Cora's unwedded wife], has succeeded . . . The jury cannot agree and are discharged! Will Cora be hung by the officers of the law? No!"

While the gambler was awaiting retrial, King went on with his program of spewing bile in selected directions, while admiring subscribers reveled. To the general run of San Franciscans it seemed that angels had opened a manhole in Heaven and dropped their city a saint.

What they loved about the *Bulletin's* editor was that he was no meek and mild halo sporter. Rather he was the dragon-fighting type, willing to take on the enemies of evil at any time. They knew of this valor from no less a source than the champion himself. "God help my assailant!" he once bragged in print. And on other occasions he taunted those who didn't like his policies for lacking guts enough to shoot it out with him.

Precisely because there were plenty of Golden Gaters who *were* ready to draw and fire, when crowded, King's words were taken at their face value. To citizens of a town with a dueling tradition, it seemed that anybody who could continue to invite attack must be a very tough hombre indeed.

Probably that conviction had made several think better of challenging him. Certainly he enjoyed a surprisingly long immunity from hot lead in a city where it was reasonably easy to find some. For it wasn't until the *Bulletin* trod on Casey's toes that anything was done about the vile newspaper manners of its publisher.

Just when James King was handed the phony affidavits, sent from New York to frame Casey, is now uncertain. All that can be said is that King published them for a personal motive, as opposed to doing so as part of a well thought out scheme. As a man with a record of having helped the Know-Nothings, James P. might have otherwise been spared.

He wasn't, because of the third and longest filament of fate in which McGowan became enmeshed. It stretched all the way to Pennsylvania, where Ned had met a brother of James King, four years before leaving for California. This was Thomas Sim King, alias Slippery Sim, alias Slant-eyed Tom, alias the Nipper Kid, alias the Dead House Cove.

"My first introduction to Slippery Sim," to quote Ned, "was in the latter part of 1845 in Philadelphia. He was traveling with Al Burtis and another noted young thief by the name of George Fish." After telling how Tom had been picked up for robbing guests of the American Hotel, where he had registered under the name of Green, Ned took him step by step to the period in which he had acted as an attendant in his wife's brothel in Washington, D.C.

The record shows that quite a few San Franciscans knew of Mrs. King's occupation and her husband's assisting role. Yet after Slant-eyed Tom went to California, she appears to have switched from madam to courtesan, a shift celebrated by Ned in a free-wheeling ballad:

> Oh, Tom King's wife of the Federal city,
>   Tom King's wife of Federal city,
> I wat you how she cheated him,
>   When he went off to the Western country.
>
> She vowed so fair, so dear did seem,
>   He little thought that she was tricky,
> But oh, the cruel, faithless queen,
>   She left her King and spread her dicky.
>
> Alas! my queen, how silly you
>   To leave thy swain, the slant-eyed beauty,
> Hadst thou to wedlock but been true
>   Thoudst now be doing good 'strangler' duty.

After a career to eastward which included service as a clerk in the Army, Tom showed up in San Francisco, in March of 1853. For many months McGowan didn't connect him with James King, for an offered reason:

"After 'Sim' arrived . . . he at once traced his steps to the Banking House of the 'great banker brother.' It was, however, all to no purpose . . . King of Wm. at that time stated to Eugene Casserly, Esq., that his brother was a bad man, had kept bad company on the Atlantic side, and he could not think of setting the example of having his brother sit at table with his family."

If James had stayed hard-hearted, Ned would have been all right; but he was induced to relent by a kinsman named John Sime and secured Tom a post in the customhouse. Then after King of William had started the *Bulletin,* the former Dead House Cove became associated with him in that venture.

James P. Casey had meanwhile undertaken to speed rising political fortunes by becoming a publisher himself, though not of a daily. His sheet was the Sunday *Times.*

Its editor was said to have been John C. Cremony. Now remembered for his book titled *Life among the Apaches,* he also edited the Sunday *Sun.*

What Cremony noticed was that although the *Bulletin* attacked other office holders, it forebore to be harsh about Tom's custom-house chief, Milton Latham. He published this finding in what was then called a "card." This was a statement of private opinion published in a newspaper. Presumably not written by a staff member, it could be and often was signed with a pseudonym.

As Cremony's connection with the *Times* wasn't generally known, he put his card in the May 11 issue of Casey's paper. Whether or not he deliberately tried to convey the impression that Ned had written it, he signed the item "Caliban."

If McGowan had penned it, there would have been the cayenne pepper that was missing from Cremony's effort. Gently humorous, it was no scolding at all, compared with James King's savaging in print. It developed, though, that a man without ruth for other people's feelings was tender of skin when it came to his own. Outraged, the *Bulletin's* publisher sent brother Tom to demand of Casey the card writer's real name.

As Ned was thought of as San Francisco's only Caliban, many assumed that he had written what the Kings objected to. Perhaps Tom thought so, too, and was in hopes of finding an excuse for feeding the *Bulletin's* stinger to a man who had made things hot for him in Philadelphia.

Casey refused to talk, when the younger King called on him. He was a man, though, who acted deceptively nervous under pressure; a trait which had fooled five later sorry Broderick men. Tom was sure he had a scared man to deal with, and began talking it up in the bars that he'd make James P. eat his paper.

Thinking he was going to be challenged to a duel or a street fight, and not owning any weapons, Casey applied to the knowledgeable Ned for both arms and counsel. After giving the details of the quarrel between Tom and James P., McGowan wrote:

"Casey came immediately in search of me . . . and asked my advice in the matter. I told him to let the thing take its course, as I did not think it would ever come to an issue of arms, and for the first time made Casey acquainted with Tom King's antecedents, and that for all I knew about him, I should judge that he must be a poltroon."

Nevertheless, Ned agreed to supply a dirk as well as a pistol. The knife was for the in-fighting that often developed in street affrays, these being no-quarter affairs.

Although when the heat was still on him, McGowan wrote that he got a six-shooter for Casey from a gunsmith, he corrected himself, when he was sure it wouldn't lead to collaring. He had slipped James P. an iron from his private stock. Nor was it a six-gun, but rather one which could have been far more readily pinned on an owner, because of its rarity. It was a "Texas five-shooter," an early type of revolver worked out by Colt, with the coaching of that redoubtable Texas Ranger, Sam Walker.

Not satisfied with the weapons procured from Ned, Casey tapped the arsenal of James McDougall for a pair of derringers. Gold-mounted bulldogs, they were, as it chanced, the match of the set regularly carried by McGowan.

On the morning of May 13, Ned did go to a gunsmith named "Natchez" Taylor, but only for the purpose of having his pistols loaded. Before the invention of cartridges, a shooter couldn't be relied on, unless freshly charged every now and then; and those who could afford the luxury had it done by experts.

Emerging from Taylor's, McGowan saw Tom on the prowl—for Casey, as he rightly guessed—and curiosity led him to shadow King. "I followed the Polecat at a short distance . . . Casey and Tom met between Moult Nickerson's and the segar store near the Bulletin office. I stepped into the segar store, to see the fun and watch the movements of the Slippery individual. The moment he saw Casey, he approached and demanded the name of the writer of the article in question. Casey all the while looking him in the eye, both parties having their hands on their pistols. King again spoke and told him he would give him until a stated hour, which he named, to produce the author. Casey stepped back and replied in a firm tone, he did not wish for a moment longer, that he alone was responsible. Tom quailed under the eye of Casey and could scarcely articulate that he thought a gentleman had written it; and turned to go away."

When King left, it was with Ned's merriment burning his ears. In addition to making Tom unhappy, it undoubtedly settled him in the opinion that McGowan was the card-writing Caliban of the Sunday *Times.*

That evening there was laughter in San Francisco's downtown saloons, with Ned in the role of mirth's harbinger. Still the general opinion was that Tom King would feel forced to do something about Casey, so a passage of arms between the two was looked forward to during most of May 14.

By the morning of that day, though, James King had heard of jeers which he felt included him, as Tom's brother. It was then that he decided to use the spurious records bearing on the publisher of the *Times.* Thus when the *Bulletin* hit the street that afternoon, it carried an editorial citing Casey as an alumnus of New York's Sing Sing house of correction.

Weighing 135, James P. went to see a man whose poundage was said to have been about 180. In place of getting the retraction he asked for, Casey was told that he would be kicked out of the *Bulletin's* sanctum, if he didn't go as a volunteer. He did that, though first warning James of William that when they next met it would be as combatants.

Along with the rest of the town, McGowan still believed that any fight between Casey and a King would involve Tom. Busy with a suit on behalf of Captain Alexander Dodge—of the schooner, *Matthew Vassar*—Ned didn't find out that James P. had become embroiled with the other brother until late in the afternoon. He was then told by Casey himself that the weapons lent him would be used in a street fight with James of William instead of Slippery Sim.

It was at first Ned's intention to stay down town and watch an affray by then expected by others, for quite a few were hopefully loitering near the *Bulletin's* office. In a while, though, he decided that Casey had changed his mind and went up Montgomery Street toward Dupont, where he had lodgings with a Mrs. Show. As he was able to produce witnesses to prove, he was not even close enough to hear the shot that was fired ten or fifteen minutes after he had gone.

There have been many accounts of the meeting between Casey and King of William. Absurd fabrications, they have ignored the testimony of witnesses and averred that James P. assassinated an unprepared and unarmed man.

The fact was that King carried a pistol, just as he often avowed that he did. Operating on the same principle as the Gatling gun, it was a five-barreled affair, and these, rather than cylinders, revolved to bring the priming caps in line with the hammer.

As for Casey himself, he honored the street affray code to the letter. He had warned King in advance of deadly intentions; and when they actually met he did the two other things required. After first shouting on-the-spot notice that he planned to shoot, he had given his enemy time to get set before slinging a shot himself.

It was only in part because he was a fourflusher, like Tom, that James of William didn't take advantage of the even break offered him. All the time he had been boasting of what would happen to any who attacked him, he had been hugging to himself the thought of the gang for whom he was fronting. It doesn't seem to have occurred to him, until the crucial moment, that Vigilantes who'd avenge him weren't quite in the same class with a bodyguard on deck in time of danger.

The man who had the best view of what took place was General James Madison Estell. Stepping out of his office about five minutes after five, the general did so just as Casey called out. Estell was on the sidewalk at a point midway between the two enemies, themselves in the street and about a hundred feet apart. Both men were wearing talmas, or short cloaks, King standing in front of the newspaper office he had just left, and Casey striding along Montgomery Street. As became men of their position, both wore plug or top hats. No weapon was shown, let alone fired, until the distance between them had been better than cut in half.

Although the Vigilantes had conducted the coroner's inquest, and doctored the data distributed to the press, General Estell published his own account of what took place: "Notwithstanding all the testimony got up under the fire of the Vigilance Committee, I now state that Mr. King was shot by Casey when they were forty-five feet apart, and after he had given him ample warning; indeed warning sufficient for him to have discharged every barrel of his revolver before Casey fired. I do not deny but that Casey would have commenced firing as soon as Mr. King, but I mean to say that Mr. King appeared to be attempting to indignantly look him down, when he should have been preparing to defend himself. As soon as Mr. King was struck, instead of making fight as he had advertised, he cried aloud and retreated into the express office, without making a single demonstration toward defense."

Believing he had a tough man to deal with, James P. had made his will that afternoon. After firing the one shot of the engagement, Casey had closed in, but let matters stand, when King retreated.

How Casey felt about the surprise ending was made a matter of record by the soon to be started San Francisco *Varieties*. This journal quoted James P. as having said of King, "Seeing he did not fire and believing him a dung hill, I did not shoot again."

The bullet he did loose hit the *Bulletin's* publisher high, to the left and in no vital spot. "The ball entered about an inch below the collar bone," according to the testimony of an attending physician named Toland, "and was one third the distance from the collar bone to the breast bone; ball went behind head-arm bone and passed out near the upper side of the shoulder blade, near the spine; the shoulder joint was not injured . . . no large artery was injured in this case."

Not decked but in state of shock, King was helped into the Pacific Express office by two who testified alike. To give the report of County Assessor James W. Stillman, "Assisted him to the express office, to the back part . . . The clerks got a mattress to lay him down on, and I then commenced unbuttoning his clothes to see where he was hurt; unbuttoned his coat, took a pistol from his pocket and handed it to a gentleman standing by."

Casey, in the meantime, had submitted to arrest, by Deputy Sheriff Lafayette Byrne, brother of District Attorney Henry Byrne, and a citizen helper named Peter Whiteman. Aside from the fact that he was a butcher by trade, all that is known of him is a notation in one of McGowan's confiscated papers. Whiteman was listed by Ned as being one of about a dozen "Philadelphians and Pennsylvanians I have loaned money to, not one of whom has ever made the first offer, or ever will, to pay."

Not a man for hard feelings on that account, McGowan had bought Whiteman a snort at the Bank Exchange Saloon, upon meeting him a short while before King was drilled below the collar bone. Soon to be explained, that turned out to be bad luck.

With everything else breaking ill for him, Ned had one bit of happy fortune, though. If Peter Whiteman was the wrong chap to lend money to, James Casey was the right lad to entrust with a hot pistol.

Although Casey let Lafayette Byrne take charge of an unfired bulldog, he refused to let go of the gun that had launched lead into and through King. As Lafayette testified, "I took from Casey, when we were going to the Station House, a Derringer pistol and gave it to my brother, H. H. Byrne. The revolver was in his other hand, cocked, and I was afraid to take hold of it."

The fact that the Texas five-shooter was never found and traced to its owner was the only thing which saved Ned from being pounced on by the Vigilantes right away. For the best proof of General Estell's charge that King had the backing of a Vigilante cadre is the promptness with which a mob went into action. When seeking blood spontaneously, mob members have to talk it up first, as a bull paws and bellows while working up steam for the charge. It is only when prepared inciters take the lead that response can be immediate, and that's what happened here.

As Washington Barrett of the *True Californian* wrote in a manuscript memoir, Casey was in danger from lynchers before he could so much as be convoyed to a nearby police station. "In less time than we are writing this account," Barrett specified, "the street was filled with persons and the air was immediately filled with cries of 'hang him, hang him—he will get clear if the officers keep him.'"

The officers had a hard time in keeping James P. Seeing that he wouldn't be safe at police headquarters, City Marshal Hampton North and Fire Engineer Charles Duane rushed the prisoner out the rear. With Casey himself helping to keep the mob off, via the two guns he was then flourishing, the three took a carriage in which they outraced pursuit as far as the County Jail.

There somebody recognized the hot gun as McGowan's and swept it out of the picture. A good guess is that it was Sheriff David Scannell, who had become San Francisco's fire chief by the time Ned got around to writing of the matter. He would not have wished to incriminate a man who was still on the public payroll of having broken with law, and that would account for not identifying a loyal culprit whose name he obviously knew.

"Although Mr. King was shot by a Colt's revolver . . . it was never produced at my trial," Ned observed. "Some friend had no doubt taken a fancy to it, as it was a very fine weapon."

At the time, though, Ned wasn't concerned about having lent a man a gun for a slightly different purpose than that to which it had been put. Nor, on the evening of May 14, was anyone worried about Casey.

The customs of the country considered, there was no reason to believe that a jury could do other than to find in his favor. He had shot a public scold; and others whom King had dirtied with ink thought of James P. as a community benefactor.

One such was District Attorney Byrne, a favorite target of King's. Meeting Ned at a restaurant the night of the shooting, he was laughing about it. He also produced a derringer which his brother, the deputy sheriff, had taken from Casey, and smilingly charged Ned with its ownership.

Having no public career to be injured, Ned let it go. For if he had told that the snub-nosed pistol really belonged to James McDougall, it could have been harmful to that friend. Political enemies of a man fighting for the senatorship which McDougall finally won, could have damaged him at the polls by picturing him as a supplier of weapons for street affrays.

As King hadn't been slain, outsiders thought the excitement in town would soon pass. They reckoned the mob as only a bunch of *Bulletin* subscribers, wrathful at an injury done to a man they had crowned with sainthood.

Yet even as McGowan chatted over the food and wine with Byrne, the strands of the entrapping web were closing about him, never to let him fully go. The enemy that James of William had never been, Tom King had moved in as ramrod of the Committee's paper. Not hugger mugger now, the Vigilantes were organizing to take over San Francisco. They could count on popular support because the *Bulletin's* editorials—of which the most rabble-convincing were those dealing with Charles Cora—had persuaded the man in the street that officials of the city and county were in league with corruption.

As of May 14, 1856, the conspiracy of the Vigilantes of that year had become a fact. From then on the fate of Judge Edward McGowan was such as he described more than two decades later:

"I have had to run the gauntlet for over 22 years—noted as a man who had to flee from his life from a Committee of Vigilance. Although tried and honorably acquitted, I dared not return to my old home for nearly a score of years; robbed of fortune, blasted in name and character, family ties sundered, and even at this last period . . . one of the daily press of San Francisco denounced me as a 'ruffian.'"

Ned got a rough deal, even for a poet. Unlike some bards, though, he knew how to shift for himself, and could dish it out as well as take it.

9

THE HUNTSMEN AND THE QUARRY

THE SAN FRANCISCO Committee of Vigilance of 1856 came out of hiding within three hours of the shot that had hit but not felled James King of William. Of those who formed the organization's founding core, Ned wrote:

"This meeting was held at the counting house of G. B. Post, who was upon the verge of bankruptcy and was willing with others similarly situated, to ward off, for a brief period, their impending ruin, and give them an opportunity to rob a few months longer, and have an excuse for delay in making remittances East, and finally rob and swindle their Eastern consignors."

The desperation of these men, then, was financial as well as political. Creditors couldn't be put off by the ruse of burning merchandise, as in the good old days of '50 and '51, for reasons already given. The only hope of cornered speculators was to play for time and a better turn of the market. Time could be bought by arranging for newspapers—not themselves—to explain to wholesalers on the Atlantic side that a state of emergency was stopping business in its San Francisco tracks. Therefore they used the wounding of one man as an excuse for proclaiming that their city was the nesting place of chaos.

They could get honest men to throw in with them, not only because they'd been brain-muddied by the *Bulletin's* editorials, but for a reason supplied by Henry Gray in *Judges and Criminals:* "The disastrous results attending the failure of several of the prom-

inent banking houses of California . . . the frauds practiced upon
the citizens of the State by bankrupt traders . . . had ruined
numbers of persons and produced a want of confidence and an
universal panic which only needed some irritating course to make it
produce disorder."

Yet whoever besides Gabriel Post was present at the first confab,
William Tell Coleman was not there. After several years spent in
New York, he had returned to California in January of 1856.
But according to his own statement, he had been too busy to mix
with his old associates of the 1851 Committee.

The leader of that group, Sam Brannan, wished to repeat in
1856; but those who formed the new gang wanted the man who
had given them a plan of procedure before. A delegation called
on Coleman, though at first cold-shouldered. But after turning
down the offered presidency, the chance to use his organizing
talent—and in his own disinterest—was once again too much for
him. A man who longed to be a Democratic senator sent word to
a group bent on wrecking San Francisco's Democratic Party that he
would agree to act as head cacique, if he was granted "authority
supreme."

Associated with this czar as officers were Isaac Bluxome, Jr.,
secretary; James Dows, treasurer; Charles Doane, grand marshal;
John P. Manrow, judge advocate; and Thomas J. L. Smiley, prosecuting attorney. The fact that neither the judge nor the attorney
had had any legal training worried none. As in the primitive
Christian priesthood, grace was conferred by the laying on of
hands.

The officers and their deputies were members of a supreme
council, forty-one strong, called the Executive Committee. Next in
rank were commissars called Delegates, eventually over a hundred
of them. Authorized to vote in such matters as to whether or not
a fellow citizen should be strangled to death, three Delegates represented the one hundred members of the Committee as a whole
by whom they were elected.

In its entirety the Vigilance Committee was divided into four
departments: financial, medical, police, and military. Coleman remembered how the 1851 Vigilantes had sometimes been thwarted

by National Guard units as well as posses. The 1856 Committee was chiefly made up of those belonging to their army, and roving storm troopers.

Enlisting in the organization, which began the night of the fourteenth, was done with such zest that there were several repeaters. Preserved is the original roster of those willing to affix their names below a pledge of which one word is now illegible: "I do solemnly swear to act with the Vigilance Committee and second . . . in full all their actions as expressed by the Executive Committee." The names of J. B. Reely, F. W. Bayliss, Charles A. Taylor, H. S. Whetstone, and Augustus M. Heslep appear twice. As for M. J. Burke, M.D., he was so eager to apply the rope cure to human illnesses that he got on line three times.

For it was on hanging that the joiners were determined from the first. Yet the front of a move to gain political control by violence, where it was not a mere swindling dodge, was a constitution. Worked on all night, it was ready for adoption by the morning of May 15.

"Whereas," the preamble reads, "it has become apparent to the citizens of San Francisco that there is no security for life and property, either under the regulations of society as it at present exists, or under the laws as now administered, and that by the association together of bad characters, our ballot boxes have been stolen, and others substituted with votes that were never polled, and thereby our elections nullified—our dearest rights violated— and no other method left by which the will of the people can be manifested.

"Therefore, the citizens whose names are herewith attached do unite themselves into an association for maintenance of the peace and good order of society . . . That the name and style of this association shall be the Committee of Vigilance for the protection of the ballot box, the lives, liberty and property of the citizens and residents of the city of San Francisco."

How well the ring leaders and their dupes had worked themselves up into an amok fury can be gauged from their reaction to a mildly worded censure of the course they had taken. John Nugent, sole owner of the *Herald* since he bought the interest of co-founder John E. Foy in 1851, had been a Vigilante in that year. But when five years older, he knew better. A morning paper, the *Herald* brought this message to San Francisco breakfast tables on May 15:

"We see that a number of highly respectable merchants—some of them our warm friends—have called a meeting of the old Vigilance Committee for nine o'clock this morning. We wish to be understood as most unqualifiedly condemning the movement."

To this expression of personal opinion, the men who claimed they didn't want people's "dearest rights violated," reacted by snatching copies of Nugent's paper from stores, stands and newsboys, and burning them in the middle of downtown streets. They also agreed to take their advertisements out of what had deservedly been San Francisco's fattest journal.

The *Herald's* editor didn't sell out or scare, but those of the *Chronicle* and *Town Talk* fished a new viewpoint out of that episode. Frank Soule and Pat P. Hull respectively, they flopped from anti-Committee to pro without bothering to shift gears. As the *Alta California*, the *True Californian*, the *Globe*, and the *Call* had been lined up with the *Bulletin* from scratch, the *Herald* was the only daily in the camp of Law and Order.

With a lone gun barking in opposition, the Vigilantes set out to murder Casey, because they had to hang somebody or disband. They had advertised themselves as reformers united to crush a crime wave, and the only crime they could see—that they wanted to—was the winging of King by James P.

The *Bulletin's* publisher had meanwhile been moved from the Pacific Express office to a makeshift hospital room in a building known as the Montgomery Block. Having thrown off shock by the next morning, he was very much on the mend. The message given newspapers, as of 11:00 A.M. on May 15, was that "Mr. King is most positively out of danger."

That didn't discourage the Committee, which expanded with the swiftness of Japanese flowers in water. "Within 24 hours," as Coleman remembered, "we had 1500 members . . . each man was to be known only by his number . . . Within two days after the first meeting 2500 men were enrolled and equipped with arms, while drilling was carried on constantly day and night."

In addition to veterans of America's 1848 war with Mexico, there were many hundreds of European soldiers in San Francisco. Mostly of France and Germany, they had been drawn to California by the prospect of joining filibustering ventures. Not planned by Americans, these were schemes to invade Mexico which had the backing of France's Napoleon III.

Because American officials had objected to the use of United States soil as a military base by foreigners, the would-be filibusters were marking time by the Golden Gate. Guns of a sort for them were likewise on hand. Doubtless in the hope of palming them off on French leaders, a speculator named George Law had bought five thousand Army surplus flintlocks. Supplemented by rifles and batteries of cannon, turned over to the Committee by joining deserters from the National Guard, they were the firearms of a military force which eventually numbered about 5700—mounted as well as foot troops.

It wasn't half that large when Sheriff Scannell became alarmed for Casey's safety and called for a posse to man the jail. No less than six persons who earned listings in *The American Dictionary of Biography* rallied to the defense of James P. They were the explorer, Edward F. Beale, then acting as California's Indian Agent; Joseph G. Baldwin, author of the wonderful *Flush Times in Alabama and Mississippi;* John Coffee Hays, Indian fighter and Mexican War hero; Hall McAllister, distinguished attorney; William T. Sherman, general-to-be; and Edward D. Baker, later to represent Oregon in the U. S. Senate. The *Dictionary* could well have included also present Eugene Casserly, in time sent to the Senate by California. Then there was one more who belongs in said work, and has been wrongly denied a place, in the person of Edward McGowan, poet and adventurer.

The efforts of this remarkable Law and Order group were nullified by the poor judgment of Governor James Neely Johnson, on the one hand, and the duplicity of the Committee's Executives on the other. Arriving from Sacramento on the evening of May 16,

Johnson called on the Vigilante chieftains, who had by then hived up in a stronghold on Sacramento Street officially known as Fort Vigilance. Because of an outwork made of sacks and sand, though, it was popularly styled Fort Gunnybags.

With the governor, when he entered this keep of defiance to law was his militia general for northern California in the person of Sherman. Having given up his captaincy in the Regular Army, he was San Francisco's representative of the St. Louis banking house, Lucas, Turner & Co.

Because Sherman was present, there are two versions of how the talk went, when the Governor of California and the president of the Vigilance Committee faced each other. Coleman's ran to the effect that Johnson slapped him on the shoulder and told him to "go to it"—meaning that he thought it was fine for the Vigilantes to slay as they saw fit. While conceding that the governor had begun by being friendly, the general said that he had secured a commitment in Casey's behalf.

In a May of 1856 letter Sherman affirmed that Johnson had proposed a trial for Casey, presided over by a Judge Norton, a jurist of unquestioned probity, as all present conceded. He furthermore offered the Vigilantes the privilege of monitoring the selection of jurors, so that no suspicion of packing could cloud the trial's result.

To this Coleman agreed that nothing could be fairer. But later that evening he made the counter proposal that a detachment of Vigilantes should be admitted to the jail, to make certain that Casey would remain in custody.

That was guile with snake all over it; for at the time, the problem wasn't to keep James P. from getting out of the lockup, but to prevent men who wished him no good from getting in. Ever since its door closed behind Casey, glowering mobs had been from time to time milling in front of the jail.

Johnson took the hook, though, as Ned found out at first hand. "On the evening of the sixteenth of May . . . an event occurred never to be forgotten or sufficiently deplored. On that fatal evening, when there was yet hope that the majesty of the law would

be respected and a popular outbreak prevented by an exhibition
of firmness on the part of the Sheriff and his posse, the Governor
of the State, doubtless actuated by the best of motives, suffered
himself to be influenced by weak counsel, and relying on the bad
faith of seditious and designing men, encouraged the Sheriff . . .
to admit within the walls of the jail a party of men connected
with the band of conspirators then organized under the name of the
Vigilance Committee . . . Several of us threw down our arms in
disgust and left the jail. I went down Montgomery Street into
Barry & Patten's saloon."

It was here, early in the morning of May 17, that he first
heard there had been Vigilante mutterings against him. McGowan
took no stock in the chat until he had made his way home. There
he found that messages, not all of them signed, had been sent to
his landlady as well as himself. One and all they implied or warned
him outright that he was next on the minds of the Committee after
Casey.

Doubtless first put forward by Tom King, the ground was that
Ned had been accessory to the murder of the not yet dead James
of William. Having learned in 1851 how little the Vigilantes asked
in the way of evidence, when their teeth were set for a lynching,
McGowan began to look to himself.

"On Sunday, the eighteenth of May, I rose late and went
cautiously and well armed to a different barber's shop from the one
where I had been in the habit of getting shaved. On coming out I
observed the house tops in the vicinity of the jail crowded with
people, and ascertaining that a demonstration was about to be
made I secured a position where unobserved I could witness all
that occurred."

What he saw, and what Governor Johnson and General Sherman watched from a more conspicuous lookout, was a Vigilante
regiment advancing toward the county jail. Arrived, soldiers
wheeled a cannon in front of the door. Courtesy of this passport,
Coleman and an Executive Committee member named Miers
Truett entered. Coming out with Casey a few minutes later, they
got in a carriage with him and drove off to Fort Gunnybags.

Although Ned didn't wait to see, they were back in an hour for Charles Cora. They could have made a third trip, had the Vigilantes been as willing to war on Protestant Know-Nothings as on Catholic Democrats.

"In the County jail at the time," James O'Meara reported, "was Rod Backus, a young cousin of Phil Backus, an auctioneer of considerable prominence in mercantile social circles. Rod Backus had shot dead a man [his name was Oldman] whose face he had never seen until the moment before he shot, a dozen paces distant. It was in Stout's alley. It was a murder, a wanton murder, without provocation, excuse, extenuation or palliation whatever. Rod Backus was a frequent visitor at a house of the demi-monde in the alley, and one Jennie French was his favorite . . . Jennie said to him, 'Rod, that fellow has insulted me, shoot the ———.' At the word, Backus drew his pistol and fired."

Content with the two prisoners in hand, though, a group who dubbed themselves San Francisco's "purest and best" citizens, began trying both Cora and Casey for murder. Why they were so sure that James King wouldn't live is an interesting question. For when Casey was arraigned for first-degree murder, doctors in attendance on the man he had shot were still sure he would recover.

Ned meanwhile was lying low, and changing burrows. After seeing Casey dragged toward doom, he had his meals brought in to him for two days. Then on the night of May 19 he decided to move across the street.

"Here I received several secret messages . . . begging me to be on the alert and trust no one," he recalled. "I also received many offers to take me into the country. I listened to all but accepted none and kept my own counsel."

While McGowan was so playing his cards, the trials of Casey and Cora were taking different turns. James P. was given what the Vigilantes described as a "fair and impartial trial" in secret court sessions at which his only well wisher was himself. Pending the delivery of a corpse, his judges had to mark time, but toward the end of May 19 they were given the good news that James King had taken a turn for the worse. "Of William" slid downhill from there on, and at 1:45 P.M. on May 20 he both passed sentence on Casey and died himself.

The trial of Charles Cora, though, ran into an unexpected snag. Some of the Vigilante jurors had perhaps talked to witnesses who had told how the gambler had been forced to shoot Richardson in his own defense; or some of them may have had firsthand knowledge of the bad disposition ascribed to the Deputy U. S. Marshal by O'Meara. But for whatever reasons, the Committee's jury was hung as high as that of the Law and Order court which had tried Cora the previous January.

According to the manuscript memoir of Prosecuting Attorney Smiley, only a "bare majority," voted the gambler guilty. That wasn't enough, even though the Committee's constitution had done away with the law stipulating that conviction can only be achieved through the agreement of all sitting in judgment. In capital cases—and the Vigilantes weren't interested in any other kind—the ruling was that the prosecution must persuade two-thirds of those voting.

They pronounced Cora guilty anyhow, of course. Had they confessed to their following that they could do no better than an authorized court, they would have had to quit.

Yet they waited for Casey to get in the pot, too, before they did anything about the gambler. Recalling how they had wowed the mob by stretching Whittaker and McKenzie simultaneously, they planned to offer spectators another double feature.

It took place the night of James King's death. Appreciating the value of pageantry as keenly as Stalin or Mussolini ever did, Coleman called for the execution as the climax of a torchlight parade. The gallows consisted of platforms extending from windows aloft in Fort Gunnybags. Gazing upward at that symbol of the Committee's might, the satisfied customers saw Casey and Cora dropped through traps provided for the private use of each.

The Executive Committee had promised a still gullible governor that after disposing of Casey, and of Cora for makeweight, they would let city and county officials carry on from there. Refusing to do as agreed, they had to name other killers, in a town which was powerful short of them, unless they wished to string up some of their own troops.

They had to please San Franciscans, as well as defy California's government, for men who depend on the support of a mob must be forever in the business of giving their followers something new to get excited about. Recognizing their problem, the Vigilantes had begun working up charges against their next victims before the first two were hoisted.

Selected were Ned McGowan and a man that the Committee knew only as "Wightman." Both were named as leagued accessories to the murder of James King.

The case against Ned was based on (a) Cremony's "Caliban" card, (b) Tom King's assertion that McGowan had been in cahoots with Casey, and (c) McDougall's derringers. A friend until the ice got thin, Henry Byrne had voiced dark suspicions about the one which had been turned over to him.

There were difficulties, nevertheless. The derringers had not been fired, the weapon which had been could not be found, nor had anybody seen Ned within a half mile of the shooting. To press an accessory charge, some positive link between the accused and the crime must be established, and that's where "Wightman" came in.

A man named Robert Somerville had seen McGowan and Whiteman drinking together a half hour before an affray of which Peter was one of the witnesses. It was therefore urged that Ned had sent Whiteman to watch a shooting of which he had been the planner.

The Committee had taken the trouble to build up a case to that extent, because Ned had gone underground, as described, by the time they were ready to reach for him. They therefore pressured a grand jury into indicting McGowan, as well as doing so themselves. That was a good dodge, because if Ned didn't turn up to face the indictment, he became an outlaw. As he chose not to put himself where the Vigilantes could get hold of him, he was from then on in a squeeze between them and the Law and Order authorities they were in rebellion against.

Legal and lawless, the indictments against McGowan and a man whose first name they didn't so much as know, were leveled on May 21. Because he was so faceless, Peter Whiteman had no trouble in slipping off to Sacramento. Ned, on the other hand, was one of the best-known characters in a town whose every route of exit was watched by the Committee's sentinels. As it was even more dangerous for him to remain than to stay in the city, however, he arranged to be driven out of San Francisco the next night.

But anxious for his safety or not, McGowan was still McGowan. After having been given the miss-in-balk by "the charming Fannie," he had turned his attention to one Eliza Greenwood—also coveted by a Vigilante named John M. Freeman. Mrs. Greenwood was accessible without going into the street, because she lived in another part of a building whose court was served by a connecting balcony.

Via this utility, Ned called on Eliza in order, as he noted, "to get some little things of mine," and to drink a champagne farewell. They were enjoying this sweet sorrow when Freeman, who seems to have been paying for the apartment, entered without knocking.

No doubt amazed at finding a man whom he knew his gang meant to seize, Freeman yet called for another bottle and told Ned not to worry. McGowan had his own notions, however. "I thanked him," he remembered, "at the same time thinking that a knife, revolver and pair of derringers with which I was armed were a better protection."

Returning to his lodgings, he there awaited allies who soon came. But Ned did not then escape from San Francisco on account of an unforeseen development. When he and the four with him had hastened to where he supposedly had a means of flight, they didn't find it.

"Before we reached there," as McGowan explained, "the heart of the friend who was supposed to drive me had failed him. He dare not risk incurring the displeasure of the Star Chamber."

So it was back in the soup for Ned. Still his first try at a getaway wasn't wasted motion. As he afterward learned, he had been out of his quarters but a short while, when they were raided by Vigilante police.

10

THE BREAKING OF BRODERICK'S WING

FORT GUNNYBAGS WAS bounded by Front, Davis, California and Sacramento Streets, on the latter of which it had a hundred feet of frontage. In its civilian days it had been a warehouse. When taken over by the Vigilantes, its ground floor was used as drill room, an ordnance depot and headquarters for military personnel. On its other story were offices for the Executive Committee, courtrooms, and cells for prisoners.

On the roof, as pictures show, stood armed guards. What they were watching for, nobody thought to jot down. There was no doubt as to the purpose of the big orb painted on the building, though. This was Coleman's "Big Brother" glim, there to let passers-by know that there could be no secrets from the Committee. With no apologies for jumping God's claim, the Vigilantes called a fake peeper "the All-seeing Eye."

Helping it out, after the Committee was fully organized, were the eyes of some 8000 members. Nearly 6000 of them were enrolled in the several infantry regiments, the two cavalry battalions and the one of artillery which made up the army. The rest were police, strong-arm men, jailers, commissary workers, clerks engaged in taking down testimony or collectors of funds to meet the outfit's outlays.

There were never better hat passers than the hangmen who roved San Francisco in 1856. As Treasurer James Dows noted,

"The expenses of the Committee were heavy, but we had no difficulty in meeting them."

Assembled in strength and supplied with war sinews, the Committee waited to see what the governor was going to do about their denial of his authority. This turned out to be nothing effective, though Johnson and Sherman tried.

As the Vigilantes had been handed the National Guard weapons belonging to most of San Francisco's armories, the militia commander applied for weapons to the Regular Army general in charge of the Department of California. John Ellis Wool had been Taylor's second in command at Buena Vista. But though he had been staunch nine years earlier, John Ellis was not all wool in May of 1856; or at least according to charges leveled by Sherman and echoed by Johnson.

General Wool's headquarters were across San Francisco Bay at Benicia, which was also the seat of his department's arsenal. Visiting him on May 30, the governor and his war chief explained that what had seemed but a lynching spree had become a rebellion of which no end was in sight.

To go by the statements of both his petitioners, Wool gave his verbal promise to furnish them with all the weapons needed. Whereupon Sherman told the governor, "That's all I wanted to know."

What he meant was that he now felt fully able to cope with the Vigilantes. Included in his outlined strategy was a plan to place a battery of heavy guns on Rincon Point and shell San Francisco from there, if that's what it took to make the Committee back down.

Wool himself declared that he had never made a hard and fast commitment. If he had, he must have begun worrying about the rule against interference with civilian affairs, on the part of United States military commanders. Pending word from the War Department, he decided to let the cits look after themselves, if they could.

Whether or not he was to blame for his stand, he had an also distinguished imitator. United States sea power was represented in San Francisco Bay by Captain David G. Farragut, acting Commodore of the Pacific Squadron and Commander of the Mare Island Navy Yard. Although later making gestures in favor of Law and Order's defenders, he apparently did so only after he had received some sort of instructions from Washington. Until then he did nothing, even when kidnapping by sea was pulled within easy range of his men of war's guns. Well, if he hadn't played it cozy then, he might have been out on his maritime ear, and never got to say "damn the torpedoes" eight years later.

Still Farragut's failure to save American citizens from abuse was less crucial than Wool's. The aid of the Captain was never depended upon by the Governor of California, while J. Neely had made personal application to the General.

When Wool turned Johnson down, it enormously increased the Committee's confidence. It likewise wrecked that of northern California's militia commander. Without giving him proper advance notice, as the governor complained, Sherman stepped out of what he saw as a hopeless picture.

When that early June event took place, the Committee were well advanced with goals spoken for by the editorials of James King. From time to time William's boy had mud-daubed Catholic priests and nuns. As already stated, his paper had steadily beslimed Democrats. After their prophet had passed on, the Vigilantes made a single package of his two chief tenets by declaring war on Democratic adherents of the Papacy. By doing so, they not only practiced what pleased Know-Nothing extremists; they hacked at the strength of a man they didn't yet feel able to get at in person.

The man was David Broderick, and how they undercut a leader, of whose widespread popularity they were at first respectful, was summed up by O'Meara. "All banished were pro-Broderick Democrats but Duane, who was a Whig but yet felt kindly toward Broderick."

The journalist also told of those who were allowed to remain: "So many of the committee were of the vile stamp, notorious gold-dust operators, who robbed the honest miner of his 'pile' by bare faced fraud; mock auction sharpers; high toned frauds and swindlers of low degree; and others who neither toiled nor spun but feasted and fattened. All these found in the ranks of the Committee their own security from the incarceration and banishment enforced in the case of so many less culpable than themselves."

General Sherman had as harsh things to say of many enrolled among a crew who blandly gave themselves out to be "the purist and best" of San Francisco's citizens: "The idle and vagabond sought the power in existence for an easy support, and through the Vigilance Committee they became what ward politicians are at all times. Even Sydney convicts became judges . . . and sent around San Francisco their absurd writs, with a big all-seeing eye impressed thereon as a great seal."

Shanghai-ing is a better word than banishing for what the Committee did to the men the printed eye was fixed upon. For they thrust American citizens aboard ships which carried them clear of California, and in some cases out of the United States entirely.

And the Committee's own papers show how little the Vigilantes could find to the discredit of the Democrats they chose to imprison and keep in irons pending shipment. Typical of charges which prove only the meanness and arrogance of the accusers, is a saved deportation order involving Billy Mulligan.

"Whereas the evidence we have heard establishes conclusively that Billy Mulligan, Yankee Sullivan and Martin Gallagher have for years been disturbers of the peace of our city, destroyers of the purity of our elections, and active members and leaders of the organized gang who have invaded the sanctity of our ballot boxes, and perfect pests to society,

"Resolved, that William Mulligan, Yankee Sullivan and Martin Gallagher be transported out of the territory of the United States at the earliest practicable moment, and that they be warned never to return to California, under penalty of death."

Yankee Sullivan missed the boat, because he was murdered in his cell on May 30. His real name Francis Murray, Sullivan had been America's heavyweight boxing champ, taking the title away from John Morrissey. Forty-five in 1856, he was no longer the darling of prize-ring fans. He was still a man of his hands, though, and willing to do something about it, when pushed around.

The Vigilantes said he had stabbed himself with a table knife, for fear of being sent back to Australia. Sullivan was not the escapee from Botany Bay they tried to make him out. He had spent all his life in England or the Atlantic side of America before coming to the Pacific Coast. The lie they tried to hide behind but swears to their guilt.

It is not enough to state the principle that the kidnapper whose victim dies, while lawlessly held out of reach of help, is as certainly a murderer as any who work with shot or poison. Two men who had themselves been imprisoned and roughed during the Committee's reign of terror agreed that Sullivan had been rubbed out. Of him Alfred A. Green wrote, "I do not think he committed suicide." Of the same dead man, J. Reuben Maloney was quoted as saying, that he "in making resistance to manacles, received a blow either from a knife or one of the sharp short swords worn by many of the Committee . . . such is surely my opinion."

In *Judges and Criminals,* Dr. Gray concurred. With reference to Yankee Sullivan, the doctor declared that he "had been cut with a sabre by a noted French thief, who was on guard over him in the cell where he was confined."

There were many French thieves among the Vigilantes. Some of the foreign soldiers welcomed by the Committee were only veterans because of the European practice of making felons do time in convict battalions. Others who joined the Purest and Best were in San Francisco on account of a circumstance set forth by McGowan:

"The present Emperor of France . . . wishing to rid himself of the lowest class in France, consisting of 'Chiffoners,' 'Chousinents,' and in fact the canaille of Paris, instituted a National Lottery. Tickets were sold for less than a cent. The premiums consisted of outfits and passage to California. As arranged by Napoleon, the prizes were drawn by the most degraded, vicious and abandoned of these characters."

Many of them not wanted at home, either, there were more Germans than French enrolled under the signet of the "all-seeing eye." According to the count published by the *Herald* there were 1512 Prussians and Germans, 451 French, and 180 English and Scotch for a total of 2143.

An enormity that angered Ned beyond measure was that these unnaturalized foreigners were licensed to grab American citizens and herd them aboard ships for export. That rat play began the day after it was known that General Wool was not going to furnish munitions to the forces of Law and Order.

On June 6 Billy Mulligan, Charles Duane, Wooley Kearny, and John Coony were shipped off on a Pacific Mail Line steamer variously referred to as the *Golden Age,* the *Golden Era,* and the *Golden Gate.* Probably the line had a series of *"Golden"* craft, hence the uncertainty as to just which one had been used. There is no doubt as to what happened, though. All these Irish Catholic adherents of Broderick were taken to New York.

That was at least an American port. Embarked in the *Live Yankee* the same day, Billy Carr, Edward Bulger and Martin Gallagher didn't fare so well. They were dumped on the then foreign shore of Hawaii, survival their problem.

Gallagher, for one, had an additional worry. The wife and small children from whom he had forcibly been separated had the problem of how to get by without his support.

How many of the exiled were wrenched away from families is something that can't now be ascertained. At least one more was a married man with progeny, though. The *Herald* of June 18 reported that the capture of T. B. Cunningham was made to the tune of shooting which imperiled the lives of his wife and several youngsters.

Home breaking, ruining financially, banishing—the big day for these villainies was June 20. Ten men were then taken from confinement in Fort Gunnybags and marched to the tug or whitehall boats in which they were borne to the *Sierra Nevada.* Aside from Cunningham, these were Terence Kelly, John Lawler, James Hennessey, Bill Lewis, Frank Murray, Alexander Purple, Tom Mulloy, Billy Hamilton, and Jack McGuire. Their offenses consisted of being Irish Catholics who were stalwarts of Broderick's Democratic machine.

For some reason John Crowe was allowed the privilege of boarding the *Sonora*—likewise on June 20—without an escort. Other Democrats, their race and religion abhorred of Know-Nothings, were allowed to make for the hinterland under their own power. Many more Broderick men slipped out of town before they could be nabbed by the Committee's goon squads.

The tradition that the Vigilantes scared countless felons into leaving San Francisco is pasteurized hogwash. All the town's criminals who weren't too lazy to work could hustle about in the service of what Ned called "the Hog's-eye," and many of them did.

Under the rule of the Committee San Francisco was a rogue's never never land. Paid for what they were accustomed to being punished for, rascals reveled in the luxury of chasing men with pistols while the sun looked on. Or also by daylight, they broke into houses and dragged their owners where they had no lust to be.

For thus doing, they won civic garlands—thanks, Ben Jonson—as well as money. Whatever was beastly was praised by the Committee's six dailies. Of these the *Bulletin* was recognized as the official voice of the stranglers.

There was a difference of opinion as to whether Tom King wrote any of the *Bulletin's* mixture of scurrilities and hymns to indecency. Some said he had none of his brother's writing ability and was but the director of what were known as the paper's "six practiced pens."

What that term meant was told by McGowan, when writing of a *Bulletin* operative called Theodore Hittell. Of a man who was later to market a history of California, Ned reported the following anecdote:

"A sneaking, inquisitive, penny-a-liner, who would rather ruin an honest man's character than lose an 'item' or take the trouble to enquire into the truth of what he writes, saw a Federal officer writing with a pen made of an eagle's quill, and asked what kind of feather it was. 'This, Sir,' said the official. 'This, Sir, this is one of the six practiced pens from a Black male bird."

Having taken the *Herald's* place as the most widely read paper in town, the *Bulletin* was almost as effective a destroyer of Broderick's Democratic wing as were the Committee's gangs of pistoleers. If these got rid of the Boys, who had formed the core of David's organization, the Black male bird sheared away the casual voters who had for years been in his train.

Horrified to learn from the *Bulletin* that Broderick's ward heelers were no better than bolts shot from Hell, men who had long been his supporters yielded their allegiance. In job lots, next, they resigned as Democrats and turned to the alternative offered them by the Vigilantes.

This was a gimmick of Coleman's called the People's Party. It was, as its priests told the congregation, a political group so pure of purpose as to be above politics. The proof of this was that it had risen above the thinking of America's founding fathers and substituted for their crass concepts a set known as "higher law." A new name for expediency, it sounded like a sending from the stars and was so accepted by the Executive Committee's growing tail of dupes.

The showpiece of the campaign to break Broderick and build up the People's Party was Ned McGowan. After his specifications had been altered through the indictment for murder, they could hardly have been better for the Committee's purposes.

Here was an ex-judge, betraying the true nature of Law and Order officers by flying from the system of justice in which he claimed to believe. Here was an Irish Catholic Democrat, differing from the ones the Vigilantes had dutifully banished but by being even worse than the rest. Here was walking depravity, taking the form of one of Broderick's chief advisers.

Of course, he would have made a better exhibit at the end of a rope. So the Committee sought him as though treasure, while Broderick—fully aware of the stakes—worked under cover to foil McGowan's deadly pursuers.

The play that followed can be likened to a flounder, its eyes on one side and dredging blindly with the other. Ned's team knew where their man was but had no strength to fight for him. The Committee was all powerful but had no clues to go on.

To scour with the blind side of the flatfish first, pursuit can be followed through the newspapers. Not all were against Ned, for there was John Nugent of the *Herald*. By far the best fourth estater in San Francisco, he fought the Committee by spoofing as well as denouncing it. He was also an able red herring dragger, as he showed in his issue of May 25:

"We learned, at a late hour last night, that Judge McGowan, whom the Committee are now hunting, left this city on the Steamer John Stephen, on Wednesday last. He was put aboard some distance outside the Heads in a complete state of disguise, having shaved off his moustache and darkened his complexion."

In the same issue Nugent undertook at once to josh the Vigilantes and show them up as men of no bowels: "The detective police of the Inquisition, the amateur 'Buckets' of the Vigilance Committee . . . were wandering about the city early on Saturday morning in search of subjects, but we regret to state they finished their labors by sunrise without securing another victim for sacrifice and practical illustration of the philosophy of hanging . . . At four and a half o'clock, Mrs. Catherine F. Hewett, the proprietress of the Washington Saloon on Washington Street between Dupont and Kearny streets, was awakened by a loud noise apparently proceeding from the entry of the house occupied by her. She immediately observed a number of persons in the entry, and feeling greatly surprised and alarmed, went to the door of her bedroom and asked them what they wanted. Whereupon one of them replied they had come to search her house. She then ran to the window and screamed, whereupon one of the persons who entered took hold of her and placed his hand over her mouth, so as to prevent her making any outcry. She was so terrified by the conduct of the persons so entering her apartment that she fainted and became for a time wholly unconscious. Some one in the party then threw a quantity of water over her person; and after they had remained in her room for some time, they left the house—and stated previous to their departure, that they had made the visit by authority of the Vigilance Committee in search of Edward McGowan."

The storm troopers also made a raid on the premises of Irene "bitter water" McCready, in search of Ned. Irene didn't faint. Not having forgotten how she had reimbursed herself on the score of the ship line's general average charge, she embarrassed the puritanical thieves of the Executive Committee by declaring that their officers had walked out of her brothel with a diamond studded watch.

With its reputation for infallibility at stake, the Committee's all-seeing eye was being worked over time in Ned's connection. Meanwhile a squad of interviewers asked all dragged or willing comers for news of McGowan, and at length found a man who appeared to have a hot tip. A David Wallace reported that he "saw McGowin talking with Joseph Bratman on Clark St. Could get nothing from Jos. in relation to it . . . Next morning Bratman Jr. and boat was missed . . . Jo's boat is named Star of the West."

Actually she was called *Queen of the West,* according to Nugent, who had the satisfaction of reporting the sea chase that followed, in the *Herald* of May 27: "Toward the close of yesterday considerable excitement prevailed. The Committee having received some information that McGowan has been conveyed on board of some vessel which was to put to sea this morning, chartered the steam tug, Martin White . . . The chase was anxiously viewed from Telegraph Hill . . . The schooners were the Queen of the West and the Francisco. In a short time the Martin White came alongside . . . By this time the excitement in town became intense. It was rumored that McGowan had been captured, and a rush was accordingly made to the wharves to obtain a glance at the ubiquitous individual . . . At length the Martin White hove in sight. The people rushed. She came alongside the wharf. A large number of the parcels of the Committee came ashore. They brought with them an ominous looking box, about six feet in length, wrapped in blankets. The rumor was immediately circulated that the aforesaid box contained the mortal remains of the ubiquitous McGowan . . . The box was placed in a cart; it was conveyed to the rooms of the Vigilance Committee . . . five thousand people witnessed the sight. In concluding this account of the aquatic sports of the Committee . . . we are of the opinion that the box over which so much parade was made did not contain the remains of McGowan, and that it was filled with tower-muskets, warranted by the maker not to explode."

The other newspapers were as dour about Ned's skill at noose dodging as the *Herald* was pleased. Leaving Tom King out of the reckoning, Ned had been on good terms with all the leading journalists of the city. Yet these men now wrote of him as though he were a black dog they'd always suspected, in place of a lad they had rejoiced to belly up to the bar with but a week or so before.

A case in point was Pat P. Hull, the last of the string of legal studs run through by the celebrated Lola Montez. Once a particular friend of Ned's, this flapjack undertook to run a brutal cartoon of the Committee's wanted man in *Town Talk;* and in the issue of May 23, he stepped on a down man in this manner:

"This ubiquitous individual, who appears to have as many hiding places as a cat has lives, was reported last evening as having been taken at the State Marine Hospital, which in common with other reports proved to be without foundation . . . We are of the opinion that if the Committee do track the fugitive to his lair, it will be when he is napping, as his cunning and ingenuity are proverbial."

It could be gathered from Hull's item that McGowan had been a hit and run desperado for years. Actually it had been only six days since he had stepped down from the role of a jolly lawyer with a taste for high living.

Formed in chief by the *Bulletin's* six practiced pens, the legend of San Francisco's monster had attained full size—and public acceptance—in another ten days. With only two weeks of mileage as a fugitive behind him, an honest man of kindly parts was thus presented by the Black male bird of June 2:

"Should Ned McGowan fall into the hands of the Vigilance

Committee and receive the punishment he so justly merits, he would a tale unfold that would make the quills of a porcupine stand erect. We think the porcupine comparison quite applicable. The naturalist tells us it is the most destructive of all animals, and lives on the bark of trees, and when it has attacked a tree never leaves it until it has completely stripped it of all the bark on trunk and branches. And so with these political leeches, they will hang on, and return so long as there is a drop of blood to be drawn from this outraged community. Out upon these heartless hypocrites! In our opinion, these men, Iscariot like, would sell their best friend for even less than thirty pieces. Creditors of Adams & Co.—did it ever occur to you that the speediest way to get the $100,000 out of the hands of Palmer, Cook & Co. would be to find the whereabouts of Ned McGowan. They would let your, as well as the city and county money, flow like water ere they would run the risk of his disclosures."

In brief, all financial as well as political frauds stemmed from McGowan, already established as a schemer of murders. "What I tell you three times is true," as the Bellman affirmed in *The Hunting of the Snark*. Daily servings of smear convinced subscribers that somewhere in the city lurked the cause of all its ills, and that by catching him these could be cured. It wasn't long before hatred of McGowan became a cardinal point of religion with they of San Francisco.

For that reason the hunt became ever more intense, instead of wearing thin after just so long. Besides those of the Committee who sifted neighborhoods for Ned, every other citizen was a volunteer sleuth, hopeful of being first to spot the town's corner stone termite.

In spite of rumors to the effect that McGowan had been seen elsewhere, the Committee didn't believe that anybody could squeeze through the picket lines in depth with which they had ringed their city. Twenty-seven days after he'd been found with Eliza Greenwood by John M. Freeman, Vigilante patrols were still vainly beating San Francisco. Finding that fun, John Nugent wrote an item he headed A DARK SCENE:

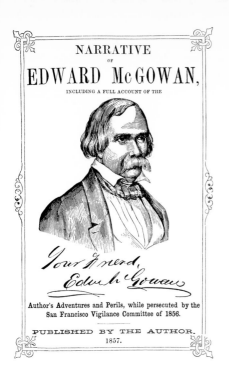

NARRATIVE
OF
EDWARD McGOWAN,
INCLUDING A FULL ACCOUNT OF THE

Your Friend,
Edward McGowan

Author's Adventures and Perils, while persecuted by the
San Francisco Vigilance Committee of 1856.

PUBLISHED BY THE AUTHOR.
1857.

*1. Ned McGowan: a sketch apparently
made at the close of his ordeal of 1856–
57. Compare with the sketch made in
1893, which portrays him as having a
strongly aquiline nose. (Courtesy of the
Bancroft Library)*

*2. David C. Broderick: a photograph
probably taken about the time that the
man who would be senator, at length
achieved his ambition in 1857. (Courtesy
of the Bancroft Library)*

ASSASSINATION OF JAMES KING OF WILLIAM BY JAMES CASEY.

The above brutal murder occurred on the 14th of May, at the corner of Montgomery and Washington streets. Mr. King was crossing the street diagonally when Casey asked him, "Are you armed?" and throwing off his cloak at the same moment, discharged his revolver, and again cocked it and held it in readiness to use again. Mr. King staggered into the Pacific Express office, exclaiming, "O! I am shot." Casey picked up his cloak, and was hurried away by his friends to the station-house, whence he was afterwards conveyed in a carriage to the county jail.

3. Typical Vigilance Committee propaganda. Actually Casey fired from much farther away, after having given an armed opponent ample warning. (Courtesy of the Bancroft Library)

4. James King before and after meeting Casey. The lower half of this bit of Vigilante propaganda shows the bullet hole in King's chest. (Courtesy of Henry E. Huntington Library)

JAMES KING OF WILLIAM—The Patriot Martyr of California.
Editor of the SAN FRANCISCO EVENING BULLETIN, who was murderously assassinated by JAMES P. CASEY, May 14th, 1856.

PORTRAIT OF MR. KING AFTER DEATH,
SHOWING THE ENTRANCE AND EXIT OF THE FATAL BALL.
Entered according to Act of Congress, in the year 1856, by JAMES M. HUTCHINGS, in the Clerk's Office of the U. S. District Court, for the Northern District of California.

5. *William Tell Coleman. An undated photograph, but the style of his clothes suggests a period close to the time of his assumption of Vigilance Committee leadership. In 1856 he was thirty-two. (Courtesy of the Bancroft Library)*

6. *The cannon-point seizure of Casey and Cora. Actually Casey and Cora were not removed from the County Jail together; it was an hour after the first was seized that the carriage—which was really an open one, with the pleasure of the spectators in view—returned for the second. (Courtesy of Henry E. Huntington Library)*

THE REVOLUTION OF THE PEOPLE,
THE COUNTY JAIL IN SAN FRANCISCO BESEIGED BY THREE THOUSAND CITIZEN SOLDIERS, ARMED AND EQUIPPED.
SURRENDER OF JAMES P. CASEY & CHARLES CORA.

7. *Fort Vigilance—a sketch made from a photograph, as photoengraving was a process then three years short of discovery. Though no work of art, it demonstrates why the Vigilante stronghold was known as Fort Gunnybags. (Courtesy of the Bancroft Library)*

8. *The lynching of James Casey and Charles Cora drew a good house, in spite of being staged after midnight. The smaller of the pair, Casey, can be seen as the dangler at the left. (Courtesy of the Bancroft Library)*

Execution of CASEY & CORA,
by the San Francisco Vigilance Committee
May 22ª 1856.

"On the 18th of June, 1856, a party of armed men might be seen slowly wending (As G. P. R. James would have said it), up Clay street, in the city of San Francisco—the Queen City of the Pacific—to Stockton. Having arrived in front of a low shanty on the west side of the street, they halted and drew up in battle array. The noise occasioned by their movements attracted the attention of those residing in the neighborhood, and window sashes were thrown up and night caps protruded in every direction. Having formed in front of the dwelling, three individuals, who by the number and variety of the warlike implements each carried, seemed to occupy a position of command, ascended the rude steps. Rap, rap, rap. The knocking was repeated until the echo reverberated through the whole neighborhood. At this stage of the narrative, though we should lay ourselves open to the charge of being literary 'Marplots,' we would state that the beleaguered shanty was occupied by a colored gentleman, whose only offense against the peace and dignity of the Commonwealth was that he, in the pursuit of a legitimate business, took in the shirts of the ubiquitous McGowan and washed them . . . Not having been able to poke anything out of the piles of dirty clothes with which the house was filled, the armed band retired and searched several other houses in the vicinity, making no distinction between white and black. Whether they were searching for McGowan or a dozen superfine shirts which he is said to have left behind in his flight, could not be ascertained."

With that episode a week back in history, the Committee had yet to find a trace of Ned, not counting clothes of his that he wasn't inside. The Vigilante press by then had begun to take serious notice of formerly scoffed at reports that he had made his getaway.

NED McGOWAN NEAR CARSON VALLEY, ran a heading of *Town Talk* on June 25. "This notorious individual is said to have been met by a Mr. David J. Barnes, from Missouri, at a place called Silver Creek, just below Carson Valley. Mr. Barnes had been wintering at Bear River, on his way to this State, and on his way across the mountains met a man at Silver Creek called Judge

McGowan, who in company with five others was spending his time in hunting."

A fugitive for five and a half weeks, at the time of that fossilized gossip, Ned wasn't as far away as the Committee had commenced to fear. Still believing that Law and Order would be restored, he was biding the time when he could again show his face in the city of his choice. While waiting for it to be deloused of lynchers, he was taking it easy and sardonically following the chase for him in the columns of newspapers. He hadn't always been in such a cozy haven, though. On his way to it he had left a wake dappled with hot spots.

11

THE CHASE AS NED KNEW IT

TO FLOP THE flounder over to its seeing side, Ned wrote a here followed account of what it was like to be on the run from men he sometimes had to brush past, while flitting to balk their venomous intentions. Although the main account was written while the snakery through which he had to pick his way was still rank in his nostrils, he later added data which might once have tipped friends a black bean.

It has been stated that McGowan's first try to leave Vigilanteland was killed by the chickening of the man supposed to drive him. Because friend Freeman had learned where he had been holing up, Ned did not go back. Instead he took over the apartment of a crony named Rynders, known to be in Sacramento. As William Stater had diggings in the same shebang, this chum could bring in groceries for two without drawing notice.

For the ten days of May 20–29 Ned remained in Rynders' Commercial Street quarters. Of this period he observed, "The hunt for me had waxed sufficiently hot, as I had been unable to execute any maneuver by which to delude my pursuers into the belief that I had left town."

Waiting for the pressure to let up, he was in that worst of all corners: forced to do nothing while knowing that the next clock tick might bring mortal danger. He couldn't watch the street, for he could not afford to show himself at a window. Only at night did he dare stir about premises he had to keep darkened. After eating, he could leave no crumb to tell any searchers that the apartment wasn't vacant. Most of each day he spent under a bed.

Soon even the furtive night visits of most allies ceased to lighten the loneliness. "After the first few days," McGowan wrote, "I requested my friends not to come near me any more, and indeed the request was almost needless, for there was a ban upon me, and by this time it seemed to me that my very touch was leprosy and my breath poison. I bade them have no fears of my being hung. I had no less than ten shots and a good knife always about my person. In a miserable state of mind I remained . . . eagerly watching for the first chance of escape and reading the surmises as to my whereabouts in the daily papers."

All the while Ned's life was in the hands of quite a few men, yet none dropped it, out of fear or for gain. The Committee grilled at least two rightly suspected of knowing McGowan's whereabouts. But neither Tom Finlay nor Billy Mulligan caved; and Billy was told that squealing would excuse him from deportation.

Aside from Stater, who kept him supplied with food, drink and newspapers, one man remained in touch with Ned. Colonel A. J. Butler was in daily liaison between the fugitive and Broderick.

The colonel and Stater would rap three times, to let McGowan know that somebody he could trust was at the door. On May 29, though, a stranger used the manual password.

"I feared from an incident which occurred," as Ned described a ticklish occasion, "that my hopes and fears were about to be brought to a speedy termination. I heard at the door the usual signal made by friends when they visited me—I opened it, and found a strange Frenchman who asked in his own language where Gustave was . . . From the scrutinizing manner in which he eyed me, I felt sure he was one of the Committee; and notwithstanding my disguise, which consisted of a Mexican or California hat, face browned and moustachios blacked, I feared that if he had ever seen me before, I was detected . . . He had no sooner gone than I quitted my room and entered a water closet at the head of the stairs. Knowing it to be impossible to escape by the street, and fearing that my hiding place was known, I here determined to make a stand, and if any armed body ascended the stairs to take me, to commence shooting."

In all likelihood a Committee frog, the man who had asked for Gustave didn't call the storm troopers. It can therefore be said that he failed to pierce Ned's disguise. That was hardly surprising as he probably had nothing to go on but the picture of Ned which the Committee had picked up from *Town Talk* and distributed as a handbill. Presenting McGowan as just the ugly mug to do the things told of him by the Vigilante press, this was sound propaganda. But as an aid to catching a man they were after, it was useless. Bad parody, it bore no resemblance to the real thing, as an honest image demonstrates.

Nervous about the Frenchman's visit, though, Ned shifted his stand to a spare room of Stater's. That night, or rather early in the morning of May 30, Vigilantes in quest of him came near enough for him to hear their chat:

"About two o'clock A.M., it being very dark outside, I was standing in my friend's room without a light and with the windows raised, and actually heard a party of my pursuers talking about me in the street below!" One of them Ned was able to identify as H. A. P. Smith, a former legislator from Marin County, with whom he had had a friendly conversation but a few weeks earlier. "Among others I heard Smith, whose voice I recognized, exclaim, 'The damned old rascal, I'll have him before five days more.'"

Bored to the point of desperation, Ned finally took the first of two chances. Like most San Franciscans of that day, Stater was an addict of costume balls. Finding a police uniform which more or less fitted him, McGowan strode forth in it the night of May 31. If exercise was all he got, he hadn't, as he said, stepped from hiding just for that:

"My object in incurring the risk was to get possession of some private papers I had left in my office, but I was unsuccessful, the Committee having been there before me and taken everything they could find."

It turned out that Ned had been recognized on the way back by men who were seemingly afraid to close in on San Francisco's ogre. Thinking he had not been marked, however, McGowan was on the town the following night.

"While lying under the bed in my friend's room," he wrote of this June 1 event, "I had observed a false face or mask, such as is generally used at the fancy balls given by the French *artistes*. I was now very anxious to get possession of some correspondence which had passed between a gentleman (one of the foreign consuls) and myself . . . I had left this in a little dressing bureau in my rooms, and fearing that if it fell into strange hands it might injure him, I determined to make a second sortie . . . My fool-hardiness may be wondered at, but the gentleman was my friend and wrote the notes for my protection. I should have destroyed them but not having done so, my duty in justice to him was if possible to get them . . . I cut the nose out of the mask, blacked it and putting it on with my California hat sallied out."

But when he reached his old quarters, his landlady told him what a close shave he'd had, following his farewell champagne with La Greenwood. Swooping just a quarter of an hour too late, Vigilantes had stolen the papers he had left there, in common with the ones rifled from his office.

The letters Ned was seeking had been written him by Guillaume Patrice Dillon—probably christened William Patrick in his native Ireland—who was the French consul at San Francisco. The only one still to be found among the Committee's papers—if that's the proper way to describe a document the Vigilantes could claim but by the authority of theft—reads thus:

28 Nov. [1855]

My dear Judge:

I have arranged the matter as far as Madame Perrier's complaint is concerned. She will not appear against you. On the other hand, you must not call at her house until you have seen me. As for M. Chauveteau, he has nothing to do with this matter & you must not bear him any ill will.

I dine with Dr. Bowie, you will find me there or at the Consulate.

Always yours,
Dillon

The correspondence bore upon the "charming Fanny" episode, then, and Ned's fear was that the Vigilantes might try to involve the consul in what the Committee's newspapers were now calling "the infamous gunpowder plot." McGowan didn't realize how much of a chance he had taken, in a vain effort to do the right thing by a chum, until he learned, the next afternoon, that he had been seen in the course of his first outing.

The June 2 issue of the *Bulletin* contained this ominous item: "It is now pretty well ascertained, reports to the contrary notwithstanding, that this noted individual has not left the city. It is asserted positively that he was seen as late as Saturday night and followed by some members of the Vigilance Committee. But he again managed to secrete himself and eludes their most vigilant search."

Knowing that the vicinity would be ransacked, now that the Committee at length had a clue to his whereabouts, Ned saw that he had to make a break for it. In preparation for such an emergency, Colonel Butler had found a hideout just beyond the city limits, along Mission Dolores Road. The house must have belonged to a kinswoman of the colonel's, for McGowan identified her as the widowed sister of General Benjamin F. Butler. The problem, though, was how to reach her premises in a patrolled city, where every departing vehicle was subject to search by a series of outposts.

Finally, as Ned stated, it was realized that he had but one take-it-or-leave-it choice. "After much time had been spent in consultation among my friends as to the best plan to be pursued, it was at length decided that my own proposition was the best—which was to disguise myself and walk boldly forth through my enemies. Accordingly arrangements were made for me to leave my hiding place just at lamplight on the third of June."

In detail the scheme called for walking well past the patrolled section of Mission Dolores Road to a point where a livery stable owner called Pat Hunt would be waiting with a carriage. As incoming vehicles were not searched, nor their passengers suspect, it was reasoned that Hunt could drive McGowan to his new refuge without drawing flies.

That leg of the journey promised no squalls. It was the lone trip to where the stable owner was waiting that called for a double ration of guts. Even thinking about it must have been hard on the pulse, while Ned was making his described preparations:

"My face, hair and moustachios were blacked with pomatum and shoe blacking, my stomach was drawn in and confined with a pair of French stays, and I had an overcoat with a Derringer in each pocket. I also had on a slouch hat, and a pair of Derringers in my pantaloon pockets, together with a six-shooter and a knife in my belt."

Then he was for it. Especially hard was keeping from looking self-conscious while passing men who knew him well. Several such were lounging in front of "Whipple's club house," as he made his way up Commercial Street as far as Kearny. There he had to show unconcern, when brushing by some Vigilante cavalry patrols. What it was like to have to do that is part of McGowan's written legacy:

"The starlight that glistened back from the sabres of my enemies was not more quick and sudden in its coming and going than the changes of my thoughts from hope to fear and back again from fear to hope as, marking every incident around me, I walked unquestioned and unheeded through the meshes of the net my persecutors had thrown around me."

The carriage in which Ned had thus earned a ride drove back toward town and deposited him at what he described as the residence of an oldish widow, who was a pillar of the Baptist church. As that wasn't the sort of company the Committee expected McGowan to keep, his asylum was well chosen.

He didn't get overconfident, as he made clear. "The front part of the house was not inhabited, and the next morning . . . I took up two of the planks in the floor of the kitchen to provide myself with a hiding place in case of necessity."

He thought he was going to have to use it that same day, for a window showed him Vigilante troopers approaching in force. It developed, though, that a nearby field had been picked as a cavalry training ground. They were close enough, too, for Ned to recognize in one of the commanders the man who paid Eliza Greenwood's rent.

At first a cause of alarm, the troopers came to be a source of entertainment to a man in need of ways of whiling time: "I used frequently to see the Light Brigade drilling, with John M. Freeman and Frank Baker in command . . . A pretty looking set they were! charging and slashing around, and mowing down fictitious enemies with the most brilliant gallantry imaginable. I could not help wondering how long these heavy-set Dutchmen and tape-selling *Bayards* would have kept their clumsy seats if charged upon by half a dozen well mounted and determined men."

There was little else to snap the monotony, so McGowan amused himself by doing some writing. Although he wrought in prose, too, his best effort was a ballad about the abortive sea chase of him, reported by the *Herald*. Before writing it, he had been interested to learn how the Executives managed to have men, ready for instant duty, always on hand. It was accomplished by offering free beer and food in premises close to Fort Gunnybags.

With this strong-arm bait, the Vigilante sachems kept on call what had been the city's loafers. Now ennobled by enrollment with the Purist and Best, they were still known to Ned as "lunch-eaters." Not of his coinage, the term meant the deadbeats who used the purchase of a five cent beer as an excuse for digging into the free lunches which it was the practice of most saloons to lay out, to give real spenders ballast enough for drinking at large.

When taking pen in hand, Ned had the above in mind. Nor did he overlook the Committee's described monetary mooching:

In San Francisco town a Vigilance Committee,
Composed of the best and purist in the city,
Spent other people's cash and raised great commotion,
To catch old Uncle Ned, they sailed on the ocean;
Thirty of these *braves*—all Lunch-eaters, too,
Were selected from among this bold Vigilante crew.

> To catch old Uncle Ned,
> It was more than they could do,
> For he knew how to dodge
> That assassinating crew.

They sailed in the morning, on board the Martin White,
To be hailed with glory, on their return at night.
Soon they fell in sight of the little, low back schooner
And they steamed it all around, to reach her the sooner.
Then they stood to their arms, each loafer had a firelock,
Commanded by Captain Smith, a second "Colonel Pluck."

> We must catch this old codger,
> It's what we've been sent to do;
> He's a cunning artful dodger
> But can't dodge this one-eyed crew.

Said the Captain, if he resists, we must shoot him through
the body,
Then we'll box him up and hobernob a toddy!
Soon they run aboard of this little craft, for she was no
clipper:
With "Deliver him to our charge, or we'll hang you, Mr.
Skipper."
Then the Skipper fell on his knees and begged this noble
band
Not for to take his life—he, too, was of Yankee land.

> To catch this artful dodger
> They ransacked the little schooner,
> But didn't find the old codger,
> Because he wasn't in her.

They retreated for the steamer, and steered for San Francisco,
But didn't take that hobernob, as they had agreed to.
Each sucker sneaked below and smiled behind the door,
And said when we get back, won't the boss bloodhounds be
sore.
Soon they landed at the wharf, with a "queer looking box"
Not with the body of old Ned but some old firelocks.

To catch old Uncle Ned,
It was more than they could do,
For he knew how to dodge
The awful Hog's-eye crew.

When giving himself that vote of confidence, McGowan still looked on his troubles as temporary. He continued to be of good cheer until California's administration made a pathetic try to restore order in San Francisco by force of arms.

In support of the National Guard, the War Department made an annual distribution of weapons to every state. In 1856 California's share was what Sherman dismissed as a "few stands of muskets." The actual number was 113—plus one sabre that the Federal Government somehow managed to spare—but as compared with the thousands of shooting irons shouldered by the Committee, they cut as little ice as the general implied.

Friendly to the forces of Law and Order was Colonel Richard Ashe. Also called Dr. Ashe, he was stationed in San Francisco as a United States naval agent. On that account he was hep to matters governmental, and on an unnoted June day he went to Benicia to see General Wool about the due issue of guns. Wool's reply was that they, the curved sword and a bullet mold or so were available when called for.

Hitherto with a policy of picking no bones with Uncle Sam, meanwhile, the Committee had only taken charge of the National Guard arms that had been voluntarily put at their disposal by joining ex-militiamen. Volney Howard, who had replaced Sherman as commander of Northern California's home troops, planned to take advantage of this immunity. Perhaps because it was never clear to him, either, a haze lies over the strategy to be followed; and no one has ventured to guess why Howard thought the musket pittance would overawe a large force bulwarked by batteries of artillery.

Let it go. The general somehow meant to capitalize on the fact that such men as remained loyal to the State were still in charge of armories, now supposedly due to be enriched by the War Department's dole.

To collect it, Ashe—himself a National Guard commander—sent three other militia officers in the persons of J. Reuben Maloney, James McNab and John G. Philips. Setting forth across the bay in the schooner *Julia* in mid-June, they half accomplished their mission. On their way back from Benicia they were captured by seagoing Committee police led by John L. Durkee and Charles S. Rand.

These took over the *Julia* on the evening of June 20. Up to that time the Vigilantes had merely defied the state administration's authority; they had avoided any act of aggression. Now they confiscated weapons turned over to California by the Federal Government and arrested National Guard officers, active in the line of duty.

Arraigned in Fort Gunnybags the morning of June 21, the three were soon dismissed, however. It has often been stated that their rearrest was sought, because they had repaired to saloons where—in terms proper only for fishwives and novel-writing serious thinkers—they aired their views of the Committee. That's a French duck.

The facts are that they took a much more practical course, while the Executives had no such silly motive as chagrin at being cursed by enemies for wishing the National Guardsmen lagged anew. A careful observer of all then going on in San Francisco, General Sherman told what took place in a letter to his bank's St. Louis headquarters, dated July 2. Of Maloney, Philips and McNab he wrote, "These men went before the U. S. District Court and filed a complaint against Durkee for a piracy on the waters of the bay, and the committee, finding themselves about to be embroiled with the United States Government, discovered that Maloney was a bad character, a ballot box stuffer and accordingly issued their orders for his arrest."

The Vigilantes tried to seize McNab, who reported in court that he had escaped by taking refuge on a Federal vessel. Philips seems to have sought the protection of the Deputy U. S. Marshal, though all that can be asserted is that he was never reported as captured a second time. Yet Maloney was the man the Committee really wanted out of the way, as Sherman indicated. As J. Reuben was to prove when he had some of the Executives clinked in New York, he was an aggressive litigant. Filing suit against Durkee was doubtless his idea, and almost certainly done in his name as commander of the *Julia*.

In this capacity, too, he went to report to Colonel Ashe, as the man who had detailed him to sail to Benicia for weapons. In his role of Naval Agent the Colonel had an office in the building which housed the Banking firm of Palmer, Cook & Co. Among the several with Ashe at the time were Hamilton Bowie, a man of some political prominence as well as an M.D., and Judge David Smith Terry. Once a Texas Ranger under Hays, Terry was acting as California's Chief Justice, while Hugh Murray was vainly trying to repair gone health.

Because downtown San Francisco was swarming with pro-Committee newspapermen, nothing of importance to the Executives could happen there that wasn't soon known in Fort Gunnybags. By mid-afternoon the choker chiefs on duty not only knew about the piracy suit but where Maloney had gone after filing it. Without waiting for the formality of a writ, the Vigilante officer of the day despatched three of the Committee's peelers to haul J. Reuben in. Of the trio the only one worth naming was a bag of grief for whoever met him called Sterling A. Hopkins.

It seems generally agreed that he pimped for his sister; the evidence isn't quite so clear that he did likewise for his mother. He had asked for the privilege of slipping the noose over Casey's head; and while the clock was ticking away an enemy's last moments, Hopkins had amused himself by rubbing his vengeance in.

As above stated—and probably because 33 Bluxome wasn't in the Committee's fort when word of the emergency was sped there —Sterling didn't have the usual eye-stamped paper to flourish. So it was without even this parody of a warrant that he tried to make an arrest in the presence of the Chief Justice of California's Supreme Court.

The owner of strong convictions, and not a man to watch when he could play, Terry was one of the Committee's most active opponents. On June 4 he had sought to hook the Vigilantes by issuing a habeas corpus writ for the then not yet deported Billy Mulligan. The dilemma he hoped to cause stemmed from Section Nine of the American Constitution's Article One. "The writ of habeas corpus," this specifies, "shall not be suspended unless when, in case of rebellion or invasion, the public safety may require it." That guarantor against the tyranny of being held incommunicado is the corner stone of the nation's law, and Terry's aim was to force the Vigilantes to declare themselves. As there was no emergency in San Francisco which was not of their fashioning, he hoped to make them either bow to the Supreme Court of California or voice open defiance of the United States at large.

Not yet ready to challenge the Federal Government, the Executives sidestepped by moving Mulligan to another lockup and inviting Sheriff Scannell to case Fort Gunnybags. But Terry didn't quit trying to defeat the Committee, for he was known as Johnson's chief adviser in the Governor's campaign to restore municipal decency in San Francisco. Just why David was now in that city has not been established, although a clue sticks out of one of the Committee's papers. This takes the form of a suggestion that Terry had forfeited his standing as a judge by having acted as a "bailiff." As that was the then more common term for a process server, it would seem that David was found to have hit town, armed with some sort of summons which he meant to present to one or more of the Executives in person.

Such a fighter for law was not one to tamely bear with an illegal arrest. With the Chief Justice's blessing, Hopkins and the two other earwigs were warped away with guns.

Expecting there'd be a sequel, Terry and Ashe agreed that the best thing to do was to take Maloney to the nearest National Guard armory. As state premises, the armories had previously been free from invasion; and on the afternoon of what chanced to be a Saturday there was good hope of finding Law and Order allies in what was a club house as well as a drill arena.

The place where they thought to win haven was on Jackson

near its junction with Dupont Street. There has been disagreement among chroniclers as to the name of the soldiery who made
it their headquarters. When the matter in hand was fresh news,
though, a firm flaunting Noisy Carrier's Book and Stationery Co.
for name, issued a pertinent engraving together with explanatory
print:

"Saturday, June 21st, about three o'clock, three or four members of the Vigilance Committee called at a room in Palmer,
Cook & Co.'s building, corner of Washington and Kearny Sts.,
in which were Reuben Maloney, Judge Terry, Dr. Ashe, and
several others, and requested Maloney to accompany them to the
Committee Rooms. He refused, and was sustained by those with
him, who drew their pistols in his defense. The deputation withdrew for reinforcements, when Maloney and his companions, arm-
ing themselves with rifles, started for the Armory of the Blues on
Jackson St."

The fortress of the Blues was not the formidable structure summoned to mind by the word "armory" in later years; and in any
case the National Guardsmen only had a piece of it. According
to Sherman, it was on the third floor of a building which mainly
functioned as the station of a company of volunteer firemen.

Terry et al. didn't reach this roost, because Hopkins, having
commandeered a horse, was back with supporters sooner than had
been counted on. The try to take Maloney by force triggered a
scuffle among well armed men. It was said by the Committee that
the bulldog that finally barked had been fired by accident. True
or not, Terry thought the bullet which whizzed past him from
behind had been meant to score. Accordingly he raised a rifle
which Hopkins jerked from his hands. Whereupon the former
Ranger whisked out his Bowie and drove it into Sterling to
larboard of his nape.

Their taste for combat lost, the other Vigilantes followed the
bellowing Hopkins off the field. His roars brought on, Sherman
wrote, "such a tumult as I never witnessed. The Vigilante bell
peeled forth its wildest clangor, and men ran, calling hang him,
hang him! . . . Crowds of people with muskets and swords and

pistols poured up Jackson Street, and a dense mass of men filled the street from Montgomery to Stockton."

In the headquarters of the Blues meanwhile, Terry and the rest had found or been joined by only six or eight clansmen. Although the others were game to make a stand, David saw that they would be sacrificing themselves for nothing gained and gave himself up.

Below an indistinct picture of Vigilantes marching off with their prisoners, Noisy Carrier ran a clear account not only of the episode's finish but of a significant afterclap: "At half past 5 o'clock . . . Judge Terry, Dr. Ashe and Reuben Maloney were escorted to the Rooms of the Committee, where they remain. At six o'clock the Armory at the corner of Clay and Kearny Sts. capitulated, and the arms were given up to the Committee. All the law and order depots of arms and munitions have been taken possession of, and several pieces of cannon and above 1500 muskets and rifles transferred from them to the Committee Rooms."

Yet if they had undertaken to destroy what power the state had retained in their city, the Executives were not glad of having been forced by mob excitement to make a captive of California's elsewhere popular Chief Justice. "All over the state," as O'Meara declared, "the feeling for Judge Terry was very strong. Harm to him would have precipitated a domestic row, which would have caused immense sacrifice of life."

Although spooked by having Terry on their hands, the head Vigilantes didn't dare lose face, with a following they had given a taste for executions, by letting him go. They knew—and at one time it came near happening—that if they didn't lead the dance, they might end up jigging on air themselves.

For a few days they tried to wriggle out of the squeeze they were in by getting David to resign. Had he done so, they could have boasted to their followers of having cleared the bench of an erring Chief Justice, while dodging the risk of lawlessly trying an influential man. But fortified by a wife who said she had rather see him hanged than back down, Terry stood pat. The Executives next did what they couldn't duck: about June 25, that is to say,

they announced that the trial of Terry for first degree murder had
already begun.

The man most dismayed by the news, if Terry himself can be
left out of the reckoning, was Ned McGowan. To him, as a
student of the philosophy behind every clause of the U. S. Constitution, the arraigning of an elected high justice by a kangaroo
court stood for the fall of risen man.

It now seemed to him that there was no hope of better days for
California, or for himself while he stayed there. So when Colonel
Butler brought him the news, he asked Broderick's liaison man to
tell his chief to provide travel funds back to Philadelphia, and
guides for an overland leg as far as Mexico. Because of the murder
indictment, Ned couldn't risk using any California port, or boarding any ship that might hold passengers who would recognize him.

If Broderick's power was crippled, he yet could get things done
which most could not arrange. After dark on June 27 McGowan
once more walked to where a buggy owned by Pat Hunt was
waiting. By it he was borne to a rendezvous with two men. Not
having met either before, Ned was introduced to James Dennison,
of Half Moon Bay, and his native Californian brother-in-law,
Ramon Valencia.

One of them led the horse meant to carry Ned out of San
Francisco County and on south for hundreds of leagues. But
eager as he was to get clear of Vigilanteland, he now recalled the
good years since his coming as a Forty-niner. He felt sad, as he
wrote, "at leaving the City of San Francisco. An hour before I
was all anxiety to turn my back on it forever, but when the time
of parting came, involuntarily my mind returned to the many
happy days I had passed there . . . turning my head toward the
city, notwithstanding the dreadful plague spot that marred its
beauty, I bid it a sorrowful and yet affectionate good night."

His take-off chanced to be in the vicinity of a tavern—one
later celebrated by Bret Harte in his parody of Poe's *Ulalume*—
of which Ned also had pleasant memories. As soon as Hunt was
out of sight, McGowan told Dennison that he wouldn't leave
without saying good bye to his "old friend William Shear, the

proprietor of the Nightingale." This turned out to be a sentimentality worth having, for when Dennison entered the Nightingale and told its owner who awaited him in the dark, Shear brought out "two bottles of his best old brandy" as a farewell present.

The horseman who rode off thus happily freighted was one who, up to that time, had taken luxuries for granted. He was, to use his own words, "very fat," nor had he been used to exercise even before his recent six weeks of forced inactivity. Then to cap his list of disqualifications as a man for open country, he had been a complete townie for all of his forty-three years save the few days spent crossing the Isthmus of Panama seven years aback.

Riding through California's rugged Coast Range is not the easiest way for a tenderfoot to learn about nature's side of the world; but that's what lay ahead for a waif whose recent experiences had already turned his hair, and the beard he'd grown as some measure of a disguise, from mostly black to mostly white. It was thought that by sticking to by-roads and trails, known to Dennison and Valencia, that the three could get beyond the Committee's reach at the cost of no alarms.

12

THE HUNT GOES AFIELD

WITH THE BEST of intentions his guides had given a man known to be in a hurry a lively horse. Going over a steep ridge in the dark, this prancer threw Ned, and so hard that he had at first thought his spine was shivered. He made it back to the saddle, though, and rode the rest of the twenty-five miles to Dennison's ranch on Half Moon Bay.

When McGowan finally dragged himself out of bed, he found the sun of June 28 had climbed high. He also learned that his back was still sulking, and his whole system had been jarred out of whack by his fall. The word was "mount and ride," nevertheless, and that afternoon the three were on their way again, each with a change of mounts.

Along with the bad time his body was giving him, Ned had for baggage the thought of complete defeat. All that he had amassed in the way of associations, high professional standing and monetary gains had been taken from him: the fruit of seven years blasted, and even the right to build again in California denied him. But it wasn't in McGowan to mope; and he was, besides, a poet getting his first good look at America out of doors.

"After crossing the Santa Cruz line," he revealed, "I was struck with the splendor of the scenery. Living so long pent up among the brick and mortar walls of San Francisco, I was prepared to enjoy with a peculiar zest the loveliness of nature. It was midsummer, and the plains and hillsides were decked in their gayest robes. Flowers of every odor and hue were showered lavishly upon the landscape, and the sweet breeze that came to our nostrils laden with their perfume, also brought to our ears the songs of a thousand birds, who, in the recklessness of their joy, seemed to mock my sorrows; and I confess, as I bounded along on my active little horse, drinking to the fill of nature's fresh, delicious charms, I forgot that I was a fugitive."

Because of the late start, he only bounded for thirty miles. A ranch at a Spanish settlement called the Piscadero (which has since dispensed with "the"), was their stopping place for the night. Passed off as a priest, on his way to make a tour of California's southern missions, Ned met with a warm welcome there.

He needed the coddling he got, for June 29 turned out to be a rough day. Reaching dry, hot country, a man used to the salt coolth of San Francisco didn't do well. "The heat and fatigue of the day," as he noted, "had thrown me into a burning fever."

It was forty miles from the Piscadero to Santa Cruz. Short of it, McGowan waited for the others to scout the town, in order to judge whether it would be a safe halting spot. While seeking a place to lie doggo, Ned found a means of relieving his thirst which was new to a lad with a nice tongue for vintages. Running through a meadow was a ditch holding water which his need made acceptable, despite a certain drawback.

Typically he analyzed it by quoting from a play by George Colman the Younger. "I had to drink every few minutes, notwithstanding I discovered from the singular taste of the water that, in the language of Dr. Ollipod, 'the cows had been there.'"

Afraid that McGowan would be recognized if they lingered in Santa Cruz, Dennison ordered a dash through it, and a ride of fifteen miles beyond. Because of Ned's enfevered condition, they covered only twenty miles the next day, but by the following morning, he was ready for hard and long saddle hours.

"I now began to get accustomed to riding which at first had fatigued me dreadfully," he said of July 1. With Valencia and a

local guide driving two extra mounts apiece, they "started away
at a slashing pace."

They made ninety miles over mountain country that day and
closed it off by sleeping out. In view of what was to come, it is
worth remarking what McGowan made clear: for him this night
under the welkin was a first.

"We pitched our camp near an Indian's hut, and having pur-
chased of him a rabbit and a piece of mutton, we cooked and ate
our supper . . . It was a beautiful summer night, and I slept as
quietly under the stars as ever I did under the canopy of a luxurious bed."

He and his companions had reasoned that beyond Monterey
County they would be safe, because of having left the zone of
American settlement. They therefore weren't jittery about the town
of San Luis Obispo. Arriving there, after having logged eighty
miles on July 2, they put up at a hotel.

Not much later it was entered by some other Americanos, one
of whom took more notice of him than Ned liked. Striking up an
acquaintance with this fellow, McGowan ended by deciding that
his identity hadn't been guessed. In this he was wrong, for at San
Luis Obispo he had one close miss that he never knew about.

The man was a peace officer named William H. Lent, and
among the surviving Vigilance Committee papers is a deposition
he wrote concerning this encounter. After stating that he had been
told that travelers from the north had hit town, Lent thus proceeded:

"As I went into the fonda, I saw three men sitting at the table
eating supper—one of the three I recognized as James Dennison
(whom I had known at Sacramento) one was a native Californian
—the third was a stout man at least forty years of age, dressed in
a check shirt, a loose gray mixed cloth coat considerable worn—
which fitted him very loosely—had wiskers [sic] of three or four
weeks growth—had a sharp piercing eye . . ."

After saying that he had no doubt that he had found Edward
McGowan, Lent told the Committee of his intention to quiz Dennison. He also explained why he never got around to it.

"I was then called out of the fonda to act in my official capacity (Dep. Sheriff)." When the peace officer got back to the hotel he was given news which made him feel that he could take his time about investigating and arresting Ned. "I was then informed by the Blacksmith of the place (who had just come in) that the party alluded to were going to have their horses shod in the morning, consequently they would not be able to leave before 9 or 10 o'clock. I then went to bed, thinking I would see them in the morning."

The fact that the smith of San Luis Obispo was a busy man on July 3 meant saved neck for McGowan. Learning they couldn't get early service, he and his siders agreed to have the shoeing done in Santa Barbara. So by the time Lent once more looked for them, they were Spanish leagues away.

That was their longest ride and the one that took them over the harshest terrain. After some forty miles of it, the rough going and the heat brought Ned's fever back. He had it for company the rest of a 115-mile jaunt, with the crossing of Santa Inez Mountain at once its high and low points.

"Before commencing the ascent Dennison told me to recall to mind the worst hill I had ever travelled up, and then add a hundred per cent to it." A mountain they crossed in the dark lived up to its reputation, for leaving the crest of Santa Inez was as hard as reaching it. Ned was grounded twice on the way down and had a nasty accident of a different sort. "My eye-sight which is miserable at night, came very near being rendered permanently useless in one eye by a piece of wood that ran into it."

Even Dennison was unhorsed by Santa Inez, but as there was no place to stop, they carried on. "At length, after stumbling and sliding down the tortuous trail in the darkness . . . we reached the plain below and rode toward the Refugio Ranch, where we arrived about nine o'clock in the evening." As they had left San Luis Obispo early, Ned had by then been in the saddle—and out of it a couple of bad times—for about sixteen hours.

But he was up, and with bounce, the next day. Dennison and Valencia went into Santa Barbara, at once to scout that port and to have the horses shod and bolstered with oats. At loose ends,

Ned celebrated the Fourth of July with a ranchero who was as innocent of English as McGowan of Spanish. "However," as Ned philosophized, "we got on tolerably well, and for want of better employment I got the old Don as drunk as any patriot on that glorious day could have desired to see him."

At Refugio McGowan also met Pedro Ortega, master of another ranch known as Arroyo Honde. Ned didn't take to Pedro, although he had an attribute which was in time to put them on intimate terms. Ortega belonged to a fellowship led by a knave of trumps called Jack Power; seemingly his right name, though often given as Powers.

Jack seems to have come as near to the style of Robin Hood as any Western outlaw. According to the reminiscences of Horace Bell —who knew his subject, as he did not in the instance of Ned— Power was also like Robin in having roguehood thrust upon him.

Born in Ireland, and well educated either there or in New York, Jack had come to California with Stevenson's regiment in 1847. When mustered out, he became a horse breeder in the neighborhood of Los Angeles. He did well in a region where he was prized for his friendly ways and skill as a sportsman, until the law tried to take his property and his living away from him.

Land titles were chancy things in that California day. Even in towns it often turned out that people had bought from those without the right to sell; and the buyer usually had no recourse but to credit his loss to experience.

In this Power was different. For when, in 1853, the Sheriff of Los Angeles County told him to get off real estate he had long been improving, Jack's response was to garrison his ranch house. And when the Sheriff and his many rode to oust him, some of the posse didn't get back alive.

Suspecting he had not yet won clear title to his freehold, Power led his chums into Los Angeles and returned home with the town's only cannon in tow. As he likewise mocked one up from a spare stove pipe, both the front and rear of his hacienda seemed guarded by fieldpieces.

That was more than the Sheriff wanted to argue with, when

he came again. Still when a county can't handle law defiers, it can appeal to the state; and unlike the Committee, Jack's dozen or so friends couldn't hope to hold off California's militia.

Whether Jack was threatened with it, or saw its use as an inevitability, he finally surrendered his ranch and shifted his base to Santa Barbara County. From that 1854 point on a once jolly sportsman began to be spoken of in sinister terms.

Some songster of the fourth estate baptized him the "Destroying Angel." That marked him as good copy throughout California, and by 1856 he was a celebrated, if misty figure. He moved freely in Santa Barbara, where peace officers had nothing to go on. Nobody could name any man that the Destroying Angel had salivated. Proof that he was the directing brain of a wide flung brotherhood of bandits had never been turned up. All the whisperers really could adduce was that Power was much with natives of a class not commonly sought by Americanos.

The banditti of Santa Barbara were no myth, though, nor was Jack's connection with them. One that was at his beck was Pedro Ortega, who tried to spring a loan from Ned on the strength of no acquaintance. But while willing to buy the riddance of a fellow who was showing more curiosity about him than he liked, McGowan was not about to show a purse abulge with the money he needed to take him East. He had been in California long enough to know that thievery was the first or second string to the bow of every non-hidalgo native.

The day ofter Ortega's visit, or July 6, Dennison sent word for Ned to join him at a Santa Barbara hotel. Glad to leave Refugio before more nosy moochers checked in, McGowan set forth in a carefree mood. "I had now ridden nearly 500 miles from San Francisco," as he pointed out, "and certainly thought I had a right to congratulate myself on my escape from all peril."

He also put more faith in his changed appearance than events justified. In spite of his whitening beard and the patch over his injured eye, a whole string of people spotted him.

The first of these was waiting on the porch of the inn Dennison had picked. "I rode up to a hotel and restaurant kept by a French-

1 walked boldly out Kearny Street, and as I went found many a fearful reminder of my peril in tramping hoofs and clashing sabres.—*Page 33*

9. Illustration from the Narrative *showing Ned escaping from San Francisco disguised as a Californio. (Courtesy of the Bancroft Library)*

10. This picture is the only indication that the exiling of the named members of Broderick's wing of the Democratic Party was perpetrated at night. (Courtesy of Henry E. Huntington Library)

Published by the NOISY CARRIER'S BOOK AND STATIONERY CO., 87 Battery Street, San Francisco.

SHIPMENT OF THE PRISONERS.
Charles P. Duane, Martin Gallagher, Billy Mulligan, Wm. Carr, Edward Bulger and Woolly Kearny, sent from the country, by the "Vigilance Committee of San Francisco," at two o'clock, A. M., June 5th, 1856.

JUDGE DAVID S. TERRY, STABBING S. A. HOPKINS, OF THE VIGILANCE COMMITTEE, SAN FRANCISCO, CAL.

11. Judge Terry sheathing his Bowie in Hopkins. Actually it sank home near the nape rather than close to the throat. The man behind Hopkins has a brace of multi-barreled revolvers, of the kind found on James King after Casey winged him. (Courtesy of the Bancroft Library)

12. Jack Power and Ned after Power's timely arrival in Santa Barbara. "Huestis" is seemingly the name of the engraver, not of the Narrative's *illustrator. (Courtesy of the Bancroft Library)*

" Judge," said he, " there is no time to be lost; will you trust yourself to me ? I will protect you as far as I am able."—*Page 72.*

13. *The San Francisco* Herald's *John Nugent. An undated picture, but the cut of his clothes indicates that it was taken later than the criminal reign at which he so boldly scoffed. (Courtesy of the Bancroft Library)*

JOHN NUGENT.

14. *Ned and the furious, if chivalrous rattler, as portrayed by the illustrator of the* Narrative. *(Courtesy of the Bancroft Library)*

I ran off a short distance, and, peering through the dim starlight, I could see its outlines as it lay coiled near the blankets rattling its tail.

EXECUTION OF HETHERINGTON AND BRACE
The Murderers of Baldwin, Randall, West and Marion. July 29ᵗʰ 1856.

15. *The sub-caption of this picture (The murderers of Baldwin, Randall, West, and Marion—July 29, 1856) is the only evidnce that Hetherington was accused of doing away with a now unidentifiable "Baldwin." The imputation is rendered further suspect by the charge that Brace slew Marion, whereas he was hanged on the score of having supposedly helped Marion slay West. (Courtesy of Henry E. Huntington Library)*

16. *This sketch of McGowan at the time of his death is a better piece of workmanship and probably more accurate than the one made in 1857, shows him possessed of an aquiline nose rather than the straight one of the earlier picture. (Courtesy of Henry E. Huntington Library)*

NED M'GOWAN AS HE APPEARED AT THE TIME OF HIS DEATH.

man," Ned recalled, "and before I dismounted, saw that I was recognized by one Albert Packard . . . Finding I was recognized, I thought it best to put on a bold front; accordingly I dismounted and took a seat beside him."

The place turned out to be swarming with former San Franciscans. When Ned entered the dining room, one A. F. Hinchman nodded. A Captain Bache, of the Coastal Survey service, was also on hand. Unknown to McGowan, meanwhile, he had been marked by Harvey Benjamin Blake. That was the bad hap, for Blake raced to find Sheriff Russel Heath.

What Ned didn't understand was the extent of the Committee's influence over the entire rest of the state—in Spanish-speaking California as well as the parts where Americans had been the first to brush the Indians aside. So though he didn't like being known where he had hoped to go unnoticed, he didn't guess he had stepped in sinking sand.

As Dennison and Valencia had not shown up by the time he had finished lunch, McGowan decided to wait for them in a bedroom of which they weren't the only tenants. He was soon joined by George Parkinson, another contributor to the papers of the 1856 Vigilantes.

"On Sunday the 6th Inst," this fellow deposed, "a person arrived at Santa Barbara and put up at the City Hotel . . . I subsequently saw him lying down in a room in which I had a bed . . . I went to the bar with him and drank with him—he wished to have a bath—I informed him there were no bath rooms in Santa Barbara. We walked down toward the beach where I had recommended him to go for a bath, and when we had got some distance on the road to the beach I saw men running in various directions, upon perceiving this the person I first mentioned avowed himself Ned McGowan."

The bath story was as good an invention as any. On the spot because of having tried to help a wanted man, Parkinson naturally didn't wish to say that he had actually been sent to McGowan by James Dennison. Nor did he choose to tell hangmen that he was against them on personal grounds: a friend of his named James

Cusick had been among the Irish Catholic Democrats who had fled San Francisco just in time to duck deportation.

So Parkinson had been willing to warn McGowan of mounting thunderheads. And he had undertaken to guide Ned to where Dennison was trying to arrange for secret quarters until darkness offered a chance for a getaway.

The reason Ned hadn't already been nabbed was the refusal of Sheriff Heath to summon a posse on Blake's mere say-so. It was complained of the officer in letters sent to San Francisco that he insisted on making sure—no doubt from the editor of the Santa Barbara *Gazette*—that McGowan had been indicted as a murder accessory.

But the news of what was afoot had winged with the speed it can only muster in a small town. Hence the stir mentioned by Parkinson and McGowan's statement that as they left the hotel, Santa Barbara "was by this time alive with people running to and fro." He added that, "We walked about two hundred yards before we reached the place for which we had started, and I noticed with gloomy foreboding that I was the object on which all eyes were turned."

The owner of the cubby where Dennison had hoped to hide Ned had got the word, too. The shed or whatnot was padlocked.

Waiting by it, Dennison could think of neither another refuge —or route of escape from a mob whose shouts told that they had at last been loosed for action by the Sheriff. Yet Ned was to meet one more Santa Barbaran whom he had formerly encountered in San Francisco.

"At this moment, when I was about giving up all for lost, a horseman came dashing toward me at full speed, mounted on a beautiful animal, magnificently caparisoned. He reined up in front of us and, springing to the ground, said to those who were with me, 'The party is made, and the hunt is up for *him*,' pointing to me.

"I recognized the speaker at once. It was Jack Power. Bandit and Destroying Angel though he may be, he was my guardian angel then, and may Heaven, which sent him to succor me, be merciful to him in his hour of need . . .

" 'Judge,' said he, 'there is no time to lose. Will you trust yourself to me? I will protect you as far as I am able.'

"Parkinson and Dennison didn't want me to leave them, but I knew Power's desperate courage well and would have chosen him out of the whole state for a partner in a desperate fight . . . In less than three minutes Dennison was arrested, but I had vanished.

"Jack ran with me about twenty yards up a street at right angles with the one in which he found us, passed me through the window of a house, rolled me up in about forty yards of carpeting he had found lying on the floor, told the woman of the house, in Spanish, what he had done . . . and then rushed out and joined the pursuit after me, louder than the loudest . . . It was all done in less time than it has taken me to tell it. I had, in an instant, as it were, been snatched from certain death.

"As I afterward learned, there were at least a hundred men in pursuit, some mounted and some on foot, armed with guns, pistols and swords . . . The din was terrible, the tramping of hoofs and yells of the mob as the chase swept, pell-mell, up one street and down another . . . now roaring past the very house in which I was lying and next dying away in the distance . . . They ransacked Santa Barbara but came not to me. *Jack Power* was leading them."

Ned had another useful ally in the person of a Don named Pablo de la Guerra, a Democratic state representative whom McGowan had met in the course of his frequent visits to the capital. To create a diversion, this thoughty cove told the dingo pack that he had seen a man dashing into the tules: a marshland—sun dried at that season—studded with cat tails.

What resulted was told in the *Alta California* of July 10 under the heading, McGOWAN AT SANTA BARBARA.

". . . While this officer [Sheriff Heath] was satisfying himself that there really was an indictment against McGowan for murder in San Francisco, Ned's friends became alarmed and ran him off to the fastnesses of a swamp. The sheriff collected a posse and started in pursuit; but it being near night it was not possible to enter the swamp to make search with any prospect of success, so he set his posse around and set fire to the tules."

"Diligent search was made all afternoon," declared a concurring letter, published in the *Bulletin,* "and a large patch of tules, where it was supposed he had secreted himself, set fire to; but all in vain. So we returned, very much disheartened at our failure."

Nothing could better illustrate the truism that the mob spirit is as easy to pass on as mumps. Ned had been but a few hours in a town where he had a nodding acquaintance with a few and had harmed none. Yet a crowd of its citizens drew heart ache from their failure to hang or roast the enemy of a band of men—hundreds of miles thence—of whom most of them knew nothing, either.

Without knowing that the flames sprang from an effort to cook him, if he wouldn't surrender, McGowan had heard them crackle. "I, of course, was ignorant of what was going on . . . I thought the town was afire. I lay still, though, preferring to be scorched a little, and even burned, rather than fall into the hands of that cruel mob . . .

"It was one of the hottest days I ever experienced. The heat of the carpet and the excitement nearly killed me. I was tormented, too, by the myriads of fleas of which the carpet was full."

He was also tormented by thirst and had his own notion as to how it should be quenched. When Power at length came back, Ned begged him for some water laced with brandy. But Jack told him, "Lie still, or directly you won't have any throat to drink with."

That warning was due to the fact that some of the mobsters had commenced a house to house search. A moment later, indeed, Power sprang to intercept an arriving party.

Hearing them in the next room, Ned crawled out of the rug, pistol and knife at the ready. Jack's glibness made them unnecessary; but Power had heard McGowan stirring, and shoved him out of sight in the nick. Ned slithered under a bed just as leaving mobsmen passed a window through which they could have glimpsed their prey but an instant agone.

Then Ned was given the water he craved, albeit laced with soapsuds instead of brandy. For the woman of the house had been bathing her tots, and Jack, with his foot, nudged the pan she had used within McGowan's reach. Kipling had not yet written *Gunga Din,* but Ned anticipated the soldier of the song by vowing that the filthy water he lapped like a dog was the most welcome drink he had ever had.

Afraid a second searching gang might be more insistent, Power next rushed Ned into an adjoining garden. When McGowan was belly-down in a furrow, Jack sped on, though first whispering that he'd be back as soon as dark made a sneak from town feasible.

"And who shall describe the agony I underwent in that long, lonely watch?" Ned asked. "He who has not stood as it were, in the full flush of life and gazed into his tomb; he who has not felt that a breath, a shadow, the crackling of a twig, might open to his burning eye, the mystery of the HEREAFTER—can form no idea . . . of the weird phantoms that peopled those two dreadful hours."

A man in that predicament could not have been blamed for overlooking beauties astray around him. Being a poet, however, McGowan could think on two levels at once:

"It was a heavenly night. A cool breeze played gently round my throbbing temples, but it brought no balm to me. I could only feel in its freshness the icy hand of death and mistook its fragrance for the odor of the charnel house. Flowers were springing round me, but as they waved in the pale moonlight, I only saw funeral plumes. A little stream was trickling near me, and its gurgling ripple broke like a death rattle on my ear . . . So fearfully had my mind been wrought upon by the horrors of that day that I really *was,* in fancy, on the confines of the spirit land."

When darkness had deepened as far as the moon would let it, Power and the two Californios who were with him took Ned to a then empty adobe house on the outskirts of town. Saying he would return after moonset, Jack led the other two away.

Although clear of Santa Barbara, McGowan was not otherwise well off. The place where he had been left turned out to be a general rendezvous for rogues. Of a pair who showed up to spend the night, Ned had to cool one down with a pistol before the gom would quit demands for money.

When several hours overdue, Power still hadn't showed up. The two fellows who had done so had meanwhile begun sleeping off their loads of booze. Not liking their company, and fearing that something had gone awry, Ned decided to pull out rather than risk being stranded in a house he couldn't leave after sunrise.

After he had slipped out of the window, just before dawn, he knew nothing but his own name. He was without guide in a strange region. He didn't know where he was in relation to Santa Barbara. He had no destination, nor any plans beyond going into hiding on the wooded heights of the nearest Coast Range hill.

In the way of shelter and bedding, he had not so much as an overcoat; he had left his at the City Hotel. Perhaps his matches had been in one of the pockets; at any rate he had none now. As barren of food as of equipment, Ned could afford to seek no place where his money could have supplied him with these lacks. It can be said of him, then, that he had been reduced to the condition of a migrant game animal, forlorn in a bad foraging zone.

There was just light enough for him to see where the highlands lay, when he set out on the morning of July 7. A peculiarity of Western mountains is that they are like men in being relatively without foliage in their lower reaches and sprouting the heavy crop toward and on the culmen. Climbing to reach thick chaparral, Ned used his knife to carve out a lair for himself.

A summer peculiarity of Southwestern hill country is that the elements can be hot enough to boil the blood by day, and chill enough to freeze to the bone of nights. Not thinking of this last, McGowan had made a tenderfoot's mistake. Sweating in the course of a stiff ascent, he had peeled off and given the winds his long johns.

A few days before he had thought he was roughing it, when he spent a night on the ground cocooned by blankets. That night, when he had made his shivering way to the warmer air of the valley, he was glad to burrow into an oat stack.

Aloft when the sun was up, and alow after dark—that's the way it went on July 8; and he had not eaten since the sixth. Like a hibernating bear, he had been living on his fat; but upon awakening on July 9, he knew he couldn't flourish on that diet much longer.

Stealing toward an isolated ranch house, Ned found an old woman in front of it, to whom he applied for food. Although with the surname of Robbins, she could speak no English. She had married a man who could, though, and had a daughter who had done the same thing. Señora Robbins was, in fact, the mother-in-law of the Harvey Blake who was Ned's most zealous local foe.

Knowing nothing of McGowan herself, she readily agreed to sell him breakfast, as well as some bread and meat for the road. If that was a good break, a bad one was not far to the rear. While Ned was on his way back to the high chaparral, Blake paid the señora a call. When, in the course of chatting with Harvey, she described the man who had recently bought food of her, a flagging hunt grew hot again.

Up till then, they of Santa Barbara had believed that Ned had managed to ride out of reach. The news that he was afoot in the county not only cheered the hearts of local killers; it was relayed to the Committee.

The Vigilantes had, in the meantime, learned of McGowan's whereabouts, even before letters informed them of the try to burn him out of the tules. On July 9, or the day of Ned's breakfast chez Robbins, the *Bulletin* ran a story headed: NED McGOWAN AT SANTA BARBARA—The People in Pursuit—Expected Apprehension:

"We are indebted to the purser of the steamer Sea Bird, which arrived here this afternoon from the Southern Coast, for the following important and interesting information in regard to the notorious Ned McGowan. Ned has been tracked at last. We trust that by the next arrival from Santa Barbara the scoundrel will be brought hither, to meet the fate he so richly deserves, and which his companion in guilt, Casey, has already suffered."

From arrivals on the *Sea Bird* the Vigilantes also got the chagrining word that Ned had been coolly resting in the suburbs during weeks in which they had sifted all San Francisco for him. The *Alta California* carried an item relative to the furor in Santa Barbara which ended on a plaintive note:

"It was now ascertained that the fugitive had been accompanied to the place by two men, one a Californian and the other an American named 'Jim Dennison,' who had acted as guides either from the Mission of San Jose or Dolores . . . Is it possible that the scamp has been out here . . . or at the Mission Dolores, and read and heard all that has been said about him?"

More to the point was news posted by the *Bulletin* on July 10: "The Schooner Exact was chartered by the Committee, made ready for sea, ten members of the Vigilance police having been placed upon her, and last evening about ten o'clock . . . she was towed out beyond the Heads by the steam tug Hercules and proceeded on her voyage with all the sail she could spread upon her masts."

The Vigilantes on the *Exact* had a choice of missions. If Ned had been arrested, they were to dicker with Santa Barbara authorities for illegal possession of his person. If McGowan had been lynched, they were to bring the body or head back to San Francisco as an exhibit. Yet if by any chance Ned had escaped, they were prepared to do something about that, too. They would up sail in hopes of intercepting him at some more southerly port.

Several days after the schooner had left, though, the Committee learned of the discovery made by Blake. Thinking that a horseless fugitive was as good as game in the pot, the Executives took three confident steps.

First they asked Sheriff Scannell to give them the indictment against McGowan which they had wrung from a protesting grand jury. Although Scannell turned their impudence down, his hand had been forced. So he agreed to send a deputy south with a document which would assure the return of Ned to San Francisco, should he be found alive in Santa Barbara.

The Committee's caciques also sent a detachment of police south by steamer. These had alternative orders. If McGowan had been captured, they were to take him from Scannell's deputy, after custody had been transferred to that officer by Sheriff Heath. If

McGowan was still at large, they were to hunt for him themselves and get the southern county's residents to pitch in with them.

To make it easier for them to get Santa Barbara volunteers, the Executives had supplied them with a reward poster. It was a monument at once of frugality and devious thinking. Although just having learned that Ned was alive, when last seen, its issuers feigned belief that he'd been slain. They were thus in position to excite more Santa Barbara interest in his capture than they themselves were willing to pay for. They threw out the lure, in other words, that McGowan would be worth more to the taker than the modest sum they put on the line.

That happened to be true; but the Executives had no knowledge of the financial standing of a man they had robbed of everything he had. Or rather Coleman didn't. He signed what was undoubtedly a product of his genius, dated July 14:

300 DOLLARS REWARD!

"It being rumored that one Edward McGowan, a fugitive from justice, on the charge of murder, from San Francisco County, who was last seen in Santa Barbara, has been murdered for a sum of money known to have been in his possession, the above reward will be paid for the recovery of his body, or for information that will lead to his discovery by applying to the office of Russel Heath of Santa Barbara county.

"DESCRIPTION OF MCGOWAN—He is about five feet nine inches tall, tolerably stout; his weight about a hundred and seventy pounds; somewhat more than fifty years of age, and accustomed to chew tobacco to excess. He has grey eyes and hair and is very dirty in his person."

Ned's comment was that he had never chewed tobacco in his life, and that about the only correct statement was his temporary lapse from cleanliness. But as he pointed out, although not in these words, a man living as a denless beast is forced to forego many niceties.

13

DODGING THE RAT CATCHERS

THE SCHOONER *Exact* sailed for Santa Barbara on the evening of July 9. Some hours later Ned finally got his bearings. Fumbling for some protection against the chill of night, he first found a road and then where it led. With darkness for friend, he wasn't quizzed by a fellow who told him he was north of a town he had thought of as being on the other side of the compass.

Stretched out in a mountain thicket the next day, he could plan future movements, where before he could only flutter like a moth when there was murk, or crawl away from the sunlight like a maggot.

Now that he knew where he was, he decided to make his way back to the vicinity of San Francisco, as the region where the Committee would now be least likely to look for him. By dark on the road again, he kept walking until the moon left him. As there was no shelter of any kind, he "then fell asleep under a tree."

The night having been a sharp one, July 11 had a bad beginning. Ned "awoke in the morning very cold and stiff, and suffered greatly till the sun came out." Also out was his supply of rations.

After he'd returned to the road at dusk, moreover, the thing he had most dreaded took place. In a stretch where there was no chance of concealment, he was met by a rider while there was still light enough for recognition by a man who had seen him before. That had happened at Refugio Ranch. Not liked there, the fellow stopped instead of passing by. In so doing he posed a problem which Ned described with his usual frankness:

"I . . . was anxious to get rid of him. How to do it without
any difficulty puzzled me. In the event of his attempting to rob
me, which I thought it not unlikely he would do, I did not want
to kill him, for it would have caused me a great deal of trouble,
to bestow his body, and horse and saddle in such a manner as to
prevent discovery."

While matters were so balanced, McGowan thought to ask the
chap if he knew Jack Power. That turned out to be the right
thing to say. Promising to bring Jack to the same spot the next day,
the Californio jogged on.

Walking in the other direction, Ned reached Refugio and
prowled in darkness until he found an adobe outhouse with no
other occupant. He didn't long enjoy solitude.

"I had lain there but a few minutes," he said, "when I heard
voices conversing in Spanish." Of the two speakers one stepped inside and "lit a match which for a moment lighted up the place but
he didn't see me, and immediately his companion went away;
whereupon he fastened the door on the inside and laid down."

Ned's roommate was another on the lam, hiding out at Refugio after having broken jail in Santa Barbara. Learning that
later, McGowan only knew now that the soul so near his own
yearned for a hermitage.

"Soon afterward another came to the house and tried to gain
admittance, but my companion refused to let him in . . . I waited
till I thought my fellow lodger was asleep and then stole softly
to the door."

The rest of the night he was hived in a willow copse. He was
"nearly chilled through" when he could see well enough to take
to the road once more. July 12 turned out to be a good day for
him, nevertheless.

Not trusting the faith of a man met at Refugio, Ned foxed it
past the point to which the fellow had sworn to bring Power, and
watched for horsemen from a spot closer to Santa Barbara. But a
chap who turned out to be a henchman of Jack's did bring his

chief to rendezvous, and the bandit king again had the answer to problems he doubtless understood by experience.

After sending his follower for another mount, Power took McGowan to a ranch house nestled in the mouth of a gulley. Called Arroyo Honde, it was the home of Ned's old Refugio acquaintance, Pedro Ortega. With the Destroying Angel's eye fixed on him, he agreed to feed, house, and hide McGowan until the heat was off.

Thirty-five miles from Santa Barbara, Arroyo Honde was a good hiding hole, as there was near natural cover for Ned to take to, when the house had visitors. Pedro himself wasn't often one of them. He devoted most of his time to missions of an undiscussed sort, leaving the management of the ranch to Señora Ortega and the eldest of several sons.

There were a couple of vaqueros, too, and through one of these McGowan made his whereabout known to a Don whom he had mixed with at state political conventions. It was a wise step, taken just after the *Exact* had reached Santa Barbara, and not long before the *Sea Bird* turned the town rank with more chokers.

Well fed and rested, McGowan had devoted the day of July 16 to placid loafing. After retiring for the night, though, he was told of the Committee's long reach for him:

"About two o'clock A.M., I was awakened by the sound of horses' hoofs. The visitor turned out to be General [J. M.] Covarrubias. He had ridden all the way from Santa Barbara to inform me, that a deputation of twenty or twenty-five of the Vigilance Committee had arrived that evening from San Francisco."

Their leader was Selim E., son of Samuel "Old Oaken Bucket" Woodworth. Earlier he'd had an adventurous career akin to Melville's, featuring as it did stints in the South Sea Islands. During the Civil War he became a naval commander of some note. When in Santa Barbara he was of a piece with the rest of the Committee, which is to say that he was at war with decency.

To the De la Guerras, one of whom was Mayor of Santa Barbara, Selim represented himself as having been deputized to capture McGowan by Ned's old crony, Sheriff David Scannell. This sleeve-dealing got him nowhere, though, for he was outslickered by one of the mayor's kinsmen. The same Pablo de la Guerra who had sold the local posse the story that Ned had been seen plunging into the tules now again knew what to do. This time he regaled the Vigilantes with wine, and while thus making his guests think him a sympathizer, he sent a messenger to Covarrubias.

The word brought by that hard riding amigo made an outdoorsman of McGowan once more: "As soon as it was light, I took my blankets and water, with provisions sufficient to last several days in case circumstances should cut off my communications with the house." Thus equipped, Ned made a hillside roost which was far more comfortable than the ones he had known before.

His courier was a small Ortega boy named Avellino, whose comings and goings drew no notice. Faithful in keeping Ned posted, he had little to report for the first two days, but on July 19 he brought the news that an armed Americano was at the house.

Whoever he was, he took advantage of a time and place where every residence was an inn by spending the night there. When he had gone, McGowan was hopeful that his hunters had crossed Arroyo Honde off their list of his possible hiding places. Late in the afternoon of July 20, as he recalled, he moved his camp to a more convenient spot.

"I came down from the mountain and prepared to sleep in the canyon, which was warmer and pleasanter." It had, though, at least one other occupant. "After I spread out my blankets . . . I went to the house to pay a visit to the Señora . . . It was very dark when I got back, and as I was about getting under my blankets, I felt something crawl along my body and coil itself up beside me. I of course knew what it was, and as I was springing from the blankets the reptile began to rattle . . . Thank Heaven, however, it had given me warning, and I could not help thinking that in that respect, it was more chivalrous than the blood-hounds of the Committee."

July 21 he spent quietly but not the twenty-second. "About an eighth of a mile from the house was a clear cold spring" in which Ned bathed every day. He had just stepped out of this fresh air tub, when Avellino rushed up to tell him that Vigilantes were on hand.

Pedro Ortega being home at the time, Ned sent the boy for his father. From him McGowan learned that there actually was but one Vigilante, his companion being a local man who had undertaken to act as guide. Having first searched the house, they were now accepting its hospitality.

Ned now saw a chance to crack back at his foes. Implicit but nowhere stated, is the fact that his pistol and derringers had become useless. Or perhaps he had discarded them, after their charges had been shaken loose in the course of his rough country rambles. All that can be affirmed, though, is that he used a gun to back a bandit off during the early morning hours of July 7, and two weeks later he was clearly without one on which he could depend.

"As there were only two of them, I suggested to Pedro the idea of capturing them," he declared. "One of the men, Pedro told me, had left his gun leaning against the house, outside the door, when he went into breakfast. I proposed to Pedro to walk into the house and engage them in conversation while I should manage to get the gun and shoot the San Francisco man, and we would then capture Meacham"—this being the Santa Barbaran's name.

Having thus written, McGowan underscored the fact that he meant nothing but business: "Reader, be not startled at this avowal of so bloody an intent. A cruel and relentless war was being waged against me by a set of lawless miscreants; I was myself hunted with guns like a wild beast, and it was as much my natural right to turn and rend my pursuers, if I could, as it is that of a bear or a wolf to destroy, if he can, the huntsman who has wounded him."

Ortega was afraid, though, or maybe he was already thinking of a jump to the Committee's side of the fence. At all events he killed Ned's scheme by refusing to help.

The next day a nephew of the ever-ready Pablo de la Guerra rode to tell McGowan that the *Exact* had dropped its hook at Santa Barbara a second time. The schooner was then on the way back to San Francisco, following visits to several other ports.

From young De la Guerra Ned learned that T. D. Johns, commander of one of the Committee's regiments, and James F. Curtis, the Vigilante police chief, had left their posts in order to deploy parties in chase of him.

Partly through their efforts and partly through the natural spreading of mob-mania, McGowan had become game for all Southern California. On July 19, for instance, the *Bulletin* had been happy to report the dedication of Los Angeles: "The news all relates to the movements of the Hon. Judge McGowan, and the chances of his capture . . . In all probability this noted veteran scoundrel will be in this city, in the hands of the Vigilance Committee, within the next ten days . . . The letters of our Santa Barbara and Los Angeles correspondents show that the whole Southern country is up and in eager chase after the fugitive."

There is no accounting for Power's role, except to say that he was a good man as well as a bad one. But anyhow this angelic if destructive friend was one reason why the notion prevailed that Ned had left Santa Barbara County. Eventually learning of a diversion in his favor, McGowan wrote that, "Jack Power had started off in as suspicious a manner as he could in company with an old Spaniard disguised as me, taking the road to Los Angeles, and had been hotly pursued by . . . eight or ten lunch eaters."

As early as July 16 a letter to the *Bulletin* from a Los Angeles correspondent held what was offered as positive news of Ned: "The Vigilance Committee boys are now close on Ned Mc-Gowan's trail, and you may expect them up with him by the next trip of the Sea Bird. When last heard from, he was on foot and hardly able to walk. He stopped at the Mission of San Buena-ventura on Wednesday . . . to get his breakfast. They immediately sent news into Santa Barbara to that effect. Eight good men, on picked horses, are now on his track . . . The vaqueros and In-dians are scouring the country, between Santa Barbara and Los Angeles. At Los Angeles Judge Hayes has issued three Bench warrants for his arrest, and sent one to San Diego, one to San Bernardino, and one to the Ferry on the Colorado River, thereby closing every avenue of escape. Ned's race is run; the fox is earthed at last."

That was published by the *Bulletin* on the nineteenth. Yet the Black male bird of July 20 was not as confident as it had been but the day before. The practiced pens had meanwhile examined an issue of the Los Angeles *Star* and found the confusing information that, without being arrested, Ned had made himself at home in that town.

"We next hear of him . . . being in Los Angeles," some *Star* operative wrote. "The report was general—nobody seemed to doubt it—yet we could not discover any one who had seen him."

Neither could Selim Woodworth, Colonel T. D. Johns, Police Chief Curtis, and the rest. Back in San Francisco as of July 25, they got the horse hoot from the *Herald* of the next day.

"MCGOWAN NOT CAPTURED," Nugent chortled. "There is an old legend related somewhere about the King of France who with a large army on a certain memorable occasion, marched up a hill, the name of which has not yet been rescued from oblivion, and after having performed this feat, marched down again. So with the schooner Exact. It spread all sail . . . for Santa Barbara— arrived there—anchored there—landed the Vigilance Committee Police there . . . took them again on board and steered for this port."

The papers of San Francisco next heard from correspondents who had seen Ned in Sonora, or when he was about to cross the Colorado via the ferry near Fort Yuma. Nearer to home, a Golden Gater had noticed him sitting in at a play staged in the city's plush Metropolitan Theatre. Most disheartening to the Vigilantes, though, was a *Town Talk* item of July 31:

"It is stated that letters have been received in this city from Philadelphia, stating that Ned McGowan was at his own house in that city. Such a report may prove correct."

With all these tales in mind, and also on July 31, John Nugent went gleefully to bat again: "This wonderful genius, this 'jack o' lantern' politician with the white hat—this apocryphal hero of the Jack Ketch Committee—has again made his appearance upon the stage, lifted his white beaver and exclaimed 'Here I am, Mr. Merryman.' As a traveler, he has thrown Humboldt and Mungo

Park entirely into the shade. At one time we hear of him enjoying the laborious acting of 'that eminent American tragedian' at the Metropolitan, and in the same breath he arrives at Santa Barbara, is recognized, retires into the Tules . . . is pursued by an enthusiastic deputation of the One-eyed Committee who return in disgust—when presto! change, the Hon. Edward McGowan has arrived in the city of brotherly love, and is quietly installed in his family mansion . . .

"P. S.—Since writing the above, we have just heard the rumor that a telegraphic despatch has been received from the Feegee Islands, announcing the arrival of the Hon. Edward McGowan. Quere—Where is Ned McGowan?"

At the time the *Herald* asked that question, Ned himself could not have answered it. He knew that he was no longer at Arroyo Honde, but that was about the extent of his certainties.

After learning, on July 23, that the *Exact* was again at Santa Barbara, he stayed in a chaparral hideout, although breaking the boredom via occasional visits to the ranch house. By this time he had lived as quarry so long that he had developed a wild animal's hushed way of walking and quick eye for danger.

On that account he escaped being seen by a stalker on July 27. Easing downhill, Ned found a discreetly prone man, his eyes fixed on casa Ortega.

Withdrawing and moving camp, McGowan stayed hugger mugger till he stole forth to replace supplies gobbled by a coyote the night before. Luckily he was as careful by dusk as by day.

Of this second sortie he wrote, "I had not gone far before I heard footsteps and immediately got out of the way. I observed two men, one of whom was Pedro, go to the place where I usually hid."

Staying away from there himself, Ned was up with the birds on July 28; and none too soon at that. Just before sunrise he saw three men sneaking uphill. After they gave up their search and went back to the house, the man they had missed began slogging in the other direction.

When squeezed out of Arroyo Honde by Ortega's treachery, he

had as equipment his knife and a blanket, and as supplies a small piece of dried meat. Yet these didn't seem too inadequate, in view of his plans. For unlike his first tour as a waif, he had a destination in mind; and by then he knew enough about the lay of the country to get there unguided.

From Covarrubias he had learned that a Dr. Nicholas A. Den, a rover from Ireland who had become the county's wealthiest rancher, was in strong contempt of the Committee. As the doctor had, besides, voiced outrage at the treatment meted McGowan— a fact seemingly imparted by Pablo de la Guerra's nephew—Ned had determined to ask of a stranger the boon of asylum.

With the sea his guide for part of the way, McGowan reached Den's mansion on July 29. Although the doctor was absent, his wife fed the fugitive and gave him the writing materials he next requested. His purpose was to write a note to a man he knew he could count on.

> Gen. Covarrubias
> My Dear Gen'l:
>   Circumstances over which I had no control have forced me to again become a wanderer, "houseless and helpless." I am writing this from the Doctor's, and will endeavor to be in the vicinity next Sunday. Try to see me. Your friend,
> Le Juge

Having plenty of time to kill, McGowan commenced drifting about in the mountains. Still a wilderness greenhorn, he made two mistakes. The lesser of these was getting lost. The serious one was losing touch with a water supply in a hot country's dry season.

There was famine to go with thirst, despite the fact that Mrs. Den had supplied him with bread and meat. He was so parched, when awaking on July 30, that munching dry rations was out of the question.

His agony increasing as the sun screwed up the heat, he gave the day to a quest as desperate as vain. Being cooler, night brought some relief, but then the sun again began its work of shriveling him like a raisin.

But after he'd thus withered until near the failing point, a patch of moist, fallen leaves at once gave him hope and tantalized him. If the stone beneath them didn't fight his knife, there were technical problems to be solved before he could shift from dying to living:

"At first I could not find where the water was weeping from . . . The rock was very soft, and I could work on it almost as easily as clay. I dug away at it and presently drops began to fall out of it into a little basin . . . I was enabled by inserting a reed which I cut for the purpose . . . to suck up a few drops of water."

It took an estimated hour and half for him to draw in enough of it to restore his body's balance. Then, for the first time in two days, he was able to eat.

This was on July 31, the day on which the *Herald* had asked, "Where is Ned McGowan?" He was wherever the crumbs of that lonely repast fell to earth. Ned could not have found his way back to the water hole, though he named it St. Peter's Spring; and in order to catch the attention of the next parching soul that might stray that way, he marked it with a cross made of poles.

It was downhill pulling from then on. On August 1 he found a stream. In due course it led him to the Pacific—and a feast of raw mussels, unaccompanied by the wine he was used to, when scooping mollusks from the half shell. He had his bearings, however, and on August 3 he was again at Den's hacienda.

He was welcome, though the introduction to his chosen host was managed on the run: "On reaching the garden, I was met by the Doctor, his wife, little Kate, Gen. Covarrubias, and eight or ten servants. The Doctor at once seizing me by the hand and exclaiming—'It's no time to talk,' hurried me through the garden and into the house. Just as we entered it the Doctor pointed through an open window to five armed men who were riding along the road to Santa Barbara . . . 'There they go,' he exclaimed, 'the rat catchers! They dare not search my house.'"

The rat catchers in this case were not Vigilantes, but a local party headed by Blake. Such volunteers could break into lesser households without a search warrant, but they didn't wish to argue with Den's twenty-five male retainers.

Ned had therefore picked the safest haven Santa Barbara County could afford him. But because of the warrant in Sheriff Heath's office, he could not let his whereabouts be known. A cot was placed for him deep in a field of towering California corn stands, and to it he retired after a drinking bout with Den and the general.

Of August 4 McGowan reported, "I had a slight head ache, when I awoke, but a drop of good brandy before breakfast, and the hot coffee made me all right . . . I found my place of refuge very comfortable. The corn was so tall that I was continually shaded from the sun except at mid-day, when I made myself an awning by fastening the corners of a sheet to four corn stalks."

Among the luxuries which he now enjoyed was a regular supply of San Francisco newspapers. Having conned a rich array of dreams about his flight, he decided to give his enemies a giraffe laugh, through a letter to the *Herald*. Not unsuitably, for it turned out that the Den household was temporarily out of ink, Ned wrote with a fluid of which the base was gunpowder.

State of California, August 8, 1856

Editor of the San Francisco Herald:—I desire to reply to a query in the Herald, dated about the 31st of July, in which the writer . . . asks the very pertinent question, 'Where is Ned McGowan?' In the words of the immortal Squibob and the somewhat well known Mr. Webster of Marshfield, 'I am still alive!' and claim the reward for my body (when they catch me!) . . . For the past few months I have played the 'Game of Life' very low down but have always kept the deck in my own hands. I will not say I stacked the cards on the 'purest and best,' or that I have held more than four aces in my sleeve at one time, but in this last deal my native talent has been brought out in bold relief, and by a little dextrous shuffling of the papers I have managed to win every trick. I acknowledge it was a very tight game at Santa Barbara —six and six on the last game, and I turned up Jack— mighty good pun, if understood.

In the town where these jibes were eventually aired, there had meanwhile been many developments since McGowan was last on its outskirts. Although the newspapers had enabled him to keep track of some of these, others were then known only to the Committee and certain of its victims.

14

THE PLANNED PACIFIC STATE

JUST HOW SOON the Vigilantes began to think of themselves as masters of all California is not now plain reading. It was early, though, for the edict of banishment bearing on Mulligan, Sullivan, and Gallagher did not merely say that they would be killed if they tried to return to San Francisco; it specified that their lives would be forfeit, if they were again found anywhere in the state. In as much as Yankee Sullivan was murdered on May 30, the edict could not have been issued later.

It can be said, then, that a fortnight after their official organization the Vigilantes had notions which could have been no part of the original conspiracy. The hopes of the desperate men who in secret egged on James King could have compassed no more than what has earlier been stated here. Item, they wanted political dominance in San Francisco. Item, they wished to stall off their creditors, while seeing what plums might be raked from civic chaos.

Except for Gabriel Post, the names of the men who stood ready to act, as soon as King was shot, cannot now be declared. Like Coleman himself, the members of the Executive Committee had not necessarily belonged to the initial cadre at all. They were the boldest and most efficient of a tribe of frontier opportunists. They not only hopped on what had the looks of a going band wagon; they took it over and gave it direction beyond the thinking of men who had mostly been trying to keep themselves from sinking.

The ones who shouldered their way into permanent control of the Committee can now be realized from two sources. Ned wrote in detail of his old *Panama* shipmate, George Ward, and a few others who will be noted later. The rest are only known individually because they lived long enough to be persuaded by Bancroft to write or dictate memoirs. Among the officers who complied in the 1870s were Coleman, Isaac Bluxome, James Dows, and Thomas Smiley. The rest were Charles V. Gillespie, Miers Truett, Clancy J. Dempster, O. B. Crary, James D. Farwell, and James N. Olney.

Perhaps there were certain ones who packed more punch than some of these; but by dying too early to meet Bancroft, or by escaping Ned's wrath, they robbed themselves of criminal credit. As faceless men are due no quarter from history, the remainder of the forty-one Executives will not be given a listing.

But after some weak ones had been shunted from membership —and founding father Post was an early casualty—the men who settled in control were predators on the peck. Having taken over the city and county of San Francisco without so much as having to fight for either, they began wondering how much more they could shoplift. When the state failed to move against them, they began to see it as feasible to dissolve California's government and substitute their own rule.

Feigned horror at San Francisco's moral state remained their screen, their excuse for staying in power while they built up local strength and wrought with guile elsewhere. Toiling clerks daily took down testimony from queues of citizens, damning their neighbors to no purpose. The papers of the Committee show that charges ranging from body snatching to buggery were placed in their files; but except in one case of expediency, nothing was done about any of them. Unless something was placed to the account of an Irish Catholic Democrat, the Executives weren't interested. They were too busy with crime in the mass to concern themselves with individual torts.

The head of the state they now had designs on was only twenty-eight. An honest man, too young to have gained a grasp of thieves' logic, he saw in the Vigilantes well meaning men who were undertaking the right thing in the wrong way. So on June 3 the Governor of California tried to bring them back to grace by issuing a proclamation:

"Whereas satisfactory information has been received by me that combinations to resist execution of legal process by force exist in the County of San Francisco in this state and that an unlawful organization styling themselves the Vigilance Committee has resisted by force the execution of criminal process, and that the power of said County has been exhausted and has not been sufficient to enable the Sheriff of said County to execute such process: Now therefore I, J. Neely Johnson, Governor of the State of California . . . do hereby declare said County of San Francisco to be in a state of insurrection."

At that time Johnson still thought the military resources of the state would be equal to the situation, if his proclamation of outlawry didn't jar the Committee into disbanding. It was not until two days later that he learned that General Wool was not going to supply his administration with the needed arms.

Johnson has been blamed for not promptly assembling California's legislature. While he certainly should have tried, it is doubtful if enough representatives of the other counties would then have voted for action against San Francisco's usurping regime.

The tale of San Francisco's horrible crime wave had been spread through the provinces with all the authority of a nearly united metropolitan press. Only subscribers who got their copies by mail now saw the *Herald*. As the owners of express services were all Vigilantes, they refused to carry Nugent's paper, for distribution by newsstands in other towns.

That was one reason for the general belief in the nobility of the Vigilante cause. Another was the Committee's diplomatic corps. Some of these were the salesmen who ranged the state for San Francisco's large mercantile houses. Naturally all stranglers, they spoke accordingly. There were, in addition, special delegates, sent to call on newspaper editors and fellow weight-packing residents of the provincial counties.

Many of the gold camps were rough, ill-organized towns, where the lawlessness imagined for San Francisco was a hard reality. Citizens of such places not only began holding the Committee up as a model for local action; in many cases they wrote letters, inviting the chokers of the metropolis to operate in their own provincial boroughs.

Getting that reaction, the Executives answered Governor Johnson's proclamation with one they issued June 9, or just six days later. Following rhetoric about San Francisco's hundreds of killers, this manifesto said, "We have spared and shall spare no effort to avoid bloodshed or civil war; but undeterred by threats or opposing organizations, shall continue, peaceably if we can, forcibly if we must, this work of reform to which we pledge our lives, our fortunes and our sacred honor."

That last crack was enough to draw a guffaw from a weeping willow. But people throughout California who did have some notions about honor were moved by the vision of nobility forced to take distasteful action.

Few outside San Francisco had any sympathy for the genuine men of good spirit who were trying to invoke the return of banished decencies. One incident will suffice to show the hopelessness of their efforts.

On June 2 Law and Order Leaders held a mass meeting in the plaza at which Colonel Edward D. Baker was the chief speaker. But five hundred attended, as compared with the thousands the Executives could whistle up at any time. When defending the way of life sponsored by the Constitution of the United States, Baker and others were hoorahed and pelted by a surrounding mob. Their heckling reached a climax when a point was made of running the American flag up the square's flagpole.

"Tear it down!" was the shout that rose. A surging gang did tear the Stars and Stripes from the halyard; and when a Law and Order subscriber began skinning up the pole, with a view to nailing it in place, he was bombarded with rotten oranges.

Some of the men infuriated by the sight of the star spangled banner were, to be sure, foreigners. Many were not; but neither were they American citizens at heart. Their nation was San Francisco and their heroes were the numbered men of the organization hatched by Coleman's know-how to harness mob energies.

The giant frogs of the Committee's pond were not thinking of secession as yet, none the less. Missing no angles, Coleman had thought to send one Squire P. Dewey to Washington, to plead before the country's chief magistrate the necessity of Vigilante action in San Francisco.

Although the date of that maneuver is uncertain, Dewey must have been long on his way by the time Governor Johnson got around to appealing to President Franklin Pierce. Unaccountably waiting until June 19, J. Neely then despatched a message asking Federal aid in quashing the Committee's insurrection. In part because of Dewey's chatter, and in part because Pierce was more interested in the bleeding Kansans of 1856 than in the strangled Californians of that year, he signaled non-sympathy to his Secretary of State. Thumbing through the rule book for an excuse to do nothing, William L. Marcy—on July 19—put his finger on the fact that Johnson hadn't got California's Legislature to agree that an armed uprising constituted a rebellion.

It took weeks for any in the torn state to learn that the national administration had decided to take no hand in its affairs. Meanwhile the Executives kept cool and watched developments; or they did until Chief Justice Terry was foisted on them by enthusiastic backers on the afternoon of June 21.

News of the Judge's capture sparked the last effort to resist the Committee inside San Francisco. Deserted by some of their officers and many of their other comrades, sixty-eight men belonging to Company C of the Jackson Guards staged a rally at their soon to be seized armory. Learning of it afterwards, the Committee's dog soldiers hunted them, as well as fellow National Guardsmen down, and weighted them with irons.

But when they had had the fun of threatening these men with further brutalities before letting them go, the Executives had to weigh the pros and cons of trying a state magistrate for a murder which had not yet become a fact. As in the case of James King of

William, Sterling Hopkins was an assumed rather than an actual corpse when the Vigilantes charged a man with killing him.

Yet King hadn't let the side down by living, and there was no reason to believe that Hopkins would. His wound seemed so final that the Executives felt safe in hiring the best medical counsel in the city for a man publicized as a martyr.

Considering his supposed slayer, the Committee found good reasons both for knocking him off and for serving him clemency. As testified by Captain Farragut as well as James O'Meara, Terry had a following of Texans to be reckoned with—a following, as both made clear, that was capable of making San Francisco's streets the scene of war. Weighed, too, was the general popularity of the Chief Justice in the gold fields, where the balance of power in the state as a whole lay. Admired there likewise so far, the Vigilante sagamores would have found it sweet to do nothing but give David a ticket back to Sacramento.

Against these deterrents had to be set the feelings of the Committee's man in the street. Mentioned so far, these have not been analyzed. Hanging a judge would be a dear dream realized on the part of Vigilantes who wouldn't have been nearly so gay at the prospect of stringing up a state senator, say.

Most of the foreigners who had shouldered Committee muskets hated the courts of California for their part in denying French filibuster planners the right to use San Francisco as a base for forays into Mexico. Then as many were veterans of European convict battalions, they had private as well as professional reasons for loathing courts of justice.

Alien Vigilantes were, of course, not the only ones who rejoiced at having caught a certified, and warranted stretchable, Supreme Court judge. The American lunch eaters who formed another large bloc would not have been listed among the purest and best citizens of any other city. Recalling times when they had either faced the bench or taken pains not to do so, they hailed with delight the chance of seeing a member boot the gallows bucket.

As the esteem of their followers was more important to them than the good will of the provinces, the Executives quit stalling on or about June 25 and resolved themselves into a court. The Minos who presided over the trial of California's Chief Justice was the Committee's so-called Judge Advocate. Of him General Estell remarked, in a speech which first dealt with Coleman, "The next in dignity is one J. P. Manrow, who was judge of the concern—settled intricate questions of law—passed sentences of death—and did many other trifling things too numerous to mention. He was born of his mother, I suppose, somewhere in the State of New York, and is by profession an engineer—an occupation that should especially fit him for the duty of sending erring mortals to their last long home with railroad speed."

The Committee's papers include only one signed by Manrow. A gem in its way, it reads, "Resolved—that the Ex. Committee concur, whith the Delligates in relation to the perade on Monday next."

Under the guidance of this author, the trial got under way. Preliminary to it was the announcement that Terry would be killed, in the event of any try for a rescue. Yet except for the judge's watchful comrades of Ranger days, nobody seemed troubled by the proceedings. The executives had been so successful in projecting themselves as men no less upright than stern, that most in California viewed them with respectful awe.

Meeting no general protest, when arraigning a state official in their private tribunal, the Executives had grounds for believing that California was as good as in their cupboard. That conviction went hand in hand with a decision to set up a separate nation. As they could not own a state while it remained a part of the Union, a hope to be free of it was inevitable.

The scheme was more than whispered about by the date of Maloney's deportation, which was July 5. He spoke of it when interviewed by the New York *Post,* upon reaching the Atlantic side. Members of the Committee had also bragged to him of another planned coup.

When the trial of Terry drew no strong opposition, the Executives decided to reach for another, if retired, Supreme Court justice. Hugh Murray was fighting with the consumption which was wasting his once great strength; but the Vigilantes planned to kidnap him by means of a rigged grand jury indictment on a bribery charge.

What the Committee's deys and beys had against Murray was a decision of his made with respect to real estate which they had been offered a chance to bid for and had not. Instead of kicking themselves, they wished to take their spleen out on the justice who had confirmed the purchases of men who had seized the opportunities they had passed by.

In the early days of San Francisco's organization as a city, a Dr. Peter Smith had contracted to house and care for the town's indigent invalids. Finding themselves without funds to meet the bill he submitted, the city's officers raised the amount by auctioning off town property. Through no fault of the administration, the sale wasn't well attended, the bids were therefore low; and because of that more public land had to be put on the block than had been expected.

The reason for the general lack of interest was that a committee without authority to speak for the law had passed the word that what were known as "the Peter Smith Sales" would be nullified. But when the matter was at length referred to the Supreme Court, Chief Justice Murray ruled that it was proper for a city, unable to meet its obligations in any other way, to do so by selling real estate.

While this seems consonant with reason, the business men who had passed the auction up were furious. Nor did their tempers sweeten, when the city's growth steadily raised the value of lots which others had bought for small change. The profits realized can be gauged from the fact that Dr. Smith's bill was for $64,000, and according to Maloney, the land sold to cover it was valued at more than $30,000,000 in 1856. J. Reuben also specified that many on the Executive Committee were those who had worked hardest to have Murray's decision reversed on review.

By trying—and, of course, convicting—Murray on the charge of having pocketed a bribe, the Executives would have scored two points and not merely one. In addition to reopening bids for coveted land, the discrediting of Murray could have been used as an excuse for denouncing all of Johnson's administration as corrupt. That in turn would have been followed by a call for Vigilante action on a state-wide scale, its purpose to set aside California's elected government in favor of a regime headed by the senior Vigilantes of San Francisco.

Why the plan to nab Murray wasn't carried out was told by Dr. Gray. After first predicating that America's Independence Day was not celebrated in San Francisco in 1856, he said that the Committee had proposed, through its newspapers, the holding of a convention in the city, on the Fourth of July, for the purpose of revamping California's constitution. This was the Committee's first defeat, for Gray added that the provinces wouldn't go along.

Still he said that the proposition was greeted with "silence," not outcries. Perceiving they had pushed too soon, the Executives shelved their bid for the state. They weren't discouraged, though, and there was nothing in the news to make them so.

The best proof of their dominance in California was proffered by the man who would have least willingly acted as an exhibit in their favor. When all Santa Barbara swarmed in quest of Ned McGowan, and when the newspapers of San Diego as well as Los Angeles commenced yapping for his gore, the Committee had solid strength where they could hardly have counted on it. With the Spanish settlements of the south in a camp which already held the American towns of the central and northern mountains, the Executives were cocks of all walks in the state, except a few owned by the Diggers and Modocs.

In progress this while was the trial of Terry, which couldn't proceed briskly until Hopkins came through with a death rattle. Putting their trust in the pale rider, the Executives were content to busy themselves with other things as well.

Although the date is nowhere recorded, it is probably at this peak point of their ascendance that the Committee's sachems felt themselves strong enough to deal directly with the man marked as their chief enemy. Gray said positively what O'Meara was less sure about: the Executives planned to deport David Broderick.

He wasn't shipped, because he had left the city before an eye-emblazoned writ could be made out for him by 33 Secretary. Possibly Broderick had sniffed danger and fled. But he was politically through in San Francisco, and it is likely that he had by then seen the uselessness of further vying with the People's Party. With his own city machine smashed, he went forth to tell the Democrats of the rest of the state what the lords of the metropolis were really up to.

One step they took led to the only detailed report of what it was like to be a captive of the Committee. The writer was a former state representative named Alfred A. Green. Because he had come West with Stevenson's regiment, he titled his manuscript narrative *The Life and Adventures of a '47-er of California.*

Green's troubles stemmed from the Federal government's agreement with Mexico to honor the real estate grants taken over from Colonial Spain. Jack Power's lost ranch a probable case in point, the result had been uproar in all parts of California where Spanish settlement was initial. But in San Francisco a confusing deck was further stacked with a wild card known as "Pueblo Lands."

When started as the Pueblo of Yerba Buena, a huge version of the English town common had been a part of the city's makeup. Open to grazing by the stock of all Yerba Buenans, it was far larger than the portion zoned for building.

When the gold rush turned what had become San Francisco into a populous seaport, Spanish zoning was one of the first casualties. Men who found land to their liking, settled on it; or they bought it from earlier birds, as carelessly rapacious or honestly ignorant as themselves. Many of these holdings were in part or wholly in the Pueblo Land area. Yet the fact of this basic, and unwaivable, title was unknown to Gringos, while the few native Californians with a grounding in law kept their knowledge to themselves.

Their secrecy was owing to their love for the country of which they had, by force of arms, ceased to be citizens. Most educated natives cherished the dream that—with aid from England—California would be restored to Mexico. When, as, and if that happened, they stood ready to pull the rug from under unsuspecting American land claimants.

San Francisco had lost its Hispanic character so swiftly that very few of its Gringos could speak Spanish. Green though had married a dictionary, and fluency in their language invited confidences from Californios. Hob and nob with one of them, he got wind of the existence and importance of the hidden Pueblo Land papers.

Securing them from one Tiburcio Vasquez [not the renowned outlaw so named] in 1852, Green commenced trying to unload them on fleeing San Francisco officials. A city attorney was eager for them until examination showed that they would have invalidated the land titles of some of the clients he had in private practice. A mayor was hot to have the ducats before he found that they would have pried him loose from his own holding.

The months rolled by in their usual order, each finding Alfred doggedly trying to bring to public attention papers worth millions of dollars to the city—and for which he wasn't asking a cent. In the spring of 1856 he finally managed to arrange for an open forum, at which he spoke with the assurance of one who had in the meantime undertaken to study Spanish land title law. It chanced that Gregory Yale, nationally recognized as an expert on the subject, was in San Francisco at the time. With the assistance of this man, a committee formed by Mayor Tewksbury pronounced the papers genuine. The committee's report, which cited the public spirit of Alfred A. Green, was published in the *Alta California* of May 5.

The mayor did not follow the matter up, because nine days later James King of William was shot, and authority in the city passed out of the hands of elected officials. Replacing them, as directors of San Francisco, were some with spurious titles to parts of the Pueblo Land.

Not understanding that the papers Green had were but duplicates of ones filed in Mexican archives, they dreamed that confiscation would allow them at once to cover up their own false claims and to oust from Pueblo Land any whose real estate they honed to possess. So when the Committee's chiefs deemed that they would never again be answerable to any but their own "higher law," they promoted an event described in the *Town Talk* of July 15:

"Yesterday morning before six o'clock a detachment of Vigilante police proceeded to the Mission and arrested Alfred A. Green and his two brothers, John and Robert Green, and brought them into town . . . We have no means of ascertaining upon what charges they were arrested . . . They were all taken to the committee rooms, where they are at present confined."

In his narrative Green told how a *lettre de cachet* brought him, on France's Bastille Day, to the Committee's bastille. At the end of July 13, he and his expectant wife had gone to bed in their ranch house, situated some miles south of the city. Yet on account of alarming noises, they did not slumber till dawn of the fourteenth.

"Startled from our sleep, we scarcely knew what to think, but were soon undeceived by hearing voices . . . 'Here's where the damned villain lives!' Then came the trampling of many feet upon my portico, the bursting of the outer door, then the rush to my bedroom and bursting there also. My wife, who was pregnant at the time . . . knew not what to think. Feeling for her, I sprang from bed, calling out, 'Who's there? What do you want?' The only answer was, 'Seize the damned villain!' . . . Within an instant the door gave way, and I was struck down and overpowered by a number of powerful and heavy men . . . and then manacled with hand cuffs . . .

"I was thrown into a wagon, and with a group of mounted men around me was conveyed to Fort Gunnybags." There he found a brother named Daniel Green, as well as the John and Robert named by *Town Talk*. "While we were conversing with each other, a member of the Executive Committee, C. V. Gillespie, made his appearance."

Green's manuscript is rich with illustrations of how puffed with small pond pride the Executives had become. A hoity-toity thief, the hero of the county court house swindle answered a question of Daniel's by demanding, "How dare you speak to me?"

"I looked at him with something of amazement at his audacity," Alfred recalled, "for I knew something of him that was not complimentary . . . and at the same time knew that the person he was addressing was an honest and industrious man."

What Alfred knew about Charles was brought out in the course of star chamber inquisition. "I was escorted into a large hall, where I found seated the Executive Committee in a kind of semi-circle round their chairman or president, William T. Coleman. I was invited to step upon a platform . . . and make my statement."

Taking note of the Committee's avowed interest in electoral purity, Green chose the topic of ballot-box stuffing: "Although I have always been closely connected with politics in this city and county," he told the Executives, "there has only been one instance of fraud which has come under my notice and that fraud was committed by one of your members, who appears to be the most active . . . and vindictive among you."

Asked to give details, Alfred told how he had caught Gillespie, then a polling place judge as well as a candidate, making a false count in his own favor. As this failed to shock men of built-in crookedness, the subject was dropped, and the prisoner was told why he was in hand.

"Mr. Green," Coleman began, "some short time ago you delivered a lecture in this city upon the title of the City of San Francisco and her public lands. You produced there original Spanish documents. We want those archives. We have nothing against you; bring them to us, and you may have your liberty."

In his innocence Alfred had himself joined the Committee, believing its leaders really concerned with civic reform. But if a naïve man, he was one who didn't take to bullying. He told his captors that for years he had been trying to find somebody who would make proper use of the papers, and that if the Executives had had the courtesy to tell him of their interest, he would have charged not a cent. Yet he declared that as long as they had misused him, they would have to pay for the time and effort he had invested, while trying to find a home for the documents.

Not minded to bargain with a captive, Coleman snapped, "Will you give us those papers, sir?" Then when Green stood pat,

William Tell barked an order to Marshal Charles Doane. "Take this prisoner and confine him to the blackest cell we have."

This was the one, as his jailers were careful to point out, which Yankee Sullivan didn't leave alive. Other forms of mental torture were applied. Once he was told that he would be marooned on a distant Pacific island at which he could never expect a rescue ship to call. He was likewise waked from sleep by ghouls who informed him they were going to hang him forthwith.

When such persuasions failed, the chief chokers resorted to geniality. As a member of the sub-committee whose aim was to try to get Green to tell where he had cached the Pueblo Land papers, James Dows had him moved to a lighter cell than the one where Sullivan had been done in. That arranged, Dows tried the friendly, man-to-man approach. He would drop in alone for a chat at times, and once he told a foe, helpless to spread the news, just what the Executives thought they could bring off.

In that interview the Committee's treasurer revealed that when they yanked California out of the Union, their plan was to plunder it of the territories of Oregon and Washington as well. "He told me," Alfred said of Dows, "that the Committee had gone so far that there was no retracing their steps, and that they would have to separate the State of California and the Pacific Coast from the general government, and that a plan was on foot, and for the purpose of carrying it out, they had sent committees to the interior to sound the people upon it."

The Executives had become sure they could safely defy and rob the United States, because there had been no Federal reaction to an uprising now with a history of going on three months, and known about on the Atlantic side since early in June. To men whose heads had fattened on unopposed triumphs, that spelled but one thing. They thought the rest of America was afraid to take on the Coastal empire they considered as good as a fact.

So much was made clear by O'Meara's report of what took place when some Executives fared to Farragut's Mare Island anchorage to call on the captain. "The Vigilante organization acknowledged no authority superior to itself," the journalist wrote, with reference to this occasion. Having apparently covered it for some sheet, he illustrated his point by telling how James Farwell had laid the attitude of his gang on the line.

"We have proved ourselves superiors of the City and the County governments, and of the State government," he told the naval commander, "and if the Federal government dares—"

Furious at hearing such talk aboard an American man of war, Farragut sprang up at that point and shouted Farwell down. Aboard the Captain's flagship the Vigilante did find it politic to let his sentence die unfinished. But that concession didn't change the way the members of the Executive Committee felt when ashore and strutting in or out of Fort Gunnybags.

They well might have got as far as forming a Pacific state, and forcing a war they were prepared to wage in their imaginations alone. Elsewhere in California they were already so powerful that men made pilgrimages to gain their good will. Deputy Sheriff Lent of San Luis Obispo didn't explicate by mail why he had failed to arrest Ned; he journeyed to San Francisco and made a deposition at the Committee's headquarters. The same was true of George Parkinson, who felt it wise to go all the way from Santa Barbara and explain to the Committee in person that he had been innocent of any intent to help McGowan.

But there was one man, and he a resident of San Francisco, who balked the Executives scot free. Aided by doctors who worked overtime, in their zeal to save a man billed as a hero, Sterling Hopkins refused to consider his wound mortal. To the horror of men who had been officially in mourning for him, proud medics sent word that the man stabbed by Terry would soon be up and about.

A score or so years later a surviving Executive still couldn't get over the shock of that body blow. Of Hopkins, O. B. Crary moaned, "The man did not die, and that was the most unfortunate thing that ever happened."

On July 22 Terry's trial for the murder of this spoilsport ground to a squeaky halt. It was later written of Br'er Rabbit that, when hoisted high by a snare, he was at once afraid he would fall and afraid he *wouldn't* fall. The Executives were similarly of two minds now.

Afraid to arouse the wrath of followers promised the sight of a dangling judge, they couldn't free their prisoner. Afraid to let it be known in the rest of the state that they had hanged a man for a crime he manifestly hadn't committed, they couldn't scrag him.

At least they feared to hang him, pending word from their embassies afield that the rest of California was ready for secession. Waiting for the returns, the Executives passed no sentence on Terry, despite loudening demands for his execution.

When these grew so insistent that mob action seemed likely, the Executives played for more time by offering a diversionary treat. On July 30 they announced that they would hang two captives, picked up with just such an emergency in mind.

15

A RETREAT AND AN ADVANCE

A MAN NAMED Marion had, in 1854, killed a fellow of San Francisco County called Captain West. Marion seems to have been hanged for it, for among the Committee's papers is a reference to his body having been in the hands of a certain, and later to be cited, County Coroner.

While alive the murderer had had a young associate—hardly more than a boy, according to O'Meara—with the unlikely name of Philander Brace. An admitted thief in a small way, he appears to have been weak rather than dangerous.

Nevertheless, he had been belatedly tried for complicity in the slaying of West in January of 1856. Found guiltless, he was at large until the Executives saw the need of new lynchings, to prove that they were still wrapped up in reform. Notwithstanding their screams about all the killers rampant in San Francisco, they were so hard up for exhibits that they sent goons in search of Brace. Even if he had committed what they charged him with, the crime was then two years old, nor had West been slain inside the city limits.

To make up the pair they liked to offer, the Executives had to thin the Committee's ranks, for Joseph Hetherington was a Vigilante. He was, nonetheless, said to have been a highly "cultured" man. And after paying him that tribute, Thomas Smiley wrote of one of his victims, "He didn't deserve to be hung much."

Prior to learning that a little hanging goes a long ways, Hetherington had shot another real estate broke called Dr. Randall. There has been debate as to who drew first, when they met at the Nicholas Hotel in July of 1856. All the fault couldn't have been on Hetherington's side, though, or Dows wouldn't have conceded that being cultured wasn't much of a capital offense.

But whatever the score otherwise, Rand had been pistol-killed by Hetherington. Thus qualifying as a Committee foil, he was Gunnybagged, supposedly pending trial. Although it has often been stated that he was in fact arraigned, the truth is that he, and Brace as well, were given no more a hearing than unwanted kittens while the tub's filling.

It chanced that Hetherington was penned immediately to the right of Green, Brace to his left. The cells were divided one from the other by wooden partitions. As there were both chinks and knotholes in the planking, Alfred could peer into the adjoining cribs, if so minded; and could hear anything said above a whisper, whether he wanted to or not.

During the night of July 28–29 Green saw and heard plenty. As to Brace he wrote, "I saw him woke up about twelve o'clock at night. I saw armed men lead him from his cell. I saw them bring him back again. I heard him say, 'They have been condemning me without a trial.' They had been away about fifteen minutes."

After a short stretch of brooding, Brace began shouting for guards, and demanding that they bring Coleman to confront him. In a short while the Committee's president appeared, accompanied by Dows, and an Executive named Tillinghast.

"Coleman," Green heard Brace ask, "were you in earnest when I was taken forth and condemned without a trial?"

To this William Tell replied, "It was in earnest . . . You die for having violated the laws of your country."

The effrontery of this statement was too much for an admitted felon, of smaller degree, though, than the unconfessing Vigilante. "The constitution and laws of my country guarantee me . . . a trial by a jury of my countrymen, and this you have denied me," he charged in return. "You have not even permitted me to send for a single witness . . . You have deprived me of counsel."

It happened that Green thought he knew the truth relative to the murder in which Brace was accused of being implicated. In an effort to save Philander, Alfred flagged the attention of James Dows.

"Don't hang poor Brace," he recalled saying. "West, who was killed, was a friend of mine. It is my belief that Brace had nothing to do with the killing."

In reply Dows as much as said that the Executives would stamp out anybody's life to further their purposes: "Green, keep your mouth shut . . . These are critical times, and it may come your turn next."

Now out of reach of threats, Brace began shouting to everybody moving along the fort's busy corridors. To boil his many words down to few, he yelled that the chief Vigilantes were murderous cheats; foes of every principle they had vowed to uphold.

Hearing his howls from their offices on the same floor, the Executives took notice of the fact that the hangings scheduled for the morrow would be attended by all their henchmen and well wishers of the People's Party. They also saw that they could not gag a man they were hanging in the name of civic purity. A part of the show that they couldn't cut, without giving themselves away, was the traditional right of a gallows bird to cheep one last time.

In short what the Executives grasped was that the stretching of Brace would draw their followers within voice range of a man who might repeat all the image-marring facts about them which he was now screeching. And they knew he would be believed by the mob, because of the superstition that a man at doom's rim can traffic in nothing but truth.

How the Committee's hetmen canceled belief in the coffin-side charges which Brace did make, was told by Green. "One of the Committee came into his cell and said, 'Brace, you take it hard. Let's have a drink together.'

"A few minutes later," Green went on, "he became a raving

maniac. . . . His ravings continued for a short time, but he was soon overpowered by sleep. He had been narcotized."

Where Casey and Cora had been hanged by night, the new lynchings took place during the morning of July 30. Busy as the Seven Dwarfs, Vigilantes had gone without sleep in order to fit Davis Street with a gallows twenty-five feet high. Standing upon a platform, it promised a good view of proceedings even to such as were not lucky enough to have one of the box seats described by Henry Gray.

The roofs of all the nearby buildings were crowded; one so much that it caved in. But that accident didn't kill the holiday spirit reported by the doctor: "The ribald jest and the horse laugh echoed from building to building."

Master of these revels was Hangman Nixon, assisted by Jake Chappell as noose-tier. Neither of the victims had to wait his turn, for de luxe gallows offered each a private jumping off place.

Before using it, though, each was allowed freedom of speech. Given no more of a trial than Brace, Hetherington had the stamina to remain calm. He did say that Gillespie had cuffed him while he was en route to the gallows, but he offset that by thanking Smiley for the consideration shown him by that Executive. Dropped, Hetherington did not so much as squirm in protest. He made a nice monkey on a string, and everybody was pleased with him.

The crowd was disappointed in Brace, however. Showing none of the dignity expected by a quasi-corpse, he screamed accusations as wild as his language was inappropriate.

"He talked rough," Dows remembered with wooden nutmeg piety; "what people would call wicked."

Alfred Green put it another way. "The public was somewhat horrified . . . at his horrible language and conduct upon the scaffold, but here out of charity and justice to Brace, I must state the fact. It was not Brace in his right mind, but Brace a lunatic and maniac, and made so by the powerful drug he had been given."

Thus escaping credited criticism, the Executives were also relieved of pressure from within San Francisco. A mob with two hangings to clack about did not, for a while, renew their clamor for Terry's demise.

It was then, though, that the murderers began to learn that all wasn't well with them outside their city. The chief cause was the lapse from duty of Sterling Hopkins. Secondary was the roving Broderick, stumping to ram home the lesson that breachers of all laws are not to be trusted.

By trying Terry for the murder of a living man, the Executives made themselves look foolish rather than the demi-gods they had pronounced themselves. And this fall from grandeur came at the very time when their emissaries were abroad, trying to promote their leadership in a pan-California secession movement.

Although many yet clung to their dream of San Francisco's high-minded supermen, the majority refused. As Ned later wrote, "The real motives of the Committee were beginning to be scanned, the people had come back to their 'sober second thoughts,' and the state was saved."

The Executives had some sober second thoughts of their own. Farragut hadn't intervened, when it seemed that Terry had actually slain a man; but when the Committee continued to hold California's Chief Justice, after it was reported that Hopkins was up and about, the commodore decided to sit in. "For moral effect," as Sherman put it, Farragut ordered the *John Adams*, E. B. Boutwell commanding, to ride within a hundred yards of San Francisco's waterfront. Looking into the mouths of cannon which could have made smithereens of their town in jig time, the head Vigilantes forgot they had ever wanted to challenge the United States.

With the rest of California lost and the Pacific Coast nation a dissolved pipe dream, the Executives now concentrated on keeping San Francisco captive. Their problem was to free Terry without causing an explosion which would break up the People's Party. For as long as they retained that gimmick, they would be masters of the metropolis, whatever their standing elsewhere.

In the meantime the rest of their gang had chewed all the satisfaction out of the lynchings of Brace and Hetherington, and were once more calling for Terry's neck. Feeling that hot breath on their own napes, the Executives took a chance; they jumped but with a makeshift parachute.

On August 7, or sixteen days after Terry's trial ended, they announced that the Judge had been guilty of something their constitution didn't allow them to punish him for. They had, they said, convicted him of "attempted murder"; but upon inspecting their penal code, they had found themselves helpless to sentence a felon for that particular crime.

Coleman wanted to tickle the mob with a pageant by mustering the whole Vigilante army for the purpose of drumming Terry out of town. Fearing the temper of their own troops as well as that of the unenlisted rabble, others saw this as too dangerous for David, and therefore themselves. As William Tell unforgivingly charged, they held a rump session after he'd left Fort Gunnybags, and voted to smuggle the Judge out of their stronghold after dark.

At that time Miers Truett took Terry to the home of a former law partner of David's named D. W. Perley. Not much later the Devil nearly got paid.

Discovering that the Chief Justice was no longer in his cell, a guard passed news which was swiftly all over town. It brought the Committee's soldiery, four thousand strong, into the fort or massed outside.

Green couldn't see what was going on, but because of the structure's acoustics he could follow the script. "Vigilantes arrived in the building in great numbers," he noted. "I heard a great commotion on the floor underneath, also on the second floor where I was . . . From the under floor I could hear the voices of several speakers, who seemed to be members of the Executive Committee, and seemed to indicate an attempt on their part to pacify the dissatisfied members of the Vigilance Committee. I could hear statements to the effect that a U. S. man of war had drawn up, and they had to let Terry go or they would have been bombarded, and advising the members to be calm, to exercise discretion and patience."

While this was going on, Bluxome sped to the house of Miers

Truett, as the man who knew where Terry now was. Hustling to
Perley's residence, Truett told the Judge that the only way he could
dodge the gibbet was to make for the *John Adams*.

To the applause of a one-gun salute, Terry did board the warship. Somewhat later quiet was restored at Fort Gunnybags. The
Executives had had enough of their army, however, and they
moved to get rid of what had become more of a threat to them
than anybody else.

As it had by then been learned that the Federal government
was not going to suppress them—a failure which Judge Harvy
Brown cited as having much to do with encouraging Southern
secession and bringing on the Civil War—they were able to call
their rebellion off in style. After deporting three more Irish Catholic Democrats on August 15, they announced that the Committee
had performed its mission of purging the city of evil doers, and
would become watchfully inactive after first enjoying a gala.

A grand ball capped the festivities which marked the disbanding
on August 18. Fort Gunnybags was made a museum for this holiday; and, as O'Meara reported, people brought children there to
fondle, among other souvenirs, the ropes which had strangled four
men. Lumping fun for the tots with the Vigilante hop, Ned
summed the occasion up by writing, "the little girl played with the
hangman's noose, and the maiden she danced with the hangman."

In a better position to bargain by then, Green was at length
given $10,000 for papers he still didn't understand that the Execu-
tives wanted for crooked purposes. But the position of no other
Committee victim was improved by the organization's retreat from
open domination. The decrees of banishment were not withdrawn.
And, of course, no move by the Vigilantes could change the fact
that Ned had been indicted for murder by an authorized grand
jury.

Four days after all but its leaders had gone underground, the
Committee heard from the man whose own murder they had so
long and doggedly sought to compass. For on August 22 the
Herald published the letter McGowan had written in gunpowder
ink, in his home amidst the corn stalks. As excerpts from that

have been given, only Nugent's comments will be drawn upon here:

"The 'Mark Meddle' press in the hireling pay of the Saints have chased the ubiquitous Napoleon of primary elections from pillar to whipping post—they have had him comfortably corraled everywhere throughout the geographical limits of this extended area of freedom, except in their own clutches—and at last the 'old Joker' turns up, and pleasantly and convivially speaks of his hair breadth 'scapes' as coolly as if he was on his old stamping ground, Montgomery Street, and had an admiring audience of drinking friends, hoisting in his original and peculiar funds of small talk."

Although McGowan's nose-thumbing and the *Herald's* applause of it must have jabbed the Vigilantes with chagrin, they probably thought that was the last they would hear of Ned. It could have occurred to none of his proscribers that a fugitive from a rigged capital charge would find a way to get a fair hearing. Assuredly none foresaw the day when he would strike back at them. For there wasn't a Jack Ketch among them with the wit to envision the weapons he would use.

With safety no longer a daily problem, Ned had given up all notion of going back to Philadelphia. To stay in California, he had to face the indictment against him in court. It could not be held in San Francisco; there McGowan and anathema were spelled and pronounced alike. So what he had to arrange for was a shift of court jurisdiction to another county.

Simpler said than done. A change of venue could only be gained through an act of the Legislature, in a state so young that there seems to have been no precedent. Yet from Dr. Den and trusted visitors, Ned had learned of the Committee's general loss of favor and the growing strength of Broderick in California as a whole.

Week by week McGowan was under ever lessening pressure. By mid-September he felt able to dine with the Dens, and not long afterward he swapped his cot in the tall corn for a bed indoors.

As Election Day drew near, there were chuckles for Ned in the efforts of the Executives to get the governor to withdraw his proc-

lamation of outlawry without suing for peace. Still posting themselves as worthy men, the Committee's werowances kept offering
to return the stolen National Guard arms, if Johnson would first
restore them to citizenship. No longer backed by an army, they
had to rule San Francisco through regularly elected officers, nominated by the People's Party.

So it was the governor who had the upper hand now, and he
was of no mind to make concessions to men who had, among other
things, ruined him politically. He told them in effect that unless
they sent the purloined arms to Sacramento, the votes of San
Franciscans for state and Federal officers would be disallowed; nor
would their county be represented in the Legislature. That was still
the story when November arrived on schedule, and two days before
the first Tuesday after the first Monday, the Executives caved.

When the returns were in, Ned was happy on two scores. Not
counting San Francisco, there was a Democratic landslide in California. Then the news came in from the Atlantic side that his old
friend, James Buchanan, had been chosen President of the United
States.

The balloting, though, had left San Francisco officially anti-
McGowan, for sworn enemies were now legally in power. As
sheriff the People's Party had voted in Charles Doane, Grand
Marshal of the Committee of Vigilance of 1856. The Police
Commissioner was James Curtis, late aboard the *Exact* when she
cruised as part of the hunt for Ned. The Harbor Master was Selim
Woodworth, leader of the rat catchers who had fared to Santa
Barbara in the *Sea Bird*. One of the two State Senators was Selim's
brother, Frederick. The other Senator and the nine San Francisco
assemblymen were all chokers in good standing.

Yet the most significant result of the election was the comeback
of David Broderick. An utterly defeated man six months earlier,
he was California's ringmaster in January of 1857.

His first move was to show that the state as a whole had
repudiated Vigilantism. California's Legislature had never had
any official chaplains. Now it blossomed out with two, carefully
chosen. The Reverend William Anderson Scott was a Presbyterian

divine who had been burned in effigy at the very door of his San Francisco church because he had undertaken to criticize the Committee. Broderick had decided that Scott would make a suitable chaplain for the Senate, while for the Assembly he picked an Irish Catholic Democrat called Father Gallagher: the priest who had shriven Casey.

If that was a subtle means of rubbing it into the stranglers that they had failed to dominate the state, there was one whose hostility took a more direct form. As O'Meara and Ned agreed, James Madison Estell was a good man and a knowing one. Over the objections of People's Party members, he made an address, published under the long but explicit title, *Speech of Gen. James M. Estell, Delivered in the Hall of Representatives, Sacramento City California, To a Question of Privilege in Connection with the Vigilance Committee of 1856.*

As urbane as hard hitting, Estell began by telling how the purist and best operated as private citizens. "In the first place I will call your attention to the conduct of their President, William T. Coleman, whose principal occupation, since his arrival in California, has been that of creating monopolies, that he might obtain famine prices for the necessities of life."

The general explained why the leading Vigilante jurist had found it well to speed west. James Madison was in a position to do that, having been told of it by the San Franciscan who had married the sister of the Judge Advocate's wife. So of John P. Manrow, Estell said, "By some unlucky mistake, this rare Judge of the Vigilance Committee was arrested for signing another gentleman's name instead of his own."

General Estell mused upon Tom King's career as a runner for his wife's brothel, and so on. His speech was a liberal education in Chokerism offered by a man who had had a gibbet-side seat in San Francisco. By discrediting Ned's enemies it helped to create an atmosphere favorable to his hopes of being able to move as a free citizen again. And the fact that the indictment of the Committee had been lanced by a non-Broderick Democrat was useful in uniting the viewpoints of the party's two wings.

David wasn't promptly ready to act in Ned's behalf. Now that the steering wheel was all his, the man who would be senator first got himself elected. He was then in such a good humor that he allowed California to have two representatives in the upper house of Congress for the first time since 1855. As John Weller was not a candidate to succeed himself, in brief, Broderick permitted William Gwin to resume his seat in the Senate.

Those things attended to, David talked Ned's problem over with the Speaker of the Assembly. As a result of this conference, a San Francisco friend of Ned's showed up at Dr. Den's ranch on February 10. His name was Captain J. Martin Reese. In his pocket was a letter from the Speaker, dated January 27, 1857:

Judge Edward McGowan
Dear Sir:

I have had much conversation with Captain Reese and others in regard to the practicability of having a special act passed by the present legislature, granting you a change of venue from San Francisco without the necessity of your personal appearance in that county, and am of the opinion that there will be no difficulty in accomplishing it.

It is notorious that your person would be in danger of mob violence, were you to go back there, to say nothing of the absolute impossibility of your procuring a fair trial in that community, so that I cannot conceived of any honest man's opposition to a law so obviously just and necessary. I would therefore recommend to you to come as quietly and quickly as you can to Sacramento, where you certainly will be at least safe from personal violence.

Very truly your friend,
E. T. Beatty

Reese had come to Santa Barbara by boat. Ned could use no public conveyance, least of all one that would dock in Stranglerland. The journey north had to be made ahorseback in the region's coldest and wettest season.

McGowan, though, was not the overweight tenderfoot who

had ridden south eight months before. From 182 soft pounds, he had shrunk to a hard 140. Trimming down had, as he said, given him a new charge of vigor. Feeling younger than he had for years, and more mentally alert, he set forth with the purposes of vindicating himself first, and next making his foes sorry they had kicked him around.

It was a measure of his new confidence in his ability to face outdoor hardships, that he was ready to make the trip alone and without a pilot. But as Reese was the kind of lad to insist on sticking with him, they slopped and slid on mountain roads together—when they weren't fording or swimming swollen streams.

The Committee got its first inkling of Ned's maneuver, when the *Herald* published a letter of McGowan's datelined, Stockton, February 27. In part it read, "I have been invited by the Legislature to deliver a series of lectures before them . . . The subjects— 'Higher Law,' 'Soft Pork,' 'Sour Flour,' and the morality of the Chiefs of the Chokers generally."

The Vigilante press was at first loth to believe that a man their heroes had consigned to oblivion was once more asserting himself. "The ubiquitous Ned McGowan," the *Town Talk* of March 1 warned its readers, "turned up yesterday as a topic of conversation, a rumor having gained currency that he had arrived in Sacramento. The report was received with considerable misgiving."

But the *Bulletin* of March 2 confessed that it was only too true. "Ned McGowan, the ubiquitous, has actually arrived in Sacramento. This time there is no humbug about it. He puts up at the Magnolia Hotel, where during all of yesterday he was the centre of a large circle of admirers with the like of whom this city swarms at present."

By the date of that item, Ned had done two things. Of necessity he had arranged for the drafting of a habeas corpus writ, to keep San Francisco authorities from shagging him off to their city. For personal satisfaction, next, he had bought a new, white plug hat. "Richard was himself again," as he remarked of that adornment.

Richard's affairs were going well in general. On March 4 Sacramento's *Democratic State Journal* declared that, "A bill was introduced in the Assembly yesterday, the effect of which would be to grant Edward McGowan a trial in some county out of San Francisco."

Despite the squalls of that county's delegation, the bill went through, and was likewise approved by the Senate. Promptly signed by a governor who had himself known what it was to be misused by Vigilantes, it did not specify where the trial would be held. Deciding that was the prerogative of the judge presiding, in San Francisco, over that vicinity's State District Court.

While waiting to learn where he would be arraigned, Ned began writing the account of his recent experiences, so largely drawn upon in this chronicle. His work was interrupted when District Judge Hager finally assigned McGowan's case to the court of Napa County. A natural consideration was that impartiality could be expected of Napans, whose bailiwick Ned had never visited. He could not say that after May 19, the day a deputy sheriff brought him to the county seat. Housing was no problem, for he was lodged in jail.

Friends came to see him there. Enemies from San Francisco hovered at a nearby resort known as Napa Springs. Their hope was that the law would end the life they had failed to snuff illegally.

Vindictiveness was now less of a motive than vindication. Sued by some and accused by many more, the Executives stuck to their pose—as they had to—of injured civic innocence. They could not for an instant admit that they had been less than champions of virtue, or they would lose the support of the San Francisco jurors who alone saved them from getting some sort of come-uppance.

Now if a Law and Order court would but condemn McGowan as accessory to the murder of James King, they could point to it as proof they had been right in all their acts. Hopeful of this boon, they had pulled evidence out of their boot tops, and journeyed to see what it would do for them.

Because McGowan had become California's most celebrated wolf's head, his trial drew to Napa many besides his foes and well wishers. It was the one time in a small town's history when the eyes of the rest of the state were turned its way. Liking the novelty, the Napa *Reporter* crowed about it in its issue of May 23.

"The town is crowded with strangers and every hotel is crowded . . . The Honorables J. M. Coffroth, H. S. Foote, and J. M. Estell are among us . . . Hon. C. T. Botts and Hon. James Coffroth appear for the defense, and the District Attorney and Mr. Heslep for the People."

In view of the fact that the *Bulletin* had attacked the star boarder of Napa's jail, the *Reporter* gave the prisoner a chance to answer back. "We publish today a card by Ned McGowan . . . The card is rather pungent but, considering the position of the writer it is not only moderate but manly and dignified. Ned does not pretend to be altogether a saint, but he is evidently one 'who hath sat at good men's feasts,' and not the vulgar and low bred ruffian which some have described him to be."

"People of Napa!" Ned had written. "I am a stranger among you and known but to few of you personally. I therefore deem it due myself . . . to vindicate my character—or at least, if possible, remove from your minds any erroneous impressions in regard to myself . . . and prove to you that I am not the fiend and outlaw that the Vigilance press of San Francisco have for the past twelve months endeavored to prove me."

In an effort to decide the case in advance of court arguments, Tom King's paper had published an account of Ned's Pennsylvania past which made murder a logical pursuit for him. To show his true standing in his home state, McGowan had given the *Reporter's* editor a group of letters. Among them were the notes from Buchanan and Vice-President George Dallas which have previously here been quoted.

When robbed of all others, Ned had clung to these straws of respectability, and now they came in handy. "As to the letters annexed to this card," the *Reporter* commented, "there is no doubt of their authenticity. They were set up from the originals, which are still in our possession."

The county judge at Napa was the later renowned Elisha William McKinstry. Defense counselors were Charles T. Botts and

James Coffroth, two of the most respected lawyers of their era. In time to arrive at some eminence, District Attorney Henry Egerton wasn't then well known. He had a volunteer assistant in the person of a Vigilante named Augustus M. Heslep. Although sporting the title of judge, he seems to have been chiefly engaged in journalism.

Comparing the two legal teams, the Committee felt their own wasn't strong enough. At the last moment they bought the services of the man considered the most persuasive pleader in California.

Actually Henry Stuart Foote had a name for oratory throughout the nation. In a Federal Senate noted for eloquent speakers he had held his own. A historian and anecdotalist, too, he was altogether a man of impressive mark.

With him in the line-up, the trial got under way a week later than scheduled. Although the set date was May 22, the prosecution had made an embarrassing discovery. When sought for, one of its material witnesses had been found toiling in the service of San Francisco County as a member of a chain gang. He could therefore be brought to Napa only through a court order. Complying with a request for one, Judge McKinstry postponed the case till May 29.

PART III

A TALE
OF EXILE AND RETURN

16

THE BOOK AND THE BIRD

FOOTE, HESLEP, AND Egerton combined to score a goose egg. They did not so much as prove that there could have been a killing for Ned to have abetted.

The witness who cast doubt on the fact that James King of William had been slain by Casey was none other than the man who had functioned as the Committee's Surgeon-Major during the reign of terror. Whatever his philosophy in other respects, Dr. Beverley Cole called shots as he saw them, when dealing with matters medical.

Summoned to testify at McGowan's trial, the doctor came armed with charts and a skeleton. With these visual aids he demonstrated that the wound inflicted on King by Casey was chalks away from being in the mortal class. What had laid James of William low was, he said, the insertion in the wound of sponges which retained infected matter instead of allowing its discharge. In short King had been killed not by the man Ned was accused of aiding, but by the medics in attendance. Originally one of these, Cole had been overruled and aced to the sidelines by the majority of those buzzing about a healable wound.

As the trial proceeded, all but the Vigilantes were amused by the antics of two prosecution perjurors. One of these was the chain gang serf, John Butts. When not in jail for shoplifting, he was a young loafer; and in this capacity he really had seen King shot by Casey.

Learning as much, the Committee had either paid or frightened him to tell a story, of which he forgot the key part when on the witness stand. When McGowan and Whiteman entered the Bank Exchange some twenty minutes before the shooting, John was, he said, seated on the sill of one of the saloon's windows. Finding him on this perch, Casey told him to ask Peter to step outside. When requested, Whiteman obliged—and that's substantially all Butts had to say.

As Whiteman soon saw James of William plugged, the theory was that he formed a manifest link between Ned and Casey's trigger finger. But when stage fright made John forget the covering lines, there was nothing in his testimony to show that McGowan so much as knew why Peter had reputedly been summoned by James P.

What Butts had forgotten to say was remembered by the other perjuror. He, however, queered the show by contradicting John, in place of going along, with respect to other matters.

The instance of Jacob Curtis is one for a head shrinker's case book. In order to protect a fib he'd told for fun, he agreed to commit perjury, and then, when the spotlight was on him in court, dropped his original lie and came up with a variant.

Among the Committee's papers is an informer's deposition which avers that "Curtis was in my office the other day and said he was present with Wightman and McGowan at the Bank Exchange at the time the boy Butts came into the room and Wightman gave him a pistol which was for Casey." Curtis, in other words, had heard the testimony, put in John's mouth by the Executives, and publicized by them at the time of Ned's indictment. He had then made a business of telling people he had been right there when Butts—as he was supposed to have said, but did not at McGowan's trial—borrowed from Whiteman the pistol with which Casey inferentially shot James King.

At Napa, however, Jacob testified that he had drunk with Ned and Peter at a saloon called Dan's, not the Bank Exchange. He said, besides, that the youngster who supposedly obtained a revolver from Whiteman was named Jimmie, whom he described as slim, while John Butts was chubby.

So much for his direct testimony. Cross examined, he yammered in part as follows: "While there boy came in; didn't know the boy . . . never told anybody who the boy was . . . did not at one time say this affair took place at Dan's saloon . . . I say upon oath it was at Dan's saloon."

What appears to have been true of Curtis is that he had merely wished to draw attention by including himself in an event which was the talk of all San Francisco. Next he was appalled to find that he might help hang a man with what he had looked upon as a harmless yarn. Unwilling to admit at Napa that he had invented his whole story, he had hit upon the compromise ruse of changing the circumstances offered by Butts, so that he would not be acting in support of statements which he was in no position to confirm, and now wished he had never quoted.

Curtis and Butts were the only material witnesses the prosecution brought forward. The one on furlough from jail and the other with unstable wits, they wouldn't have made the best of testifiers in top form and pulling together. But as it worked out, John got tongue-tied and told the jurors nothing damning. Then after Jacob said he did and did not know "Jimmie," and that he had and had not been with McGowan and Whiteman at Dan's, there was nothing for the panel to make out of him but the pathetic liar he was.

The upshot of the Committee's try to hang Ned by proxy was related by the Napa *Reporter* on June 6: "This famous trial closed at 12 o'clock on Monday night last. The prosecution scarcely made out a case against the defendant. Indeed there was not evidence enough against him to hang a cat—and so thought the jury, for in just ten minutes from the time of their leaving the Court Room, they returned a verdict of Not Guilty."

So by midnight of June 1, 1857, a hounding which had begun one year and fourteen days earlier had come to an end. Cleared of an indictment by due process of law, Edward McGowan was once more a free citizen of the United States. Well, almost. He was free to come and go everywhere in America but the part of it where he most wanted to be.

In San Francisco it was not only the Executives and their like who refused to admit they had been wrong about Ned, the verdict at Napa notwithstanding. There were many honest dupes of the conspirators who closed their minds against all assaults of reason, as the only means of denying they had been party to atrocities. If they had confessed to themselves that they had been mistaken about a man who had escaped the Committee, they would have had to think about the ones who had not got away. They would have had to wonder about Yankee Sullivan, brought into Fort Gunnybags alive and taken out dead. They would have had to wonder if there had been truth amongst the ravings of Philander Brace, when he charged that he had not been tried at all. They would have had to wonder what the ruined victims of exile decrees had actually done, aside from being Irish Catholic Democrats.

Not being willing to face haunting realities, well-meaning men continued in the faith that Ned was a monster who had somehow compassed the death of James King by remote control. So the *Bulletin* spoke for most in San Francisco, when it described the trial which had vindicated him as "The farce at Napa."

In the city corrupted by Vigilantism, the forms of Law and Order had been restored. Yet the law of the United States remained without authority there. The banishment decrees had not been lifted. Nor could Ned return to his law practice, or regain the money and property stolen from him by the Committee.

After his trial he went back to Sacramento. Dwelling there for the next twelve months, he devoted his time to turning out one of the most remarkable bodies of writing in American Literature.

First he completed his life on the dodge, beginning with the events leading up to the shooting of James King and ending with the trial which had absolved him of complicity. Dedicated to Dr. Den, it was titled *The Narrative of Edward McGowan, Including a Full Account of the Author's Adventures and Perils While Persecuted by the San Francisco Vigilance Committee of 1856.*

Although Ned couldn't go to San Francisco, Jeremiah F. Sullivan published his book there in July of 1857. The artist who illustrated it has not been identified, but he was remarkable among a breed of free thinkers by hewing to the author's line in place of striking out in contrary directions. There are pictures of Ned making his way past mounted sabreurs, of the timely advent of Jack Power, of the snake with finer instincts than the Vigilantes, and so on.

Enough excerpts have been here offered to give an idea of the manner in which it was written. Its over-all flavor was grasped by the editor of the Alameda County *Gazette:*

"The work combines in equal proportions the spirit of John Bunyan's Pilgrim's Progress, Sinbad the Sailor and Robinson Crusoe. The changing bursts of piety and passion, the thirst for vengeance giving way to an occasional domineering thirst for brandy and water—the remorseless denunciation of rogueries in general, and the complacent explanation of the little venalities of the author have an exquisite relish of true McGowanism, while the account of his exposure to cold, hunger, thirst and mortal perils give a pathetic interest to the story that none can fail to appreciate."

None but Vigilantes, who nevertheless didn't overlook it. The Committee's sachems were in particular disturbed by it. Here was an exposure of them in book form, hailed as delightful reading matter.

But while Ned's enemies were licking this unexpected wound, he was preparing to hit them where it would hurt a great deal more. In the *Narrative* he had dealt with them as a group, and on the whole had been moderate as to language. Now he meant to take them apart individually and without gloves, in a weekly dagger sheet he called the *Phoenix*.

It has been the fashion of California chroniclers to describe this venture in original journalism as an irresponsible scandal rag; or at best a scatter fire of accusations which sometimes found a weak spot in an essentially noble body of targets. Before examining what Ned had to say about the true nature of the Vigilantes, the opinions of two other capable journalists will be put on display.

In *Varieties, a Chronicle of Life in California,* J. Walter Walsh wrote, "In May, 1856, a number of individuals resolved themselves into a lawless combination, styled the Vigilance Committee of San Francisco. The *professed* object was the detection and punishment of evil-doers—the *real* object was of a deeper and darker character—it was the subversion of the law and the Courts, and the institution of power by which a set of monopolists, speculators, defaulting bankers, usorious Shylocks, mushroom and dishonest merchants, thieving firms, cheating haberdashers, and close fisted, soulless money changers might maintain or hide their unjust acquisitions, frauds and embezzlements, and creeping, sly faced, disappointed politicians might obtain power by the turmoil."

Ace newspaperman George Wilkes concurred, in the *National Police Gazette*. "Who were the merchants of San Francisco?" he asked before answering himself on the strength of his personal knowledge. "For the most part commercial desperados . . . false pretense men and disgraced clerks . . . This is the band; this crowd of merchants, politicians, sharpers and cowards who have deposed the law in San Francisco."

Proof that these are not mere wild charges is to be found in what the Executives said about each other. Of Gillespie, it was noted by 33 Secretary Bluxome that he "left China for China's good." Of Miers Truett, Gillespie recorded in turn that, "He was in the Board of Health, and found guilty a few years ago of pilfering in one way or another."

Still it is the official papers of the Committee which reveal the nature of the Committee's makeup. The portions of them taking the form of accusations call to mind Chesterton's line about the British soldier who "knew no harm of Bonaparte and plenty of the squire." Asked to point out citizens that San Francisco would be better off without, the Vigilantes slung many more charges at members than at outsiders.

A flock of murderers had joined the Committee's ranks, according to those best in position to know. To give one example, members 344, 364, 367, and 375 all agreed that frat brother Thomas Hayes was a "well known desperate, who was arrested for murder and robbery two years ago." Tom stayed on in good standing and was awarded a certificate of membership, after the disbandment in August of 1856.

It was complained of No. 4270 that he was "arrested for rape committed on two little girls." It was furthermore complained that this Vigilante was bailed out and hanging around the Committee's club house the same afternoon.

Aside from murder, in the crime of violence class, they charged each other with attempts on the lives of wives, wife beating, rape, armed robbery and buggery, described as "indecent assault." Also in the list of falls from grace were bigamy, adultery, pimping, and the odd charge of misbehaving in a whorehouse. Crimes of deceit ranged from perjury through ballot-box stuffing, swindling, fraud, issuing hot checks and passing counterfeit.

There was also one charge in this class, unusual enough to deserve separate mention. This was "coffin stuffing," with a dash of body snatching thrown in to sweeten the kitty.

The Vigilante accused on these counts was an undertaker, formerly doubling as San Francisco's coroner, named Jerry W. Whaling. Of his enterprise there is only room to give a couple of instances now, though Ned knew some things about him that Jerry's fellow Committee members didn't mention.

As has been stated, a man simply named as Marion was the real murderer of that Captain West whom Brace was falsely charged with slaying. Almost certainly hanged, Marion came into the hands of Whaling, who divided him between two coffins. The makeweight rubble, with which the boxes were also loaded, was flavored with manure—to give the aura of authenticity as it were; and the county was charged with two autopsies and two burials instead of one. A variant of this dodge was simpler: according to Vigilante colleagues, Jerry planted a bodiless coffin, having sold to a doctor bent on research the corpse of the little girl which was supposed to have been its inmate.

The Vigilantes said to have been on the lam form an interesting list. Take the case of Dr. Josselyn, accused of having neither license nor training. An abortionist, however, he was described by a fraternity chum as an old grad of Massachusetts State Prison, who'd skipped to California to duck a second stretch.

Such were the men whom McGowan meant to arraign. When he sought for rogues among the Committee, he was not outraging the probabilities, as understood by the Vigilantes themselves. The difference was that he wished to air matters which the Executives wanted kept in the secrecy of their files.

If Ned would have given much for a squint at the Committee's papers, he knew a great deal which they failed to cover. His facilities for dredging facts about personal lives were far reaching. A lawyer deep in San Francisco's political life, a judge and the confidant of other court holders, an associate of the town's leading newspapermen—McGowan was all these. Then as a police supervisor in the East, and the correspondent of such men as Wilkes, he knew what many Vigilantes had been up to on the Atlantic side. Or if he wasn't sure, he knew where to apply for straight tips.

It was with this equipment that Ned started the Sacramento *Phoenix* on August 30. In his statement of purpose he asked anybody who didn't like what he said to come around with a gun and tell him about it:

"Before going further we wish to state that we acknowledge . . . the code of the duellist is a portion of our political creed. We are aware that in conducting a fearless and independent organ, we shall be a target at which any one may at any time be ready to launch their darts."

In what he called his "Salutatory" McGowan also announced the slant and scope of his work. He meant to publish nothing but what he thought certain. And he said that although he would welcome authentic data, he was interested in exposing none but members of the Committee.

For his purpose it was as useful to throw the spotlight on vulgar misdemeanors as grave felonies. He didn't expect to put any of his enemies behind bars. What he planned was to show up as fake the Committee's claim to a corner on virtue. That is what they had used as their title to abuse others, and that presumption was what he aimed to puncture. "We," as he put it, "conceive that the public have a right to an insight through a public organ, into the private lives of those who set themselves up par excellence as moral reformers."

Wolf as to tactics, if a bird in name, the *Phoenix* went for the throat first. The Committee had mainly used the *Bulletin* as their means of sugar coating themselves and blasting opposers. So Ned's opening move was to show how filthy a megaphone the Vigilantes had barked through.

The quoted ballad about Tom King's dicky spreading wife was dedicated to the *Bulletin's* chief, hailed as "the King of the Pole-cats." Below that were more verses for Tom to paste in his memory book:

> Raised from the stench of a charnel house,
> A bird of filthy feather, a skulking louse . . .
> May the strong curse of crushed affection light
> Back on thy carcase with reflected blight!
> And make thee in thy leprosy of mind
> As loathsome to thy self as all mankind!
> Thy name—thy human name—to every eye
> The climax of all scorn—should hang on high.

Under this tribute was the first of a series titled *McGowan's Lives of the Stranglers*. It was subheaded:

"The Life of Thomas S. King, Alias 'Slippery Sim'

> From the earth's center to the sea
> Nature stinks of thine and thee!
> The Fratricide! The Bawd's Pimp

Who Lives on the Bones of his Brother and the Flesh of his Wife,

Alias 'Slant-eyed Tom,' Alias 'The Nipper Kid' Alias 'Dead House Cove!' "

But having thus caught the reader's eye, Ned briskly told what he knew about King's past. As an outline of Tom's pre-California career was given in another chapter, it will be here omitted.

Next to the Dead House Cove, the *Phoenix* stood most in contempt of Gillespie. In his life of that strangler, McGowan gave the details of thievery in the Orient, only hinted at by Bluxome when stating that his fellow Executive had left China for China's benefit. While making a break for California, after having just missed the distinction of being part of a Chinese chain gang, Charles probably hadn't expected to win a bard's notice. He did, though. "Caliban, Poet Laureate to the Purest and the Best," contributed to the *Phoenix* lines about him which were dedicated to "George 'Robespierre' Ward":

> In Crime's gilt frame Gillespie I display,
> Thy villain's face unto the light of day . . .
> Thy heart's the resting place where Murder hides,
> Surrounded by his fears—his hopes—his guides . . .
> Conspicuous murderer, e'en when all were so,
> Bloody, crafty, base and a *coward*, too,
> Thou chief of traitors, round that scaffold's stand,
> Who to thy victim dared to raise thy hand . . .

That was a reference to the fact that Gillespie had struck Hetherington, while by the platform supporting the gallows. As the doomed man was, of course, bound, "dared" was a well-chosen verb.

Yet the *Phoenix* was by no means always severe with the Vigilantes. Many of the short items, composed as outliers of the main articles, evinced a blither spirit. An example of this gentler mood was the bird's reaction to the news that one Frank Wheeler had opened a gymnasium for women by the Golden Gate:

"Frank is now teaching the young ladies of San Francisco healthy bodily exercize, and how to *create* muscle. In the good old times before the reign of the Stranglers, the sweater's wife . . . in Commercial street, where she kept a bagnio, instructed young gentlemen in the pleasant operation of *relaxing* muscle . . . although the after claps are sometimes rather disagreeable."

Or at times the *Phoenix* would offer advice, even to members of the Executive Committee. No doubt on good authority, Ned be-

lieved that Chancy Dempster had ordered the hazing of Yankee
Sullivan, which ended in murder, when the old battler resisted.
By way of pinning this on a man known as a chronic churchgoer,
McGowan gave him a troubled conscience and told him how to
cure it:

"Can't the revivalists do something to alleviate the sufferings of
this poor wretch, Dempster? The ghost of Sullivan follows him
waking and sleeping. *Strychnine* is a good antidote for keeping off
ghosts—take a little, 'pious cretur' and become one yourself."

Although Dempster rejected that advice, an extraordinary number of Vigilantes—by Ned's cheerful tally, forty-three—did make
away with themselves at this period. The chief cause seems to have
been despond over the failure of the rebellion to raise them out of
bankruptcy. Actually it worsened business conditions in San Francisco, for Eastern wholesalers became leery of extending credit to
merchants holding forth in a city billed as crime ridden.

Of the many firms which collapsed, one was that of Gabriel B.
Post. In his premises, as has been shown, the Committee had held
its initial meeting. By the next year, though, this merchant prince
had become such a pauper that he was at length glad to take a
job as assistant keeper of San Francisco's County Jail.

Before getting that foothold in security, Post had taken his fall
from big-shotism so much to heart that he had tried self-murder.
Although he had failed at this, too, the *Phoenix* thought that with
practice, he might succeed. In the way of encouraging him Caliban
dedicated to Gabriel, A New Song, *The Choker Suicide:*

> A Choker was wending his way one night
>   Through the darkness so dreary and lone;
> When his traitor heart with a sudden fright
>   Jump up in his throat with a groan.
> The Commandment Divine he had broken,
>   His brother's blood wickedly shed;
> For the First time his conscience had spoken
>   And filled him with fear and deep dread . . .

> He thought of how many of the murdering crew
> Who engaged in this red crusade,
> Have departed this life—the victims, too,
> Of Conscience that long will upbraid.
> In terror thus rolled the thoughts of the past—
> On the future he could not dwell;
> In fear and dismay of his hour—the last;
> It had come—by his own hand he fell.

The record doesn't indicate that Post obliged with a second try. Yet the news of the day supplied the *Phoenix* with other satisfactions. Executive U. P. Hutchings was sued by a fellow Vigilante for passing a hot check in the amount of $2500. Executive Jules David was bounced from the banking firm of Abel Guy & Co. for gambling with funds that were dubiously his. Ned also liked what Eastern journals had to say about the Committee's former ambassador to President Franklin Pierce.

"Squire P. Dewey," the *Phoenix* mused. "Can any one inform us, whether he has forfeited his bail of $50,000, which was imposed on him in New York, on the eve of his departure for Europe, upon the complaint of Gov. Rodman M. Price of New Jersey, for having STOLEN from him certain moneys arising from the sale of property in San Francisco? Will Theodore Payne, his partner in the swindle, answer? Do, Theodore, if you please."

To mend slumping financial fences, Coleman, Dows, and Truett had gone East. Apparently it hadn't occurred to chronic law breakers that they were not as immune from punishment elsewhere as they were in their citadel. But when they landed in New York, they were arrested on charges leveled by men they had banished to that city. They were calaboosed, too, pending the raising of bail, which in Truett's case was said to have escalated to a cool $280,000.

Abreast of the former Broderick men who had been shipped to the Atlantic side, Ned exchanged letters with *Phoenix* fans who were pressing suits against the said Executives. In one received note the writer averred, "The affidavits you sent on about the robbery that Coleman committed in Placerville in 1850 will be of great service here in the trial."

In explanation, McGowan wrote, "Our correspondent refers to the robbery of two barrels of pork (hard) by William T. Coleman, worth at that time $200 a barrel. Coleman was arrested, gave bail and fled in the night to San Francisco."

To the exiles across the continent, the *Phoenix* was a joy. To Californians throughout the state as a whole, it was a source of whoops and chuckles. Whether rejoiced in or not, it was read by everybody in the town below Telegraph Hill.

Happy Law and Order lads waved the paper at debunked yaks, as one by one the *Phoenix* picked them out of the ranks of the Purest and Best and dropped them where they no longer felt the urge to sing "holier than thou." Ned's enemies all read his writings, because of the kind of men they were.

Churchgoers exposed as living off the earnings of whores weren't glad of it, though they loved being able to join the laugh at those helping them hold down a pew. So the Vigilantes bought the *Phoenix*, both to see whether their past or present had escaped notice, and to have something on friends, if that's the word.

From his own and truer allies, Ned had a considerable amount of volunteer aid. Most of it was confined to digging up data, though; the feathers clothing the *Phoenix* were nearly all his. There were some general contributors. General Estell gave facts in denial of a Black Male squawk to the effect that he had illegally farmed out a contract for managing San Quentin penitentiary. For another example, the chap who had married Manrow's sister-in-law wrote that the Committee's Judge Advocate had logged time in New York's Tombs prison, for having seduced a thirteen year old girl. But all the innumerable unsigned articles, and all those by-lined with such pseudonyms as "Southwark" and "Vindex," are as clearly Ned's as all the poetry, though in a couple of instances he amused himself by pretending he'd found the lines elsewhere.

Yet it is not enough to say of the *Phoenix* that it lampooned Vigilantes in prose and verse. In any one-horse newspaper the

toughest problem is how to fill the gaps in makeup, which yawn
after the main items have been assigned to their places. McGowan
had no feature service to rely on. Nor could he crib from Eastern
papers because the editors of San Francisco's dailies could beat him
to anything choice.

Ned met the situation by becoming a feature service himself. In
the same issue with slashing invective and bawdy fun-poking appeared his lovely *The Spirit of Beauty*. In another number he ran
a fine comic ballad about a couple trying to ride to a wedding
aboard a donkey:

> . . . "Come, Dobbin," says Peter, "I'm thinking we'll trot,"
>   "I'm thinking we won't," said the ass,
>   In the language of conduct—and stuck to the spot,
>   As though he had said, "I'll sooner be shot
>   Than lift up a foot from the grass."
>
> Says Peter, says he, "I'll whip him a little."
>   "Do it, my dear," says she.
> But he might just as well have whipped a brass kettle,
> For the ass was composed of such obstinate mettle
>   That never a step moved he . . .

Two or three times he ran a series of epigrams. Sample: "Why
are good resolutions like fainting ladies? They want carrying out."

Yes, but along with light snaps he could run such a profundity
as this: "The more a man enlarges his circle of light, he sees but
the more of the darkness that lies around. The wider the diameter
of light, the larger the circumference of darkness."

If a new joke occurred to Ned, it, too, would become a filler:
"A couple (not very long married) were contending about what
should be the name of their first and only child.

"William, my dear, I want to name him Peter.

"Oh, no, my love, I do not like Peter; he denied his Master.
Let us call him Joseph.

"Why, William! I can't bear Joseph; he denied his mistress."

McGowan seems to have been the first American poet to employ

Gipsies as a theme. It is interesting to note that he did not take the romantic view of this people, common to most who wrote of them in the nineteenth century:

> The Gipsy girl to her mother said,
> "I'm heavy, dear mother, like women who wed."
> "And who, my dear child, I should like to know,
> Who, my Gipsy girl, has made thee so?"
> "A gentleman fair, oh mother mine,
> A Gorgiko gentleman, fair and fine;
> Six months ago, he did it about;
> 'Twas yesterday only I found it out."
> "Thou little, shameless harlot, away!
> No daughter of mine thou shalt be from today.
> With a Gipsy lad hadst thou done so ill,
> I had called thee my dearest daughter still,
> But a shameless harlot thou must have been
> To carry a Gorgiko rat within."

Ned took pains with even the tags used to complete columns which don't quite stretch to the bottom of the page. In most newspapers this branch of journalism doesn't make for rewarding reading matter. But when McGowan tapped his mind for something of the right size, the result could be remarkable. Set as prose, for instance, as it wouldn't have fitted if arranged as verse, was this graceful bit of song:

> I met her at sunset bright,
> Her gingham gown was blue;
> Her eyes that danced with young delight
> Were of the same dear hue—
> And always when the sun goes down,
> I shall think of the girl in the gingham gown.

Notwithstanding the literary value of the *Phoenix,* the Vigilantes set no store by it. They acknowledged its effect, however.

With many of them shown up as real criminals, they could no longer feign that men charged with nothing worse than petty breaches of the peace were too villainous to breathe the same air as they did. In October of 1857, the Executives voted to withdraw the decrees and death threats lodged against the men they had banished or chased from San Francisco.

Not included in the amnesty was the man who had brought it about. If the Vigilantes had craved the wrung neck of Ned McGowan, before the *Phoenix* hopped out of the ashes they had made of his career, they were now of that persuasion ten times over.

17

A BOUT WITH THE BRITISH CROWN

AS A CALIFORNIA journalist, Ned throve in the teeth of some opposition. Once a detachment of Vigilantes swooped on Sacramento with the avowed purpose of seizing McGowan; but after coursing a town peopled by many banished Democrats, they slunk back to San Francisco. Once J. P. Manrow came to the capital, advertising a pistol he didn't see fit to use, when Ned walked past him. Causing more trouble were two lawsuits brought against him.

In January of 1858, a writ on the count of libel was issued against him, on the complaint of Augustus Heslep. The man who had volunteered to help try McGowan for murder had been described by the *Phoenix* as a "decayed skunk." While that could be taken as a mere matter of personal opinion, the bird's further remark that Heslep had debauched his own daughter was something it had to stand ready to prove.

Libel damages in any amount would have put the paper out of business. Yet the *Phoenix* but gave a cheerful chirp, when Augustus appealed to the law. To understand the ensuing lines, it's essential to know that "Dr. Plug" was one of Ned's nicknames for a foe he also referred to as "Hellslip." "The Thug," on the other hand, was a Sacramento judge, of whom McGowan was in contempt, because of the bench warmer's pro-Vigilante leanings. With both in mind, the *Phoenix* piped:

I'm a gone COON, Dr.—All's up with me!
Hellslip's after my poor bird, don't you see.
Oh, omen dire, oh, omen dread,
My poor Phoenix will soon "go dead."
Have mercy, won't you, Dr. Plug,
Save, oh save me, from the THUG

It developed that Ned's confidence in his case was justified. The upshot was described in Mortimer J. Smith's weekly, the Sacramento *Watch Dog:*

"He (Heslep) came up from the Bay on Wednesday night to prosecute his case of libel against Judge McGowan, and on the opening of the Recorder's court yesterday morning, the case was called, but the old rat not being present to prosecute, though the defendant was on hand and ready for the examination, the Recorder very properly dismissed the charge . . . After the adjournment Heslep made his appearance, but was met by McGowan . . . who proceeded to castigate the Vigilante cur in a manner richly merited. After spitting in his face and giving him a 'right hand' or two, McGowan wrenched a cane out of the hand of Heslep and applied it smartly to his back. Heslep, like all the cowardly Vigilantes . . . received the castigation without daring to defend himself, although he was armed, and was called upon by McGowan to draw."

That encounter took place on January 30. A fortnight later Ned was accused of assaulting another member of the Committee. In time to become the West's first circus owner, John Center had come to Sacramento. Oddly enough, the men who had abused so many others never seem to have been prepared for any comeback; nor was the fellow Ned had met on the *Panama* in '49 a whit more self-conscious than the rest. On the night of February 15 he had gone to the Forrest Theatre as nonchalantly as though he didn't have an enemy in the capital. It turned out that he had unforgiving ones. Spotted, John got rough handling before being allowed to creak back to his hotel.

McGowan was not in the theatre at the time, nor did Center himself say that he was. But others of the Committee saw a chance to pluck the *Phoenix*. Up the cry went that Ned had planned and launched the assault. Yet as the scene wasn't San Francisco, McGowan was easily able to win a case, filed in the hope of having him jammed in jail.

Before a judgment could be handed down in his favor the *Phoenix* had become the *Ubiquitous*. As Ned gave no explanation, none will be attempted here. The fabled Arabian bird died with the number of February 14. Seven days later subscribers received the first issue of another weekly, resembling the first in all but name.

In its twenty-five numbers the *Phoenix* had demonstrated the versatility of its editor. In the eighteen issues of the *Ubiquitous* he displayed even more resourcefulness and talent. More ingenuity was, to be sure, needed at this point. He had already slung his heaviest debunking ammunition and perforated his most notorious targets.

One new pitch was a series of puzzles, inviting readers to fill the indicated spaces with letters spelling the names of prominent Vigilantes. What follows is a portion of one of these:

"I am composed of forty-four letters. My 16, 14, 4, 37 is a licentious clergyman. My 34, 38, 41, 33 is one of the medical staff of murderers. My 31, 2, 22, 10, 23, 24, 16, 9, 37 is a noted Peter Funk [the arch type of an auctioneer's shill, created by Asa Greene in *The Perils of Pearl Street*]. My 20, 15, 43, 5, 19, 32 and my 32, 19, 29, 5, 19, 32 are two pioneer lunch eaters."

The first four cited numerals stood for the Reverend E. S. Lacy, who had preached the funeral service for James King of William and had stoked mob fanaticism by pulling an ersatz swoon in mid-eulogy. The *Ubiquitous* thus had grounds for taking an interest in the news that the minister was courting King's relict.

In verse he urged Mrs. King to yield to her wooer:

> Come, charming widow, hear thy poet sing,
> Thyself the rose, and he the bird of spring;
> Love bids him sing, and love will be obeyed.
> Be gay! Too soon the flowers of spring will fade.

And in prose Ned gave her suitor this genial slap on the back: "On the other hand, Parson Lacy, who preached, prayed and advocated

the hanging of innocent men upon the Sabbath day . . . did it to
some purpose, as it now appears there was 'more method than
madness' in his ravings, for he is about to take to his arms a beautiful and accomplished widow, and at the same time corral the
$45,000 'King Fund.' Go in, Parson, it is none of our business,
and we only now give it notice to help the cause of 'reform.'"

Another of the paper's social notes bore upon Baillie Peyton
and a January and May pair, of whom the younger produced a
daughter, named for the former Know-Nothing city attorney. There
could hardly be a neater summary of an eternal triangle,
squared by the addition of a fourth party, than the one offered by
the *Ubiquitous:*

> Where's old Harris? Horned. Where's Mrs. Harris? Diddled.
> Who's father to Peytona? That's not so soon unriddled.

Yet the time was to come when Ned couldn't laugh at man's
involvement with woman. The lead item on the front page of a
May issue was an outpouring of grief, caused by news of the death
of someone. At a guess, the person was the wife with whom, for
unknown reasons, he had not stayed mated in anything but name.
It could have been some other figure from his Atlantic side life, her
passing the reviver of old longings. The only certainty is that she
was nobody he had met in California. Replete with frank references
to his love life on the West Coast, McGowan's writings give not so
much as a hint that he there met any woman who had tampered
with his emotions.

One that had done so evoked as moving a lament as American
Literature boasts. Unlike most elegies, it has no window dressing in
the way of high sounding comparisons, fanciful names or borrow-
ings from myth and romance. It succeeds by the simple intensity of
a never lifted voice:

> . . . My sorrow seeks no lonely spot,
>   In some far desert placed;
> To me each scene where thou art not
>   Is but a joyless waste.
> Where all around is bright and fair

I only feel thou art not there,
And turn from what thou canst not share
   And sigh to be at rest.

I bow no more at beauty's shrine,
   For me her charms are vain;
The heart that once has loved like mine
   Can never love again.
The wreathing smile, the beaming eye,
Are passed by me unheeded by;
And where the ruined relics lie
   My buried hopes remain.

Life's latest tie hath severed been
   Since thou hast ceased to be,
Our hearts the grave has closed between,
   And what remains for me
In this dark pilgrimage below?
A vain regret—a cherished woe—
And tears that cannot cease to flow
   Whene'er I think of thee.

Although two following poems were melancholy, the *Ubiquitous* remained the jaunty stone thrower he had always been—but not for long. Ned gave up as a publisher without telling why. Reason says, though, that he did it on the score of being unable to push public opinion as far as he wanted to.

What his goal must have been was to make the Democratic governor who had replaced Johnson take the steps necessary to open up San Francisco and restore it to civic decency. Through a proclamation, backed by the threat of a National Guard invasion, this could have been done; and an American citizen could have no longer been denied the right to walk the streets of a United States city.

Governor John Weller did nothing, however, to alter the shameful fact that American law meant nothing in California's metropolis. Seeing that Weller did not have character enough to act from volition—and that the people of the rest of the state could not be

roused to more than laughter at the owners of San Francisco—
Ned decided to throw up an effort which had availed others but
not himself.

In the meantime he had lost out politically, as well as in most
other respects. That last piece of bad luck was due to the defec-
tion from the Democratic Party of the man who had been Mr.
Democracy in California. In 1858 David Broderick backed a Republican governor, and of the political faction of which McGowan
had been a faithful member nothing was left.

Ned and the man he had so often helped—and been helped by
—had gone separate ways as early as 1857. When Broderick returned from his first session as a United States Senator, he declared war on the national Democratic administration. What
McGowan saw was what really happened: a split in Democratic
ranks would permit the rise to power of the emerging Republican
Party. As to him this was but Know-Nothingism renamed, he and
David were through.

In later years writing of what must have been a painful matter,
Ned only said, "I was Mr. Broderick's intimate friend for eight
years . . . When he broke with the administration of Mr. Buchanan, we separated. I remained in Sacramento for a year afterward . . . We never conversed, although upon several occasions
we were inmates of the same city. Col. Butler at Mr. Broderick's request, wrote to me while I was residing in the Territory of
Arizona. I did not answer. But he was for all that a fair and square
man, one in most instances true to his promises and friends."

With no political home and barred from the only city where he
wished to practice law, Ned had to leave California. Luckily for
his need at this time, the big news of 1858 was the British
Columbia gold rush.

Although a certified Argonaut, Ned had never prospected in
California. But nine years after he had checked in as a Forty-
niner, he journeyed to join the stampede up Fraser River.

He could not, of course, sail for Canada in the easy and open
fashion of other Californians. San Francisco was the only embarka-

tion point within hundreds of miles, and it was not a city through which he could safely pass.

To test that fact, Ned first gave notice that he was going to leave Sacramento earlier than he intended to. Proof of this was published on June 20, the last time at bat for the *Ubiquitous*.

"We understand that fifteen of the Executives were on the wharf last Monday, previous to the sailing of the steamer, with their murderers, the police thieves of San Francisco. Well, gentlemen, was it a sell, or was it not? If you had not searched Mrs. Irene McCready's state room, probably people would not have known who you were looking for."

While arranging for passage, McGowan had planned to lay low in San Francisco in the home of one Joseph Palmer. Because of the folly of this man, the Vigilantes did briefly get Ned in their clutches.

Without notifying the person most concerned, Palmer decided to trust the honor of men who thought it a foolishness for marks only. Through a prominent Vigilante named John Middleton, Joseph received the Committee's assurances that McGowan would be given free passage through their city. But as Middleton had promptly tipped off the San Francisco police force, certain of its members met the boat in which Ned had fared down the Sacramento River, and thence across California's great bay.

The day was June 25, as the *Bulletin* noted when writing of one of the officers—the craftsman who had tied the hangman knots for Hetherington and Brace. Wishing authority to arrest Ned, Jake Chappell had gone to the chambers of a Justice Hall, "and after some difficulty in making out a complaint—the justice refusing to issue a writ without an affidavit—procured a warrant of arrest on a charge of libel against himself."

Whether or not committing libel, the *Ubiquitous* had remarked of Officer Chappell: "To show how well he is fitted for the part, we have only to allude to his dishonesty in robbing a prisoner in the County Jail, and later his conduct in a house of questionable repute . . . He there destroyed furniture and abused the inmates, thinking that, as they were women, he need apprehend no fear of chastisement. In this he counted without his cost, for the girls 'went in' and gave him a severe thrashing."

Of Jake's companion, James Boyce, McGowan had stated that his former occupation was that of highway robbery. When the two advanced with the mentioned warrant, Ned wanted to hold them off with a gun. But the lawyer he had brought with him—the same James Coffroth who had served as one of his defense counselors the year before—talked him into accompanying the officers to Justice Hall's court.

Coffroth went along, too, for the purpose of arranging bail. Fixed at $1000, the bond was put up by a couple of men to whom the attorney applied on Ned's behalf.

Stepping into the corridor of the Court House next, Ned found the two policemen laying for him. Boyce promptly fired the pistol he had in readiness. According to a letter which McGowan wrote the *Herald* on June 26, the only thing which kept this close-range shot from being fatal was the quick reaction of one of Ned's bondsmen. Chancing to be close enough to Boyce, Thomas Tilghman knocked the officer's arm aside. Although on that account the bullet failed to wound, the shot was such a near miss that it scorched McGowan's top coat, as well as making a hole in it.

Even the Vigilantes saw the impropriety of a policeman trying to slay a man on the doorsill of a judge's chambers. Boyce, as the *Alta California* of July 4 declared, was arraigned for the shooting. Yet he seems to have escaped punishment on the plea that, "he only meant to intimidate Ned and that the gun went off accidentally."

To go back to June 25: After his close shave with death, McGowan returned to the court room to ask, "Am I to be murdered in the halls of justice?"

In reply Justice Hall advised Ned to forget that he was out on bail and rely on the security of a jail cell. Recalling how safe Casey had been in the same situation, McGowan chose to fend for himself.

Outside the Court House, Police Chief Curtis and some of his men were lying in wait. Yet so were a crew led by Captain Reese, the stout fellow who had sided Ned on the trip up from Santa Barbara.

The jockeying for possession of McGowan's person drew a crowd largely made up of Vigilantes. Not liking the smell of hemp, Ned decided to make a break for it.

"At this point in the argument," he wrote, "I jumped from the crowd and ran down to Meiggs' wharf, followed by Mart Reese and one of the brothers Tilghman—I don't remember whether it was Tom or Fris . . . On I sped—under the wharf, out again toward Telegraph Hill—I never stopped to look behind. I remembered the fate of Lot's wife, fleeing the burning city of Sodom."

Having shaken pursuit, Ned "fell down and hugged mother earth from sheer exhaustion." When he could talk again he asked Reese and Tilghman to boat out to the Marine Revenue ship at anchor off shore and request asylum for him. Captain John McGowan no longer commanded the *Polk,* but through his brother, Ned had met her current skipper.

Perhaps in no other way could he have squeezed past the hostile port authorities of San Francisco. But when Reese summoned McGowan to the beach by an agreed vocal signal, that part of the game was won. Safe aboard the *Polk,* he "spliced the main brace" with Captain Pease, and then began scheming how to put to sea for Canada without getting caught.

Tipped off by Reese, General H. C. Cobb arranged with Captain Bob Haley of the steamer *Pacific* to pluck Ned from a rowboat off the landmark known as the Heads. This the shipmaster was willing to do, because his craft was owned by a chum of McGowan's named "Bully" Wright.

The *Pacific,* though, was not due to weigh anchor until Tuesday, June 29; and Ned's closest Vigilante shave had taken place on the previous Friday. He stayed on the *Polk* for most of the weekend, but left it about noon on Sunday, June 27. At that time, as he reported, "a boat was hoisted out, and a gallon of whiskey, provisions for several days, a double barreled gun, and small arms were put on board."

After the jolly-boat landed at an isolated point "A little beyond

Horseshoe Bend," Tilghman and the crew pulled away, while Mc-
Gowan and Reese prepared to make camp. There they were joined
by "Horseshoe Bill"—no other name given, and perhaps none
other known—the Bend's one resident.

Of a hermit who proved willing to give up solitude in exchange
for whiskey, McGowan said, "Although Bill was the Robinson
Crusoe of Horseshoe Bend, he had no 'man Friday,' nor pet goats,
but he had a faithful dog, and some pigs, which in this more advanced age answered a better purpose."

In San Francisco, the while, it was like old times, for the newspapers were again in the business of guessing as to the whereabouts of the Committee's jinx. "It is confidently asserted," said
the *Alta California* of June 28, "that the ubiquitous Ned Mc-
Gowan did not leave on the *Sierra Nevada,* but is still housed in
this city by his friends."

As of that same day, Ned reported a false alarm. Beholding
the approach of a well-manned boat, McGowan, Reese, and the
Hermit of Horseshoe Bend forted up in some coastal rocks. The
newcomers, however, turned out to be cronies, so Ned enjoyed one
last San Francisco shindig, before Bill rowed him out to the *Pacific.*

That vessel dropped its hook in the harbor of Victoria, Vancouver Island, the evening of July 3. As the next day was the anni-
versary of America's independence, Ned conducted himself accordingly:

"On the morning of the glorious Fourth, after the captain and
the purser had gone ashore, I made application to the mate to fire a
salute in honor of the day. There were two guns aboard. The mate
gave his consent that I should do so. Several of my friends were
aboard who were General William Walker's Nicaraguan heroes,
and I gave orders to Major Tom Dolan—who was wounded so
badly at Rivas—to pipe all hands belonging to the crew, and in a
few minutes the guns were manned; the mate furnished the powder; 100 guns [rounds of cannon shot] were fired.

"As volley after volley pealed out, down on the beach came
hundreds of Indians and others, subjects of Great Britain, as well

as our own inquisitive Yankees, not knowing what was up. An English man of war was lying off in the harbor, and no one for a moment imagined but we were bombarding the town, or bearding the lion in his den."

When the astonished Governor of British Columbia was finally convinced that cannon had been touched off as no more than a show of patriotism, he forbore to make an international issue of the matter. This was not, however, the last time that James Douglas was to hear of a man, of whom he was all too ready to believe the worst.

It was in Canada that Ned learned something that he had to bear with the rest of his life. Outside of California he was known only through the reports of him which had been spread by the Committee's press. His vindication in court had done nothing to change the malign reputation they had given him. Papers all over the nation had been pleased to reprint articles telling of a fugitive former judge, charged with murder. Few or none had taken an interest in his clearance, denounced in any case as a fraud by the journals of San Francisco.

So wherever he went, newspapers hailed him as "the notorious Ned McGowan." And in British Columbia the yelping was particularly loud and vicious, because the editor of the Victoria *Gazette* was Washington Bartlett, late of the *True Californian*.

Ashore in Victoria himself, Ned had a run-in with one of the Executives. While he was passing a saloon owned by a John Keenan, Miers Truett stepped to the door, owning a load he wasn't carrying well. Miers drew a pistol which a fellow called Theodore Shillaber tried to get him to put away. But by doing so the dove was making it hard for McGowan to shoot back, should Truett manage to wrench free and start firing.

"I immediately called out to Mr. Shillaber to let him come out," Ned commented, "and drew my Colt's revolver to defend myself, when Governor Purdy [a former Lieutenant Governor of California, first named Samuel] came in front of me and said, 'Judge, you do not want to kill a man who's been drinking.' I replied, 'No, Governor, I do not, nor do I want a man in his cups to kill me.' "

Doubtless the episode was given an anti-McGowan twist by the time it reached the ears of Canuck officials. Prepared for sinister news of the Ubiquitous, they took note of his associates, too. As Ned's companions were men who had also been proscribed by the Committee, they were looked upon in the Dominion as lesser outlaws, belonging to a mob of which he was chief.

For a while Ned gave lowering Canadian authorities nothing to justify their jitters. Because of flood water and other obstacles, he didn't make it up the Fraser to Fort Yale until September. The hub of the gold field, this Hudson's Bay Company trading post had blossomed into an infant metropolis.

"I went strolling around, sightseeing," McGowan remembered. "Met a number of old Californians, and saw 'history repeating itself,' in reacting the scenes of the city of San Francisco, in '49, but upon a much smaller basis."

Again like San Francisco, Fort Yale was a supply point for miners rather than a mining camp. Ned began his treasure hunting at New York bars, where he learned that seekers aren't always finders. After he, Tom Dolan, and a third partner named Raines had dug for four or five hours, they paused, to tot the gross profits and weigh them against invested capital. The books didn't look good.

To give Ned's report, "We had worked hard all the forenoon, had drunk up a bottle of bad schnapps for which we had paid two dollars and a half, and had realized ten cents. I pitched the rocks, pick, and shovel, etc., into a deep canyon running past the claim, and that finished the first day's work I ever did in the mines."

Through as a gold hunter, Raines went back to California; but both McGowan and Dolan moved to Hill's Bar. There their luck was so good that they turned up $1598 in three days. Fond of that, they stayed on as members of a mining group calling themselves the California Boatmen's Company.

A few miles upstream and on the Fraser River's other bank, Fort Yale had developed into an enemy camp. "Yale is chiefly inhabited by partisans of the 'Vigilance Committee,'" Judge Matthew Begbie explained in a letter to Governor Douglas, "Hill's Bar by partisans of the 'Law and Order' party in San Francisco."

That was one cause of what came to be known as "the Ned McGowan War." Another was a crooked Commissioner for Crown Lands called Richard Hicks. Subsequently found out and fired, he had not been challenged by any but Americans, when he wrote a letter to Douglas datelined, Fort Yale, October 28.

At a meeting held in Patrick Martin's saloon, the California Boatmen's Company had denounced the Commissioner in a resolution published in the Victoria *Gazette*. To discredit the men who had drawn it up, Hicks had but to name Ned.

"I am under the necessity of informing Your Excellency that the Notorious Ned McGowan, who is on Hill's Bar, has been trying the last two days to incite the miners to revolt, and I can prove that he asserted that 'Your Excellency had better mind your own business in Victoria, for that he was the ruler of Hill's Bar.' "

As this was just what the governor had been expecting of British Columbia's most unwanted visitor, he was prepared to put faith in a desperate appeal from another source. Fort Yale's Justice of the Peace was "Captain"—it was later found out that his claimed British service commission didn't exist—P. B. Whannell.

He imprisoned men for crimes which were none except in the eyes of a man with total ignorance of law. He was, indeed, as overweening as a Choker chief; and he was holding forth in a Vigilante stronghold. After inspecting Whannell with growing distaste, Ned stepped on him.

McGowan's chance came when the fake captain refused to cooperate with the Hill's Bar J.P. As Ned described the latter, he was "an English magistrate, who, though it sounds like a Paddyism to say it, was a French Canadian, a devilish good fellow called [George] Perrier."

Among those Whannell had illegally put in hock was one Dixon, who had been assaulted by two men brought before the Hill's Bar court. Needing the victim as a witness, Perrier sent a constable with the rhyming name of Hickson to borrow the prisoner from the

Fort Yale pokey. But in place of being able to spring Dixon, Hickson landed in durance himself.

What then happened was told by Matthew Begbie, British Columbia's Chief Justice, in a report to the governor: "Mr. Perrier, indignant at this treatment of his constable . . . immediately fulminated against his rival a warrant for his apprehension, and also a warrant for forcibly taking Dixon out of the gaol at Yale and bringing him to Hill's Bar; and having no constable to whom the execution of these warrants could be committed, he swore in Edward McGowan and one [Terence] Kelly, and I believe several others as special constables . . . These two men then, with 12 or 14 others, all fully armed—the usual weapons here being one or two revolvers and a large knife—came to Yale, suddenly seized Captn. Whannell, who himself usually sat in court with a revolver at his belt, and also the gaoler who refused to obey Perrier's warrant for the delivery-up of Dixon . . . But little remains to be told. Captn. Whannell and the gaoler were both taken before Perrier. The gaoler was discharged as having acted under orders. Captn. Whannell was fined 25 dollars for 'contempt of court.' "

The Victoria *Gazette* agreed with Ned that the actual sum more than doubled Begbie's figure. So there was enough to cover expenses at the change of venue described by McGowan: "The court and its friends then adjourned to Paddy Martin's deadfall, and put up the fifty dollars and costs for drinks all around."

Whannell turned out to be a poor loser. On December 31 he wrote Douglas: "I also have to inform your Excellency that Edward McGowan came up this day to this town at the head of a band of ruffians; broke open the Jail and liberated a Prisoner . . ."

Its worst fears seemingly realized, the British Empire marshaled its forces and began moving against Ned in January of 1859. Parts of all the warrior services were in the expeditionary force which began stemming the ice-clogged Fraser.

Commander of the whole was Lieutenant Governor Richard C. Moody, who doubled as an army colonel. Prepared to throw up fortifications afield were Royal Engineers under Moody's direct command. Captain Grant led a detachment of Royal Grenadiers. Lieutenant Mayne of the Royal Navy headed a detachment of tars with a cannon in tow. Governor Douglas had made good his threat to "despatch fifty marines and a body of police" under a territorial official called Chartres Brew. To sit in judgment over the arch-miscreant, when captured, Judge Begbie had joined the expedition.

The intelligence service at Hill's Bar had not been caught napping. Word of the coming red coats brought, councils were held and strategy agreed upon.

"We had arranged a plan," as Ned wrote, "in case of collision with the troops, to take Fort Yale and then go down the river and capture Fort Hope and retreat with our plunder across the boundary into Washington Territory—only twenty miles distant."

Although determined to resist military arrest, McGowan announced his willingness to appear before any civil court. But while waiting to see how he would be called upon to act, he breached the peace of British Columbia by cuffing a Fort Yale Vigilante named Dr. M. W. Phipher.

Colonel Moody's troops had by then managed to work their way up the Fraser as far as Fort Hope—like Yale, no more than a fur trading post. Hearing that the lion of Hill's Bar was on the rampage again, the commander sped a messenger down to the coastal town of Langley, with a call for reinforcements.

The climax of the war was the arrival of Moody and Begbie at Fort Yale on January 17, 1859. The crisis began to fold up and look foolish, as soon as the Chief Justice began making enquiries. In his letter to Douglas of January 18, he stated that all the evidence he had turned up was "all on the side of what may be called the Mr. Ned McGowan faction."

As Ned had said he would, he appeared before Begbie's civil court voluntarily and unescorted. Aware that Phipher had lodged an assault complaint, he led off by apologizing for fracturing the Dominion's peace and proffering the usual five-dollar fine.

The Chief Justice, though, was bothered by the charge that a visiting American had unlawfully invaded the court of a British magistrate and arrested him. Pleading not guilty, McGowan got Perrier to tell of putting him in the service of the Queen by deputizing him—at which point the colonel and the judge glanced at each other and laughed.

To give Begbie's version, "The next matter then came to be examined into; and although irregular, I permitted the defendants to enter into what was really the gist of their case—viz., that they were acting by virtue of a warrant from a justice of the peace, which they were in fact precluded from even questioning. Mr. Perrier was examined on this point; and on the whole Mr. Brew and I were both of the opinion that no jury would have convicted on an indictment for the alleged misdemeanor in assaulting the justice and forcing the gaol."

There was one more phase of the Ned McGowan War. Although Colonel Moody wasn't feeling well enough, Begbie and some of the expedition's officers visited Hill's Bar on January 20. In his memoir titled *Four Years in British Columbia*, Lieutenant Mayne noted of this occasion that McGowan "conducted us over the diggings, washed some 'dirt' to show us the process, and invited us to a collation in his hut, where we drank champagne with some twelve or fifteen of his California friends. And whatever opinion the Vigilance Committee of San Francisco might entertain of these gentlemen, I, speaking as I found them, can only say . . . I have rarely lunched with a better spoken, pleasanter party."

Far south by the Golden Gate, though, Ned's enemies had been by turns scurrilous as to his conduct, hopeful as to his downfall and wrathful as to the war's outcome. As usual the Vigilante papers had falsified the facts. They had reported that McGowan had been found in the wrong by British authorities; but then had to make the contradictory statement that Ned had suffered no scath.

The fraternization cited by Mayne was sourly noted by the *Bulletin*, which published a despatch from British Columbia headed NED'S COLONY. After stating that McGowan ruled in Hill's Bar as "lord of the manor," this item went on to add, "He entertains on behalf of his subjects all distinguished strangers, and this public hospitality can no more be civilly refused by the British officials than a public dinner (given by the bhoys), to a distinguished statesman . . . McGowan on such occasions drinks the Queen's health in champagne with high gusto."

With equal gusto McGowan netted a fine stake—reported in the Steilacoom *Puget Sound Herald* as totaling $47,000—while prospecting on the Fraser. The *Ubiquitous* was then ready for other parts, and when the ice went out of the river, he began following it downstream on February 26. Pausing at Fort Hope for a dinner with Lieutenant Governor Moody, Ned and Tom Dolan headed for Vancouver Island and the ship that would bear them beyond the United States.

18

SOLDIER AND SAILOR, TOO

ONE OF THE casualties of the Committee's uprising was the West Point career of James A. McGowan. The records of the United States Military Academy show that this eldest of Ned's sons became a plebe on July 1, 1855. When the exams to qualify him as a yearling came due in June of 1856, the big national newspaper story was the chase of his father on a murder charge.

Ned said that James had a good head, and in view of his heritage that can be accepted. The records of West Point say that he resigned from the Military Academy on June 30, 1856, having been found short of standards in English, Mathematics, and Conduct.

There are two possibilities, adding up to the same thing. The youngster could have been so thrown off balance by the family disgrace that he wasn't in shape for quizzes or bracing. On the other hand he might have deliberately flunked and slumped, as the best way of separating himself from an institution where he felt himself no longer wanted.

But whichever was true, James McGowan had decided to follow his father westward by 1859. Via correspondence Ned had somehow arranged for them both to be taken on as members of an expedition led by Captain Charles Pomeroy Stone. Ned had met the officer—later the Chief of Staff of the Khedive of Egypt— while he was in command of the arsenal at Benicia. On leave from the Army in 1859, Stone had been hired to make a mineral survey of the Mexican State of Sonora.

The port of rendezvous for the McGowans was Guaymas on the Gulf of California. For Ned, at least, there were hazards en route.

One of these took the form of an encounter with former Executive Jules David. As a result of an earlier meeting—treated below in Ned's comment on the second—McGowan arrived in Victoria to find that David had posted notice that he would shoot him on sight.

Not looking for trouble, Ned paid no attention to the threat, until he happened to see Jules coming his way. Of this meeting with a chap who seems to have had something of a reputation as a gunman, McGowan but said, "I stepped to one side, my hand on my pistol, my eyes on him. He made no demonstration and passed on. He and I had had a little affray a few months earlier at Fort Yale, and he ignominiously fled."

Dolan was not going to Mexico with Ned; he had determined to rejoin Walker in Nicaragua. Yet they made it together as far as San Francisco, a port which stuck them with the same problem.

Among those who had left before he was tossed out, Tom had come under the amnesty proclaimed by the Executives in October of 1857. Since then, however, he had been celebrated as an ally of Ned's in British Columbia. On that account he, no more than McGowan, could consider the Committee's town a safe place to pass through; and all southbound ships naturally called at the Coast's largest city.

Ned's solution took some shopping around on the one hand, and some correspondence on the other. Not wishing to board a steamer, where he would be sure to meet passengers who knew him, he found at Victoria a Sardinian schooner named the *Giulietta*. Then he arranged by mail for friends to send out a boat from Sausalito and land Dolan and himself short of the Golden Gate.

During the several weeks that the *Giulietta* remained moored in San Francisco Bay, Ned stayed at a ranch near San Rafael. As he was in the neighborhood of San Quentin Penitentiary, he was able to improve the stop-over by performing once more as a judge of the county owned by the Vigilantes.

While an associate of San Francisco's Court of Sessions, he had agreed that ten years was the right sentence for a burglar called "Jimmy from Town" Byrne. By 1859 Jimmy was eligible for parole, which Governor Weller said he would sanction, if one of the convicting judges would sign Byrne's petition. McGowan did so before reboarding a schooner that carried him away from a region he was not to know again for sixteen years.

Late in May or early in June, he joined Captain Stone's exploring party in Guaymas, Mexico. Besides Stone himself and James McGowan, Ned knew at least one other of the some forty members. He was Philemon T. Herbert, nominated for Congress by the Gwin faction of the Two Headed Convention; and elected in 1854.

Herbert's political career was cut short by a more serious version of the fracas which had finished McGowan as a legislator. Under provocation considered sufficient by the jury which freed him, Phil had slain an Irish waiter in a Washington hotel in 1856. The Committee's newspapers had thundered that he was a Caligula-type murderer, though, so the Democrats couldn't run him again.

Whether or not he and Ned had been chums earlier, they had become sidekicks by the time Stone's expedition reached the end of a short string. The Americans had been ranging the State of Sonora but a few weeks, when they heard from the man who had engineered the massacre of Henry Crabb's force two years before. Mistaking the mineral seekers for another group of filibusters, Governor Ignacio Pesquiera gave them forty days to get back into their own country. Feeling the brush of Crabb's ghost, Stone and those with him didn't argue. As Ned remarked, they "stood not upon the order of their going."

The beeline they followed to the American border took them across it where the Santa Cruz runs north into the United States. In other words they were in the western portion of what the Gadsden Purchase had added to New Mexico Territory in 1853.

Upriver in walled Tubac a newspaper called the *Arizonian* had been launched in 1859's March. It is possible to say when Ned reached the old Spanish garrison town, for he declared he did so just in time to witness a duel between Edward Cross and Sylvester Mowry. The first was the *Arizonian's* editor, while the second was later author of a valuable descriptive work titled *Arizona and Sonora.*

Their meeting took place on July 8. All accounts of this encounter agree that it was farcical, but McGowan's is the best. After writing that "Col. Phil Herbert, myself and my son James had just arrived from Mexico with Captain Stone's surveying party," he went on to tell how the principals had blazed away at each other with Burnside rifles until they had used up their allotted ammunition—whereupon they had rushed into each other's arms in their relief at having come through unscathed.

One of Mowry's seconds was Granville Oury, brother to William S. Oury and like him a noted adventurer. James McGowan seems to have gone back to Philadelphia fairly soon; for at the outbreak of the Civil War he was employed by a brotherly love mercantile firm. Ned and Phil Herbert remained in New Mexico, where they became Granville's allies in peace and war.

Down the Santa Cruz from Tubac lay also walled Tucson. Headquarters for Oury, it soon housed the *Arizonian,* in whose production Ned began to take a hand.

In no other connection did he mention acting as a printer. Nor elsewhere than at Tucson was he portrayed by others as practicing the craft he is said to have followed for some years in Philadelphia. Some Vigilante must have come to inspect the pickings on America's newest frontier and reported in, for San Francisco knew.

Never forgotten, McGowan was grimly marked by the Committee's press, whenever it could keep pace with his progress in exile. To that pertinacity a January 1860 item of the *Alta California* testifies: "Ned McGowan is setting type on the Arizonian at Tucson, also practicing law and drinking whiskey."

About the time that was published Ned took his thirst and his shingle to booming Mesilla, on the Rio Grande. But as a representative of that town, he was back in Tucson in April, a delegate to a convention held for the purpose of setting up Arizona as a territory separate from New Mexico.

The vertical division which eventually took place was not the aim of Ned and his fellows. Their plan was to slice the cake horizontally along the line of thirty-three degrees and forty minutes, Latitude North.

Ned was one of the seven delegates appointed to draft a constitution, and is probably its virtual author. He was likewise on the committee to set the boundaries of the territory's four proposed counties. He offered most of the resolutions approved by the convention; and in one of them he as good as voiced an explanation of the stand he took in the onrushing War between the States:

"Resolved, that we heartily approve of the pure, wise and patriotic administration of our venerable President James Buchanan, fully believing that his only aim in carrying out his Government, has been for the good of the whole country. And if some of the judicious measures of the administration have failed to become effective, it has been caused by the opposition of factious demagogues, whose only desire has been for their own aggrandisement and political preferment, and not for the public welfare."

Jumping the gun, the convention voted to consider the Territory of Arizona already a fact. Ned was elected one of the two judicial associates of Chief Justice Granville Oury. The other was Samuel Cozzens, in time to become the author of a travelogue cross-bred with romance called *The Marvelous Country*.

Like all journalists of the post-Vigilante era, Cozzens took note of the supposed desperado he had met in the Southwest. He differed with the others, though, in assigning kindly motives to McGowan:

"It was said that although Ned had killed at least a dozen men in his life, he never killed one save in behalf of some friend's quarrel."

In 1860 McGowan did stick one man under, though probably not with a do-gooder's smile on his face. In May the Pinos Altos gold strike drew stampeders to what is now western New Mexico.

One besides McGowan was called Porter. In all likelihood, he was the James Porter described in a letter to the *Ubiquitous:*

"Do you know that a man by the name of Porter . . . is at present an inspector in the Customs House? Porter is one of the crew that carried a musket in the guard of traitors who placed Martin Gallagher on board ship and banished him from his family and home."

The above would supply the motive not offered by James Henry Tevis, when telling of a duel fought by McGowan and "Captain Porter" in a volume of memoirs titled *Arizona in the '50s.* Nor did Ned supply details, other than to say that he and his foe had agreed to have at each other with Navy revolvers.

As that's about all he had to say about Pinos Altos, what he found in the way of gold there cannot be reported. No matter for his luck, he was back in Mesilla, the capital of Arizona, by fall, and in conference with Provisional Governor Lewis S. Owings re a disturbing development.

At the convention held in April, Sylvester Mowry had been chosen to lay the proposed territory's case before Congress. Although he had accordingly started off for Washington, he had somehow got sidetracked to South Carolina, whence he indirectly sent in his resignation.

In consequence there was an election for a replacement, held in Mesilla on November 7. Voting for Ned, the Arizonans living in what has since been incorporated in New Mexico got immediate action.

As most of his constituents were Southerners, McGowan hurried East with instructions soon relayed to San Francisco. No longer steered by John Nugent, the *Herald* ran a letter which specified that "Should the South separate, he [Ned] is instructed to attend the Southern convention and pledge the Territory to the Southern Confederacy, and to ask for a Territorial organization under the Confederacy."

McGowan's mission at Washington was seen as a probable lost cause, even before he started. Buchanan was sympathetic—he himself had proposed separate status for Arizona as early as 1857. But

by December of 1860 he was a lameduck President, opposed by a
dominant coalition of Republicans and Northern Democrats. Impatient with Buchanan's efforts to avert a break in the Union, they
were opposed on general principles to anything he advocated.

It chanced that when the cold Civil War first got hot, Ned's
brother, John, was involved. In periods of emergency, the Marine
Revenue Service was absorbed by the Navy. Captain McGowan
was thus in the pool of officers available for duty, when the administration decided to strengthen the garrison of Fort Sumter.
In James Buchanan's memoirs he complains that he had wished a
warship assigned for the purpose, and that officers in the service of
the opposition gave him the run around. In any case reinforcements
were shipped on the unarmed transport, *Star of the West,* with
John in command.

Clearing New York's Narrows on January 5, 1861, the side-
wheeler chugged toward Charleston Harbor. It never got near Fort
Sumter, though. Helpless to return the fire of shore batteries and
threatened with capture by an armed schooner, John got the *Star
of the West* out from under while he still could.

Ned stayed north of the Potomac until after Lincoln's inaugural
address, which he heard with dour forebodings. That was in March,
of course. By the time Lincoln issued a call for Northern troops in
April, McGowan had followed his instructions as a delegate by
attending the Confederate convention in Montgomery, Alabama.

Back in Arizona, about this time, there had been a reorganiza-
tion of the government as a specifically Confederate one, and
Granville Oury had been elected as delegate to the Congress of a
nation which wasn't permanently organized until February of
1862.

As the Confederate capital had been moved to Richmond in
May of the previous year, Ned had presumably been there ever
since. There is no record of how he was employed in the interval,
but he was ready for roaming by the time Oury finished his brief
term as a representative of Arizona. For John Baylor had come out

of Texas to proclaim himself governor of the territory, and his appointee displaced Granville on March 11.

That was the day before McGowan's forty-ninth birthday. With no military training, to boot, he might have reasoned that he wasn't first line material. In point of fact he and Oury came up with a dandy idea for getting into the Confederate service on their own terms. And they rushed to put it into effect, after first joining forces with Phil Herbert in East Texas.

What they were up to was racily described by the aforementioned Thomas P. Ochiltree in an 1888 article for *The New York World:* "At the beginning of the war, McGowan, Phil Herbert and Grant Ouray [sic] late member of Congress from Arizona, organized what was known as the Arizona Battalion, for service in the Confederate Army. This was probably one of the most marvelous commands ever got together. It was made up of experienced and desperate men—men who had lived on the frontier for years, and to whom six-shooters, bowie knives and personal encounters were every day occurrences."

In the spring of 1862 Ochiltree was assistant adjutant general under Henry Sibley, commander of the Confederate expeditionary force which had conquered New Mexico proper the year before. With the tide turning against him, General Sibley wanted reinforcements in a hurry. He had therefore picked former Texas Ranger Tom Ochiltree as his messenger to department headquarters in San Antonio.

The better to speed, Tom had taken none with him but three scouts who had also campaigned in the Comanche country through which they had to pass. En route to the San Diego–San Antonio stage road, one of the scouts was killed in a brush with the Indians; and after the three survivors had commandeered a stagecoach, the Comanches worked that over until there was little left of it.

"It was at this time," as Ochiltree wrote, "that I first met McGowan, and I met him under peculiar circumstances." After the second Indian attack, Tom and the two with him had "continued the journey with nothing to ride on but the front wheels of the coach." While so faring east in Comanche land, Ochiltree descried a westbound desert craft which turned out to have Ned, Herbert, and Oury aboard. "I had never seen any of them before, but I was so glad to see anything in the shape of a human being that I took out a canteen of whiskey I had saved through all of my unfortunate experiences, and we drank it on the spot."

A veteran unit a year later, the Arizona Battalion was under the command of Zachary Taylor's also rough and ready son. Ochiltree described a battle in which he and Ned took part as one of the bloodiest of the War between the States. That was praise from Sir Hubert. Serving with distinction on the staffs of Generals Sibley, Maxey, Green, Taylor and Longstreet, the colonel had ranged a front extending from New Mexico to Northern Virginia.

So much for preface to an account of one of Ned's exploits. "The next time I saw McGowan was in Southwestern Louisiana," Tom wrote. "I was then on the personal staff of General Dick Taylor, and the opposing force was commanded by General Banks. I found that McGowan and his companions were in the army under Taylor. Both armies were encamped on the banks of the Bayou Teche. The command of navigation was at issue and brought on the Battle of Camp Bisland, one of the fiercest fights of the war . . .

"We had only a single gun boat, the *Diana,* which had been captured a few days before from the Federal fleet, with which to dispute the passage of the river, but the circumstances were so fortunate that this single gun boat was of more value than several times that number would have been on another occasion. The Federals had a powerful fleet of boats, but as they could only engage one of the fleet at a time, the odds were not so desperate as they might have been."

Asked by General Taylor to find him a commander who would hold the river "until hell froze over," Ochiltree answered that he had the man on tap. "I knew that Edward McGowan would never give up the point as long as there was any possibility of holding it. I went to him, and he and Oliver Semmes agreed to jump into the breach, and, with 80 volunteers, they took charge of the boat."

Federal Civil War records show that Ned had the rank of the *Diana's* purser—he was probably the Arizona Battalion's finance officer—without contradicting Ochiltree's story. "I chose [Captain] Semmes as nominal leader for the reason that he was the son of Alabama Semmes and presumably knew something about ships. I found out very shortly that he didn't [Oliver had gone to West Point, not Annapolis], because one of the first things he did when he got on board was to take a piece of chalk and mark "starboard" on one side and "larboad" on the other, so he would make no mistake in giving his orders!"

Seamanship wasn't of paramount importance in a stream so narrow that it was no trick to get from its banks to the *Diana's* deck; and anyhow Semmes was not long in charge. He and Lieutenant J. Dubecq were downed with wounds, leaving Ned the only active officer on the gunboat.

To proceed with Ochiltree's account of the Battle of Camp Bisland: "After the struggle had continued for some time, I was dispatched by General Taylor with a message for McGowan and Semmes. I hurried down to the boat and got across the planking and landed on board. I shall never forget the sight. Out of 80 men 40 were dead and dying . . . The decks literally ran blood. It was at least two inches thick all over, and when I came away my boots were marked with blood as they might have been with mud after plodding for an hour along a New Jersey road. The boat was riddled with shell and shot. The boiler had been smashed, and the escaping steam mingled with the smoke of battle. But above all was heard the voice of Edward McGowan calling upon his men to continue the fight."

In the end what was left of the crew were captured, but not the *Diana* herself. Ned said they had managed to blow the gunboat up, when forced to abandon it. McGowan and other Confederate officers captured at Camp Bisland spent the rest of the spring of 1863 in New Orleans, "where they kept us in close confinement in the old slave pen. The New Orleans ladies, who could see us from the street, made such a demonstration in our favor that we were transferred for safe keeping to the Customs House."

But although they held him for a while, the combined Federal Army and Navy proved unequal to the task of keeping the Ubiqui-

tous inactive. The Vigilantes had doubtless lost track of their
scourge after he dropped below the Potomac in 1861. By the summer of 1863, though, he was in the news of both sections of the
disUnited States, on the score of having captured the prison ship
which Union officers had unwisely exposed to his enterprise.

The story can be traced back to a letter, datelined New Orleans, June 2, which was addressed to the Assistant Adjutant General at Fort Monroe, located at Old Point Comfort, Virginia. Its
subject was the shipboard transfer of ninety captured officers. Included were two cited as belonging to the Arizona Battalion. Not
of these, Captain Oliver J. Semmes was specified only as a light
artillery officer. Mentioned as staff members of the *Diana* were
Purser Edward McGowan and Lieutenant Dubecq.

As a result of this communication, Ned, Semmes, and the rest
were herded aboard the *Catawba* about the same time and taken
to Fort Monroe. But when the *Maple Leaf* tried to relay them to a
Northern prison, McGowan put his foot down.

"On the second day out," as he said in the casual paragraph he
devoted to the matter, "I communicated with Semmes and some
of the others, and managing to get possession of some arms, we
overpowered the guard . . . and ran the vessel ashore about 8 miles
from Cape Henry Light . . . We arrived at Richmond with a
maple leaf in our hats, and were at once restored to our commands."

What Ned didn't bother to say was that they had landed in a
part of Virginia which was in Federal hands. Twenty-three were
recaptured or shot in the course of the sneak through Union lines
to Confederate territory.

That detail was given when the *Alta California* of June 13
reported the latest McGowan coup. The Vigilantes were doubly
outraged by it, for with the exception of Peyton, Foote, and Coleman, all the prominent ones were Northern sympathizers.

Because some of the fugitives from the *Maple Leaf* had been
seized and interviewed, the *Alta* was able to describe Ned as the
ringleader of the revolt at sea. It also told of a scheme he had
been forced to abandon. "At first the prisoners decided to run the

vessel to Nassau as a Confederate prize." Finding there wasn't enough coal for that, however, they made for the vicinity of Cape Henry Light, as related by McGowan.

On June 18 the *Alta* picked up a story written by a war correspondent who had interviewed Ned aboard the first prison ship, the *Catawba*. Pursuant to telling of the capture of the *Maple Leaf,* the journalist gave his impressions of the man who had engineered it:

"In regard to Judge McGowan, said to be the leader of the surprize and escape . . . He is a man of great decision of character. He dislikes New England, and of course is not an ardent admirer of Wendell Phillips, Henry Ward Beecher and Horace Greeley. The wine cup has delights for him, and he is what many would call "a hail fellow, well met." . . He is fifty-two [actually fifty] and with his silvery locks, grey moustache and beard, he presents quite a patriarchal appearance."

That was the last that San Francisco heard of the Golden Era's greatest figure for over twelve years. Before he surfaced in it again, his favorite city had lost all its frontier characteristics but one. It was still politically owned by the Vigilance Committee of 1856.

19

THE CITY OF THE VIGILANTES

CITED IN AN earlier chapter, the suits against the Executives were an annoyance, when they led to imprisonment, pending the raising of bail. They were expensive; the Committee's papers show that Coleman had to appeal to grudging colleagues for financial help.

Yet the suits led to no punishments for various reasons. Brought in New York courts, the question of non-jurisdiction was raised. Then there was the technicality of whether the Vigilantes had been in rebellion against San Francisco authorities—naughty—or in revolt. As the war which had given America its independence was known as a revolution, revolters were viewed as doing the right thing.

While these points were being debated, though, J. Reuben Maloney passed away; and according to Bancroft that gave the game to the Vigilantes. His summation that "when Maloney died, the suits did, too," stemmed from the fact that J. Reuben was the only man shanghaied to New York with money enough to press the suits hard.

In San Francisco it was useless to sue a Committee member for any of that body's official acts. A gang that had complained that local juries were packed had turned into packers de luxe themselves. It was impossible to impanel twelve San Franciscans of whom some hadn't been banishers or admirers of the sport.

So nothing at all came of criminal suits. One civil case resulted in an award of damages, but the defendant was not a Vigilante. Nor, according to Ned, did the winner live long.

Of a man who had been stranded on foreign soil, McGowan wrote: "Martin Gallagher was killed by an emissary of the Committee after he had obtained a judgment against the bark Live Yankee for $3500 for forcibly taking him out of the country."

Nothing was done about the four men the Vigilantes had publicly murdered. Nothing was done about the property stolen from McGowan and others.

The efforts to bring the head Vigilantes to some sort of book weren't dropped during the lifetime of most of them. For many years Federal and state courts tried to get hold of the Committee's rosters and papers, with a view to learning the exact parts played by men who had publicly been known only by numbers in 1856. Always tipped off in time, the possessor had passed the documents to another custodian, by the time a subpoena brought him before a judge, or a search warrant made him open his safe.

It would have simplified the lives of the chief stranglers, had they felt able to destroy the books and papers. Because of knowing the bents of many of their followers, they didn't take the easy way out. Were the records disposed of, some might have levied blackmail by threatening to bleat. While the numbers could still be checked against names, the Vigilantes were all equally guilty— and equally anxious to defeat prosecution.

Thus the Executives beat the law and kept what they had snatched. They were not in all cases the ones who had ruled San Francisco at the time of Ned's flight from it. Gabriel Post, as has been said, lost out and became a flunky in the hoosegow. By 1858 John Middleton was of the Committee's baronage, although he had not had that rank two years earlier.

In a speculators' market the ability to come back was what separated the men from the boys. Coleman had been in dire straits in 1857; General Estell said the New York newspapers had put him down as being $400,000 in the red. But the true killer whales are already planning to tear off the next fortune, while watching the one at hand slipping away. It's only the mud sharks that jump out of windows or run for cover to salaried jobs, when gambles go awry.

So the men who kept their places on the Executive Committee were there by right of being cormorant cream. Coleman didn't stay president on account of the love the others bore him. Probably because he dealt too fast for them, as afore remarked the colleagues who mentioned him in their memoirs did so spitefully. He stayed in control by out-thinking the others and making more money. When the *Argonaut* published a list of San Francisco's millionaires in 1877, William Tell was the only Executive on it.

That was the year in which he again called for Vigilante action. There was no cackle about crime then; the Purest and Best were arrayed against laborers, sullen and threatening on the score of being asked to work long hours for no pay to speak of.

The story of another round won by the Vigilantes doesn't belong in this narrative. The episode was only cited because nothing could better illustrate the complete hold on the city retained by the Executives more than twenty years after Casey winged James King of William.

Who still kept Coleman company at that period isn't wholly clear. Already said, some with the stuff to have stayed Executives, disqualified themselves by dying. Remarked also, ten of the 1856 members lived long enough to be tapped for memoirs by Bancroft a decade later. Minus such high riders as Marshal Charles Doane and Judge Advocate John Manrow, Coleman, Bluxome, Dows, Smiley, Farwell, Truett, Dempster, Olney, Crary, and Gillespie carried on. These and promoted associates steered an organization which said who could and could not run for office in San Francisco for more than twenty years. The People's Party likewise said who could and could not be called for jury duty.

Through these means the Executives ordered San Francisco's political climate, and thus its moral tone. The nature of that tone has been declared exemplary by a succession of California chroniclers. Reputedly the most thoughtful of them, Josiah Royce wound up a recital of the Committee's activities in good, rousing, bedtime story style:

"And thenceforth, for years, San Francisco was one of the best governed municipalities in the United States."

The Executives themselves were not backward in boasting that they had given local ethics a tidy boost. With several such statements to choose from, one by James Dows should suffice to illustrate their practice of fluffing moral feathers:

"The Committee resulted in a political reformation, and the influence of the Committee lasted for years afterward in that direction."

An objector was Harvy Brown, the junior associate of the Court of Quarter Sessions when Ned was the senior one. In a deposition which Bancroft secured from him, but didn't quote, Brown wrote of the Committee:

"I believe it productive of more evil than anything that ever happened to this state, because it taught people that the law could be successfully disregarded."

The judgments of Dows and Brown can best be weighed through application to the record. Many years before they set down their conflicting views, Ned's *Phoenix* had published San Francisco Police records covering the years 1855 and 1857. Bracketing the year of the reign of terror, the lists showed how things went with the city before and after taking the Vigilante pill.

	1855	1857
Murders	6	9
Assaults to kill	1	6
Affrays	1	7
Highway robbery	4	4
Robbery	12	16
Burglary	5	7

In 1857 John Nugent translated Ned's statistics into an editorial: "The truth is that for purposes of good, the Committee has been a sorry and tragic failure. During the last six months crimes against life have been more frequent in San Francisco than in twice that length of time in any previous period of its history . . . Murders, robberies, and all sorts of ruthless violence have run riot in our midst. The organization has not extirpated a single evil. It has inaugurated immeasurable crimes."

One reason for the increase in felonies was the immunity from prosecution enjoyed by the Vigilantes, unless they had trod on the purse strings of fellow members. When called for hearings with respect to crimes against persons, they could afford to laugh. There was nothing so crude as asserting Committee membership in court, though. A bit of ribbon, worn in the buttonhole of a lapel, was the hardly noticeable symbol.

And even when a choker committed the sacrilege of a crime against money, he was shielded from the bite of publicity. Mc-Gowan pointed out that when Executive Hutchings was sued for a torrid check, hung on a brother hangman, the Vigilante papers didn't carry a word about it.

After the boycott finally induced Nugent to sell the *Herald,* the officials of San Francisco were under the scrutiny of no daily. Protected by the People's Party and not liable to exposure by the press, they gave the city the underworld it couldn't have under earlier conditions.

There is no underworld where there is no furtiveness. When San Francisco's bagnios operated in the best business districts, they were on the same legal level as other enterprises. Their owners were therefore immune to shakedown by politicians and/or police. The same was true of gamblers. As long as they could perform anywhere they were treated as the legitimate part of the entertainment world which they were in fact while frontier notions prevailed.

As early as 1854, teste McGowan, the Know-Nothings had celebrated their victory by voting to shoo the brothels off the main drags. The tart marts were for the first time at a disadvantage as compared with other businesses. As for the madams, they could only stay where they liked by offering bribes; or if they won any preferred locations, it was through hush-hush deals.

As such, the Know-Nothings didn't hold the reins long enough to get far with their program of cathouse zoning. But when, as the People's Party, they really took over, districts were arranged as they wished them to be. Losing all power to operate other than where city officials told them they could, the gambler and the madam ceased to be part of the community at large and dropped to the level of the underworld. It was then, to say it all, that they became the victims of special laws, which they were allowed to break as long as they paid off.

That development was but one phase of a city where corruption spread like hives. In 1855 crime in San Francisco supplied newspapers with the modest number of items indicated by Ned's citations from the police blotter of that year. By 1858 the prevalence of law-breaking encouraged a journalist to start the *California Police Gazette*. Devoted to vice and scandal in San Francisco, it had a varied beat to cover.

Prior to the Committee's reign, crimping was on so small a scale that no newspaper or chronicle took notice of it. By definition, decoying for the purpose of putting a man aboard a ship he wouldn't otherwise be on, the word had an enlarged meaning by the tarnished Golden Gate of 1861. Behind a protecting screen of pay-offs, gangs of crimps openly worked both sides of the street. That is to say, that they first created a demand for their product by kidnapping the seamen aboard an incoming ship; and next supplied with tars the shipmaster thus forced to buy a new batch or keep his cargo under hatches.

"They swarm over the rail like pirates," said the San Francisco *Times* of October 21, "and virtually take possession of the deck. The crew are shoved in the runners' boats, and the vessel is often left in a perilous situation, with none to manage her, the sails unfurled, and she liable to drift afoul of the shipping at anchor. In some cases not a man has been left aboard after the anchor has been dropped."

Never naming any, however, the *Times* told how unabashedly political leaders and officials showed their hands in this game. "Honest shipmasters, especially those in command of foreign vessels were frequently warned by 'certain interested parties,' that if they interfered with the crimps they would be denied crews when they were ready to sail."

The runners for the various houses where the sailors were kept in a stupor, until the head crimp had an order to fill, were prepared to lure, dope, slug, or force their victims to come along. They were equipped, universally, with naked girly pictures, treated booze, blackjacks, knives, and guns.

A sailor who died from rough handling, or because his system couldn't stand the hooch with which he was kept paralyzed, did not necessarily stay ashore. Many a skipper, clearing port at night or when the fog was heavy, found that he had ponied for a cadaver or so. That sort of thing went on for decades, and though newspapers described conditions, none told of the organization that sponsored civic depravity—or traced its origin back to the causative 1856 take over.

The Committee's purest and best contribution to the felonious annals of the United States was the Barbary Coast. Only Natchez Underhill and Lafitte's Galveston Island Campeachy had anything like similar standing as criminal boroughs, and both were dwarf when measured against San Francisco's entry.

Within ten years of the Vigilante crusade this social tumor had attained the dimensions it was to keep for forty more. It would have lasted longer, but the earthquake of 1906 proved to be one case where protection money was powerless to save the payers.

This quarter of the city was a snug fit between the water front and the County Jail, whose directors took no notice of the fandango houses on the opposite side of Broadway. Otherwise the Coast was made up of brothels, cribs, cutthroat gambling dens, houses where the crimps held sailors captive, and saloons whose function was to feed visiting yokels to dives where they'd be rolled.

As Benjamin Lloyd summed the civic jakes in 1876, "The Barbary Coast is the haunt of the low and the vile of every kind. The petty thief, the house burglar, the tramp, the whoremonger, lewd women, cut throats, murderers, all are found here."

Moketown and Murder Point were sections of San Francisco's Isle of Dogs; Dead Man's Alley and Battle Row were two of its drags. Of the Row it was said that it averaged a killing a week; but nobody really knew, because nobody really cared.

The only interest taken in the Coast by San Francisco's law-makers was to pass regulating statutes, in the rare instances when some reformer tried to queer the best source of revenue the People's Party had. The laws showed the city's solons were stout for reform; and beside each was good for so much more in the way of protection jack.

"I don't think the Committee lost anything pecuniarily by their actions," Gillespie smiled behind his hand. He didn't mean the Vigilantes as a body. What he was chuckling about were the Executives and their coadjutors: the moguls who kept books that were never officially audited; the merchants whose taxes and tariffs were cut by corrupted Federal officials; the employers who made a cheap labor town out of what had been the best working man's burg in the world; the men who decided how the shakedown returns would be portioned out; the ones who owned the land on which the denizens of the Coast went their malign ways.

The San Francisco of the Vigilantes was the home of the syndicates which supplied whores to the mining camps of the entire inland West, after the railroads had made large operations and the distribution of chippies a feasibility in parts distant from the Pacific. The Committee's city was also the national head-quarters of the opium trade.

The Chinese had been hitting the poppy for years without tempting others in the United States to hide out in the acedia of bought dreams. According to Kane's *Opium Smoking in America* a first for white men was racked up in 1868 by one Glendenyn of San Francisco. The city's opium dens—into which Glendenyn was followed by white women, as well as Caucasians of his own sex—were the spawners of the national plague of narcotic addiction in all its crippling forms.

The pioneer opium dives were in San Francisco's Chinatown, which was also the locus of the city's thriving slave trade. For although most of the Committee had taken a strong stand against slavery for Negroes in the South, the People's Party went to all lengths to keep Chinese girls from being rescued from enforced servitude in California.

The selling of Chinese girls to whoremongers had, like puffing opium, been practiced on a small scale in pre-Vigilante days. Yet it was not until after the fake reformation that it got to be big business.

There is nothing else in American annals which comes near rivaling the vileness of San Francisco's live meat market. Those sold were children and young girls who seldom lived to be adults; most were fornicated to death before they were twenty. Although only a couple of thousand were involved at any given time, the mortality rate demanded hundreds of replacements each year.

Various contemporary sources agree that the average age of the slaves was twelve to fourteen; but farsighted purchasers sometimes bought infants and ripened them for the market. "The girls cost $40 each in Canton," to quote Evans' *A la California,* "but are valued here at about $400, if passably good looking, young and healthy, and readily sell at that figure for cash."

By 1869 the trade had reached such proportions that the *Chronicle* referred to it as "the importation of females in bulk." The paper also told how the bidding went. "The particularly fine portions of the cargo, the fresh and pretty females who come from the interior, are used to fill special orders from wealthy merchants and prosperous tradesmen . . . Another lot of the general importation offered to the Chinese public are examined critically by those desiring to purchase, and are sold to the trade or to individuals."

The only ones who made a real effort to put a stop to shamelessness were some respectable Chinese organizations; and they were defeated by the city's politicos. The story is told in a memorial the self-named Six Companies sent to President Grant in 1874:

"Quite a number of Chinese prostitutes have been brought to this country by unprincipled Chinamen, but these at first were brought from China at the instigation and for the gratification of white men. And even at the present time it is commonly reported that a part of the proceeds of this villainous traffic goes to enrich a certain class of men belonging to this honorable nation—a class of men, too, who are under solemn obligation to suppress the whole vile business, and who certainly have it in their power to suppress it, if they so desired. A few years ago, our Chinese merchants tried to send those prostitutes back to China, and succeeded in getting a large number aboard the outgoing steamer . . . but a certain lawyer of your honorable nation . . . procured a writ of habeas corpus . . . and the courts decided they had a right to stay in this country, if they so desired. Those women are still here, and the only remedy for the evil . . . lies, so far as we can see, in an honest and impartial administration . . . even including the Police Department. If officers would refuse bribes, then unprincipled Chinamen could no longer purchase immunity from the punishment of their crimes."

Although Grant paid no attention to that pointed appeal, Ned had better luck with the President, when he made a request in person the next year. The man who introduced them was almost certainly Tom Ochiltree. As heretofore stated, the colonel had become a fast friend of the general against whom he had fought with distinction in Virginia.

After listening to McGowan, President Grant told Coleman that a citizen who had cleared himself in court had a right to hang his hat in any city he fancied. In consequence Ned boarded a train in November of 1875, his purpose to end an exile begun nineteen years and five months before.

Of the twelve years since he reached Richmond with a maple leaf for cockade, his reminiscences say but little. At the close of the Civil War he went north to take part in the long struggle to rebuild the section's shattered Democratic Party. As the only place where it retained any strength was New York City, he settled there. He spent some years in Manhattan; how many he didn't say. In 1867 he went to Albany, to attend the funeral of his old friend, Senator James McDougall. Where he spent the rest of the time, and how he made his living throughout any of this period are things he didn't find worth noting. Essentially he was interested only in his California experiences.

The epoch which had broken his life in two was unfinished business to which he had to return; hence his arranging it by what amounted to a presidential edict. As the word had gone out, Ned's return to where he had ranked as anathema was marked by no uproar.

Even the press was in general polite. The once hostile *Alta California* took occasion to check its files and erase Tom King's libel to the effect that McGowan had pocketed all the revenues he had collected as State Commissioner of Immigration. Referring back to the card published by leading San Franciscans early in 1856, the *Alta* reported that Ned was the only holder of a then extinct office who had ever voluntarily turned over to California's treasury the fees paid out by newcomers to the state.

The Committee, as represented by its president, formally recognized Ned's changed status, when McGowan, as he would have quoted, "bearded the Douglas in his hall." The occasion seems to have been some sort of a political festivity, for although sitting on Democracy in San Francisco, William Tell was zealous for it on the state and national levels.

"I met Mr. Coleman for the first time after the unpleasantness," as Ned put it, in one of his milder moods, "on his own grounds in San Rafael, at one of the famous Bullhead breakfasts. He came forward and put his arm though mine and carried me aside from the crowd and asked me if I had seen General Grant. I looked at him a moment and answered, 'Yes.' He said the General had spoken to him about me. After we returned and joined the breakfast party, he introduced me to his two sons."

For the next eighteen years the two principal actors in the most wonderful of Wild West stories shared a curious relationship. They were on good terms personally, in a word, without ceasing to slam each other when their political feud was the topic.

But the difference was that Ned was not trying to ruin any individual; he wanted vindication through the principle that a crew who'd been at odds with all law and decency must be held in the wrong. Coleman wanted vindication, too; and in order to

maintain it, he had to go on working for the personal discredit of
the writer who had ably impugned the Committee.

As 33 Bluxome said of him, William Tell was one day of this
nature and the next morning of that. To judge from his actions,
a centaur couldn't have had a more split personality.

Without leaving the People's Party, he could run for U. S.
Senator as a Democrat, which he did in 1864. He could make a
wreck of Governor Neely Johnson's career, and then write him
a letter whose tone implies confidence that they were still the
buddies they had been before the Committee went into action.
He could be openhandedly generous. Once when Ned felt an
itch to join a stampede, Coleman volunteered a stake. Or he
could be as callous as he was, when he sentenced Brace and Hetherington without so much as bothering to marshal the kangaroos.

Without ceasing to plot against Ned, such a fellow could gen-
uinely enjoy his company. And after a fashion not uncommon to
arrogance, he probably even admired the one man who had
mustered the power to have him overruled.

As for Ned's appreciation of William Tell's great capacities, he
made that a matter of record: "Had Mr. Coleman never (un-
fortunately for him), mixed himself up in this 'higher law' business, he would no doubt have been governor of the state a long
time ago, and probably U. S. Senator."

Yet financially Coleman had thriven, and because of him and
his associates, McGowan had not. At sixty-two he had nothing
going for him but valor, and a quality he told of in a poem that
is all the more moving because of the persistent hard luck of its
maker:

> How many there are who sing and dream
>   Of happier seasons coming;
> And ever in fancy, to catch a beam
>   Of a Golden Era, roaming.
> The world may grow old—and young again—
> And the hope of a better shall still remain.

Hope comes with life at its dawning hour,
   Hope sports with the infant creeper;
Hope cheers the youth with her magic power
   And when, too, the gray haired weeper
Has closed in the grave his weary round,
He plants the tree of hope on the mound.

It is not an empty, vain deceit,
   In the brain of fools created;
It speaks to the soul of a state more sweet
   Where its longings shall all be sated.
And the promise the in-dwelling voice thus makes
To the hoping soul—it never breaks.

No doubt Ned's hope had long been that if he could but return
to San Francisco, he could regain the prosperity he had been
forced to abandon there. But he couldn't renew in his sixties the
law practice and the perquisites of personal influence and political
recognition which had been his a score of years earlier. In 1877,
therefore, he turned to a new hope and joined the gold stampede
to Deadwood.

All that he told of winning by his jump to Dakota Territory
was the knowledge that the brand the Committee had burned
him with was still as fresh as it had ever been. At the railhead
point of Cheyenne, Wyoming, he had been spotted by a former
San Franciscan who gave reporters an earful. In Deadwood he
got the same dish, with more trimmings.

Half of the bad men of the West had sped to see what could
be gouged out of its latest bonanza, but McGowan got top billing.
"In the Black Hills," as Ned wrote, "a Republican paper, the
Times, stated that I had 'kept the Committee at bay single
handed.'"

Although he never mentioned it himself, one of Ned's death
notices asserted that he had a hand in organizing Washington as
a state. Certainly he didn't take part in the Constitutional Convention, held in Walla Walla in June of 1878; for in May of that
year, he was back in San Francisco.

His known occupation at the time was writing a series of articles for *Argonaut* magazine. Mainly about his adventures in Canada, these dealt with the Committee only when telling of his difficulties in squeezing through San Francisco alive.

The *Argonaut* series so interested the editor of the San Francisco *Evening Post* that he contracted for McGowan's reminiscences at large. Beginning in July, they ran serially on Saturdays throughout the rest of the year and deep into 1879.

Ned eased into stride by telling what it was like to be a Golden Gater during the city's springtime years. The logic of the calendar took him through the first Vigilante season of 1851. Without hurrying, and charmingly, he treated the next forty-eight months. Then came 1856, and he had the Committee in his teeth.

In the *Narrative of Edward McGowan* he had told the story from a personal point of view. In the *Phoenix* and *Ubiquitous* he had lashed out as a satirist. In the *Post* he wrote of what had happened objectively, and on the basis of more information than had been at his disposal in the '50s.

Yet he didn't have the field to himself in 1878. In that year appeared the first of several books aimed at making the permanent record read in the Committee's favor. For up till then nothing spoke for the Vigilantes but yellowing newspaper articles, and pamphlets as forgotten as those written against them by Dr. Gray and General Estell.

O'Meara was of no concern to the Executives, as he was yet to write of them. But on the Law and Order side there was now a bound volume, in addition to Ned's book. In 1875 the Committee had received a shot between covers from an unexpected source. A hero in California, if not in Georgia, General Sherman had published memoirs, caustic in detail with reference to the Purest and Best.

Another body, headed by another man, might have issued a volume in their own names. Such an admission that they felt the need of a defense was not, however, what was fed to the market.

20

A WREATH FOR A GALLANT MAN

HARKING BACK TO its founding as a pueblo called Yerba Buena, San Francisco celebrated its centennial in 1877. Unquestionably schooled by Coleman, the commission in charge of festivities paid John S. Hittell $1500 to produce a book billed as a history of San Francisco. Not previously known to Ned, John was the older brother of Theodore Hittell, of Black male bird notoriety.

As always, William Tell moved with the cunning that serpents are only supposed to have. Although the history was published as a Centennial item, the business and political figures who made up the commission did not cite themselves as the work's backers. To give it a cultural nimbus, they issued it as sponsored by the California Society of Pioneers.

A charter member, McGowan was able to learn from the society's directors that the ascription was false. The membership had never been asked to vote on a volume, which became theirs only through a foisting which they didn't know how to reject.

Assisted, it was said, by Theodore, John Hittell had nothing but sweet peas for the Committee: "Occasions now and then arise that justify revolt against established authority and lift them in the estimation of mankind from the lower levels of rebellion to the sublime heights of revolution."

But although he could praise, John could also blame—anybody opposed to the Vigilantes. To quote Ned, "This portion of the book . . . is full of errors, omissions and false statements and appears to have been gotten up mainly for the purpose of picking holes in the character of the deceased David C. Broderick and his friends, and to enlighten the community of the great and good acts of the Vigilance Committee of 1856."

Ned was naturally not overlooked by the Centennial Commission's pitcher. The brickbats thrown at him came in two sizes. As Broderick's close associate, McGowan was inferentially guilty of everything scored against San Francisco's former Democratic chieftain. Then he got the smear direct in passages drawn from the Vigilante version of his own career and character.

After taking time to check all his sources, Ned gave propaganda masquerading as history a going over in several articles, published in the *Post* in 1879, that showed Hittell's work up as junk on all counts—not merely the parts bearing on the Committee and its foes. In fact he blew the volume so full of holes that the Executives lost confidence in its power to stand as a believed treatment of the city's annals.

Before they found a man with a better brand of snow to bury their critic under, Ned made one more try for a stake to see him through his final years. When sixty-seven he went back to Arizona to make a pass at the silver of rough and booming Tombstone.

He was there as late as the end of February 1881, for on the twenty-fifth he was acting as lookout for Luke Short—sometimes known as "the undertaker's friend," because of usually using one shot to dispose of a man, in place of riddling a corpse—who was dealing faro at the famous Oriental Saloon. While Ned was on duty, a noted gunnie named Charlie Storms—called "Frenchie" in McGowan's account—made the mistake of asking Luke to step out into Allen Street and swap shots. After Storms had been disposed of, Short went on dealing, and Ned continued to watch for hanky-panky on the part of those bucking Luke's tiger.

Two years later, and then seventy, McGowan got a piece of patronage again. He had never ceased to work for the comeback of the Democratic Party, and in the Congress which convened in 1883, his side was at last strong enough to be able to give out some prizes. The one awarded him for faithful service was the post of Assistant Sergeant at Arms of the House of Representatives.

In between sessions he seems to have been mostly in San Francisco, though in 1884 he was interviewed by a representative of *Forey's Press* in Philadelphia. As usual his California notoriety was the chief topic, and Ned was portrayed as making another display of brittle clippings, covering matters twenty-eight years agone. But after a time, a man who'd been notched by seventy-one years asked the reporter to spare him further questioning, and for cause:

"My head aches a little, and I cannot talk any more just now. Some of the boys dropped in to see me last night, and I didn't turn in until four o'clock in the morning."

In 1884, too, McGowan and Coleman squared off in articles written respectively for San Francisco's *Evening Post* and *Call*. In the course of their journalistic jousting, Ned put his foot in the quicksand which was to swallow him whole. Voicing an old man's dream of what he would do when he could spare the time, he stated that he was going to publish a history of the Committee and its depredations running to five or six hundred pages.

Word that exposure on a massive scale was planned by McGowan made Coleman see that to destroy Ned as a witness something must be done not only about him, but his standing as a writer. If the *Post* articles were themselves ephemera, they showed how much more McGowan had learned about the Vigilantes, singly or as a body, than he had known when writing not only his *Narrative* but the barbs lanced by the *Ubiquitous* and the bird. Now he was threatening to put the *Post* material, plus who knew what else, in a volume to roost on shelves that already held his respected earlier book and *The Memoirs of Gen. William T. Sherman*.

Against this array the Committee could only pit John Hittell's shoddy history. Realizing his mistake in depending on a journalist with no pretensions to scholarship, Coleman saw that what he had to get was a man of national standing. Aside from supplying a better front, such a chap wouldn't make howlers, when not writing of the Committee, and so would be trusted when Vigilantes were his subject.

Coleman's first pick was Josiah Royce, whose position as a professor at Harvard equipped him with both high academic rank and the presumption of integrity. Royce had written a book called *The Religious Aspects of Philosophy* and was said to have been a philosopher himself. There will be no quarrel with that finding here; for philosopher merely means a lover of wisdom. The adoring coyote that howls for the moon isn't always awarded Cynthia.

At all events the professor consented to give the Committee his learned blessing; by using the same approach William Tell had also obtained strips of Death Valley which were rich in borax. And Royce was a chattel with the useful advantages of being a native son and a graduate of California's young university. An interest in pioneer institutions could be viewed as natural on the part of a deep thinker, brooding on his homeland in far away Cambridge.

In 1886 he published a work titled *California from the Conquest in 1846 to the Second Vigilance Committee of San Francisco: a Study in American Character*. The beauty of the scheming behind it was that it was almost invisible; the book had all the earmarks of an objective study of the means by which American settlers had governed themselves before California had matured as a state.

In particular it reviewed the necessities and dangers of justice as popularly administered. On the whole Royce found that it had not worked out well in other parts of the state, albeit beautifully in the metropolis—when and where it never existed.

The treachery of the work lies in the balanced reasoning with which the author treats his topic, prior to moving into San Francisco. By then he has so lulled the reader by good-tempered analysis that the enormous fallacy he's slipping over is something to be caught only through a slow and incredulous double-take.

What the philosopher was paid to purvey is the atrocious lie that the popular tribunal of the mining camp and the Star Chamber courts of the Vigilance Committee were the same thing.

The true popular tribunals were community functions. Whether well- or ill-conducted, everybody took part; and all knew just what sort of a break the accused was or was not given. The courts of the Vigilantes were closed-door affairs, of which no word reached other ears, except in the never reliable form of Executive Committee propaganda.

Quoting Coleman as gospel, Royce played hob with truth and logic in all other respects. A shot he took at Ned's book will serve for example. This peddler of hocus-pocus opined that the *Narrative* was "unprincipled." Actually it's compact of principles: the values, maintained under the direst stress, of a manly, generous and engeniused spirit.

The chap who could read it without warming to its author must at best have had caterpillar ichor, and not blood, in his cockles. Not too much can be expected of a man so handicapped, of course. If unkind to Ned, Royce hadn't mustered the savagery to blast a man he bore no personal grudge. So Coleman went shopping for eminence not so squeamish.

Resident in California was one man whose writings had earned him renown in exactly the right field for the Committee's purposes. With his five volume *Native Races of the Pacific States of North America*, Hubert Howe Bancroft had deservedly won the plaudits of critics throughout the nation. Aided by a staff he had trained, he was well advanced with a grander project: his twenty-eight volume *History of the Pacific States*. Conveniently, besides, he was in the indiscriminate business of turning out books to order for customers with enough cash.

The contradictions of this bird would have stumped Audubon. He had a passion for gathering authentic data—which he would cheerfully ignore, if somebody paid him to keep the truth behind scenes. He spared neither time, energy nor money in amassing the most valuable collection of Western Americana ever assembled by an individual; and through sheer venality did immeasurable harm to the culture of the very state with which his library was chiefly concerned.

A line on how he operated, when he had his eye on rhino only, can be gained from glancing at a prospectus for a series of brief biographies to be called *Chronicles of the Kings.* In this unctuous come-on Bancroft explained that the really important people of the West were not those who had made name and fame in any political, warrior, explorational or cultural capacity—the real Kings were those who had kept their eyes on the main chance and built up personal fortunes. The true Kings of the West, in brief, were those who could afford to shell out for immortality.

If the title had stuck, America's West would have burgeoned with more monarchs than have ever sat on the combined thrones of England, France, and Spain; but as issued in seven, fat volumes, the series bore the name, *Chronicles of the Builders.* If perhaps not the first, this was the greatest of "fame at space rates" shakedowns. Hubert Howe is said to have grossed over a quarter of a million in days when the buying power of the dollar was high and production costs low.

According to his biographer, John Walton Caughey, Bancroft praised, in the *Chronicles,* men he had put on the pan in earlier works. But of course, every historian is entitled to review his findings, and make adjustments when necessary.

This was the man Coleman approached, after Royce had flubbed half of his assignment; and the right fellow had been found. William Tell wanted a book which would accomplish certain ends, he and his colleagues were willing to pay a famous historian's price; and Bancroft was prepared to earn it by satisfying his customers.

In the work fittingly dedicated to Coleman, Hubert Howe sold the same gold brick as the philosophy professor. His theme was the pretense that the secret courts of a metropolitan clique were identical with the mass-participation operations of justice, as practiced in the loosely, if at all organized, mountain mining camps.

Attempting to do the job as a philosopher's thesis, Royce hadn't felt the need of much source material. Bancroft's library was bulging with it. He declared that he was allowed to examine all the Committee's papers, additionally; and he had the statements, secured from various figures, which have been quoted now and again in this work.

Thus possessed of a scholar's wealth, he ignored most of it, because all but the propaganda put out by the Committee testified to the ill worth of his clients. Their own official documents spoke against them at every turn; and, as has been demonstrated, so did the memoirs of all but Coleman. He had sense enough to keep a united front by praising his colleagues, while they slammed him and sniped at each other. Or else they made damning admissions as to how they had operated; confessions that showed them up as comic where not disgusting.

None of this disturbed Bancroft, who gave the surviving—and well paying—Executives the *Chronicles of the Kings* treatment. "I propose to present these men as nature's noblemen," to sing his song as he caroled it. And the laddie made good.

With equal thoroughness he excoriated all who had opposed nature's peerage. For documentation he used gossip without a shred of offered support, items taken out of context, deliberately rearranged data and inventions of his own.

He also liberally quoted the *Bulletin,* in spite of explaining that Tom King was as full of indiscriminate malice, and as little to be trusted, as a bushmaster. Although the details are not now clear, Tom appears to have betrayed some of the Executives in his rag's columns—or the Black male bird's handler may have managed to pry some backsheesh out of them, before he left San Francisco in 1859. However for that, giving King a basting was one of the minor assignments faithfully carried out in *Popular Tribunals* by Hubert Howe.

The full measure of this Jekyll and Hyde of scholarship can be found in his dealings with Alfred Green. It is to Bancroft that history is indebted for persuading Green to write a fascinating document, bristling with factuality in every paragraph. But when employed as a practiced pen, Hubert Howe didn't quote from this fruit of his praiseworthy enterprise. The only interest he took in Alfred was to tar his character, because a finally enlightened Green had testified against the Committee in certain lawsuits.

But McGowan and his book were the chief butts of *Popular Tribunals*. As the lies told of Ned's actions have already been dwelt upon, only the treatment of his character will now be mentioned.

What Bancroft undertook was to make comedy the reigning aspect of the *Narrative's* author. McGowan was portrayed as missing greatness in villainy only because he was not to be taken seriously in any capacity.

Such a man, to get to Hubert Howe's purpose, was *incapable* of writing a work of any value. Yet how seriously he himself took McGowan's chronicle can be gathered from the space he devoted to discrediting it. That point was well pushed home by Joseph A. Sullivan in his preface to a small 1946 reprinting of Ned's work:

"Bancroft allots twenty-three pages to the McGowan Narrative . . . In a negative way, Bancroft's very emphasis shows both the importance and the sting of McGowan's recital."

Published in 1887, *Popular Tribunals* antedated by a year the two-volume account of California's pioneer era which Hubert Howe marketed. With his foot in the fly paper, he did what he had to, in order to avoid angering clients with the power to ruin him. And what he had to do was to make the statements of this basic history of the state conform to the lies and false judgments which had first appeared in a written-to-order piece of complete trash.

Because of the veneration accorded Bancroft—abetted by an admired philosopher—California's culture has rested on no foundation of actualities or truth to values. Generations have been taught in book after book and article after article that all the best men of the state's early years were false or weak-minded, because they did not see eye to eye with arrant scoundrels, piloted by a perverted master mind.

Reference works faithless to the trust placed in them. Sincere writers of non-fiction are not the only ones whose best efforts have been undone by sold-out history and bogus philosophy. Creative literature has been a victim as well. A dewy-eyed novelist named John Myers Myers, for instance, was hornswoggled by the Committee's penmen into featuring the McGowan of their counterfeit coinage in a work of fiction titled *I, Jack Swilling*. Welladay.

The myth of San Francisco's bloody infancy was perpetuated by Bancroft. McGowan had been moved to scornful mirth by statements that the city's streets had been littered with hundreds of cadavers in the five years from '49 on. How absurd such figures are can be ascertained by John Nugent's alarm at the increase in violence in 1857. There were nine murders that year, and a newspaperman who was himself a Forty-niner said the town had never seen anything like the recklessness with which gore was then being spilled. As there were six killings in 1855, three dozen would be a generous estimate for the lustrum of 1849–54. Yet to make a case for the Vigilantes, Bancroft said in his so-styled *History of California* that 1200 was the correct count.

To get back to *Popular Tribunals,* the work hatched one valuable by-product. James O'Meara had up to then written nothing about the Vigilantes, but the fiction fittingly dedicated to Coleman by Hubert Howe was more than the veteran journalist could take. Desiring, as he said, to put the record straight, he wrote a serial run by the San Francisco *Star*. Titled *The Vigilance Committee of 1856,* it added up to the little bound volume which 1887 also saw published.

His exposé should have been enough to demolish the Committee's reputation, but it was formidably overshadowed. Matched against the two volume opus of a renowned historian, a slim deck of pages by an obscure newspaperman had the look of a Mexican hairless trying to take on a Great Dane. Seemingly it has been not much read or valued since. Certainly it did nothing to upset the complaisance of the Executives while they lived.

For through *Popular Tribunals* the cross-biters had taken every trick. They had remained honored for villainies through old age, and now they were sure of posterity's approval. It was so perfect a diddle that the thought of its completeness must have sweetened their declining years.

Not many of them lived long enough to see themselves eulogized in the four volume *History of California* which Theodore Hittell finished in 1897. As a *Bulletin* alumnus, Hittell but did as expected, with one significant exception. Ned had been so sealed in his tomb by Bancroft and Royce that Theodore didn't find it necessary to devote much space to hacking the enemy of hangman virtue.

But the true extent of McGowan's decline from notice was demonstrated, in 1915, through a comprehensive chronicle of the state edited by a man who had never taken the Committee's shilling. In a five-volume job supervised by Zoeth Skinner Eldredge, Ned and the *Narrative* were dismissed with a couple of sentences which show how thoroughly the very thinking processes of educated Californians had been corrupted by the Committee's apologists.

"McGowan was pursued by agents of the Committee long enough for him to reflect on the worthlessness of his miserable life." That was an attempt to explain how a book, bespeaking an opposite type as author on every page of it, could have been somehow penned by the criminal clown of Bancroft's devising. Yet the hit of the paragraph is sentence two. "Seven or eight thousand men of affairs could no longer wait for him, and there was indeed not much reason to do so."

In some monstrous but unexplained way, in other words, Ned had stopped the clock for seven or eight thousand society pillars who couldn't get on with their worthy pursuits until he had been hounded by men intent on lawlessly executing him. That combination of nonsense and depraved reasoning is the essence of the legacy bequeathed to California by the San Francisco Committee of Vigilance of 1856.

Salvation was right around the corner then. One destitute man murdered, and the world would have come around rich for a decent eight thousand, like the milk of a freshened cow. Still alive in 1888, however, Ned tried to collect $50,000 in damages from Bancroft.

All he got from that lurcher was the admission that he'd erred; a retraction which didn't cost Hubert Howe a cent. The widely sold works in which he had libeled McGowan couldn't be recalled, besides, nor was there any way to stop general belief in an admired historian's statements.

The stab for a slice of Bancroft's bankroll all but finished Ned's career. In 1889 he left his post as an employe of Congress. He was then seventy-six, and the so far discovered record tells of no more ploys.

San Francisco was where he chose to ride out years that saw his slender means draining away as implacably as his energies. Only newspapermen, seeing good copy in a fellow always pictured as a retired desperado, continued to take much of an interest in him.

"He never complained," one reporter wrote, "but took the poverty and hard luck . . . without a whimper."

The day inevitably came, though, when he could no longer keep the flag flying. "The old man has been failing for some time," the *Examiner* reported on June 4, 1893. "Recently he took to his bed, and it is unlikely that he will ever rise again. Ned McGowan is destitute, and during the days of his illness none has come to see him. Mr. Holland, the proprietor of the Commercial Hotel, where the old man lives, has done what he could for him, but Ned McGowan is past a physician's power to help."

When mental collapse followed the physical one, he was taken from a room where his chief belongings were a mass of newspaper clippings bearing on the events of 1856. What was left of him was turned over to a hospital run by nuns, under whose care the mind of second childhood remembered the prayers he had been taught in his first.

In his lucid moments, as the *Examiner* reported, Ned couldn't be persuaded to talk of his perhaps forgotten past. Yet in delirium he muttered of the amazing adventures and encounters with celebrated people which had spangled his career.

Even when dying he scored one more coup. William Tell Coleman—head of the gang which had for so long sworn to kill him, should he ever show his face in the city—left the top side of San Francisco two weeks before McGowan did.

For him the end came in St. Mary's Hospital on December 8,

1893. The funeral cortege which left St. Francis Church on December 11, included only two ancient mourners. The sole floral tribute on the grave for him in Holy Cross Cemetery was that sent by the owner of the Commercial Hotel.

"N-E-D," it spelled.

Such was the all but Potter's field passing of the most gifted man to be drawn to California by the finding of gold near Sutter's Fort in 1848. With some prescience of his destiny, as it would seem, he had written a poem he called *History of Life:*

> Day dawned. Within a curtained room,
> Fitted to faintness with perfume,
> A lady lay at point of doom.
>
> Day closed. A child has seen the light;
> But for the lady fair and bright—
> She rested in undreaming night.
>
> Spring came. The lady's grave was green,
> And near it oftentime was seen
> A gentle boy with thoughtful mien.
>
> Years fled. He wore a manly face,
> And struggled in the world's rough race,
> And won at last a lofty place.
>
> And then he died. Behold before ye,
> Humanity's brief sum and story—
> Life, death and all there is of glory.

Although they several times gained him eminence, only to be frustrated by turns of fortune, Ned's diversity of talents ended by being paid with glory in reverse. Recognition of McGowan took the form of the mudhole in history in which his enemies had steeped him. With his book discredited he saw himself leaving no monuments by which he could hope to be better remembered. The above poem is but the most desolate of several expressions of his feeling that the powers he knew he possessed had been spent to no purpose. He had neither made his mark politically nor maintained the prosperity to rank as a successful man in any other walk.

Yet his achievements were almost as numerous as the disasters which kept him from shining, while men of lesser parts seized the prizes he aspired to. When a coming crop of scholars begin rewriting California's history with truth for proofreader, they will look to McGowan, as the author of the largest body of reliable source material bearing on the era of the state's formation. When they revalue California's literature, they will allow Ned the priority as a poet and a wit that has been his neglected due for over a century. As for his *Narrative,* there is but the one thing to say. It belongs on any balanced list of the world's great autobiographical works.

All in that category, barring the journals of the quaint secret writers like Pepys, have mighty hearts as their well-springs; and that of the Ubiquitous was nothing if not such. No matter what dire haps befell him, he never soured, quit striving, lost his spark of zest or broke with the philosophy he boxed in an epigram:

> When fortune smiles, we ride in chaises;
> When she frowns, we walk by "Jasus."

So much for Ned McGowan, of all points of America's compass. He got to do a lot of walking in his day, with some running from the Vigilantes thrown in. But wherever he went—and no doubt on trails of his that haven't yet been cut, as well as on the ones here traced—he did so in his own bold, perceptive and ever spontaneous way.

BIBLIOGRAPHY

Manuscripts

Handwritten matter relative to McGowan's trial, in 1848, is held by the City of Philadelphia Department of Records.

Memoirs, written or dictated by participants or observers of Vigilance Committee activities, take the form of statements by the following figures, held by the Bancroft Library of the University of California at Berkeley: Washington Barrett, Garret G. Bradt, Isaac Bluxome, Jr., Harvy S. Brown, Richard Beverly Cole, William Tell Coleman (two items), Oliver B. Crary, Clancy John Dempster (two items), James Dows, James D. Farwell, Charles V. Gillespie, James M. MacDonald, James N. Olney, Gerrit W. Ryckman, Thomas J. L. Smiley, and Miers Truett. In the same category but much longer is the mysteriously never published manuscript by Alfred A. Green, which he titled *The Life and Adventures of a '47-er of California.*

Miscellaneous manuscript items at the Bancroft Library consist of the correspondence of the Rev. William Anderson Scott and the diaries of Walton Van Sloan, covering the years 1854, 1856, and 1858.

Papers of the San Francisco Committee of Vigilance of 1856: The bulk of the surviving ones are in the Henry E. Huntington Library, San Marino, Calif., which also holds a letter addressed to

McGowan by Guillaume Patrice Dillon, a page from the journal of Milo Hoadley, and a laconic refusal of an invitation reading, "Am sick can't come," which is the only so far found McGowan manuscript. The residue of the Committee's papers, including the original roster and correspondence addressed to McGowan in 1852–53, are held by the Bancroft Library.

Consulted Periodicals

MAGAZINES: *The Argonaut,* San Francisco, 1877, 1878; *California Historical Society Quarterly,* San Francisco, 1922–1965 (Vol. 6, or that of 1927, contains an article about McGowan called *Ned, the Ubiquitous* by Carl I. Wheat); *The Century Illustrated Monthly Magazine,* Vol. XLIII, New York, 1891, includes *San Francisco Vigilance Committees* by William T. Coleman and *Unpublished Letters of Gen. W. T. Sherman.*

NEWSPAPERS: Alameda County, Calif., *Gazette,* 1857; Harrisburg, Pa., *State Capitol Gazette,* 1843; Mesilla, Ariz., *Times,* 1859; Napa, Calif., *Reporter,* 1857; New York *Evening Post,* 1856; New York *National Police Gazette,* 1849–50, 1856; *The New York World,* 1888; Philadelphia *Forey's Press,* 1884; Philadelphia *Public Ledger,* 1847–49; Sacramento *Bee,* 1858; Sacramento *Democratic State Journal,* 1856–57; Sacramento *Phoenix,* 1857–58; Sacramento *Ubiquitous,* 1858; Sacramento *Union,* 1858; San Francisco *Alta California,* 1855–58, 1860, 1863, 1875; San Francisco *California Chronicle,* 1855–56, 1858; San Francisco *California Police Gazette,* 1858–61; San Francisco *Chronicle,* 1869, 1893; San Francisco *Evening Bulletin,* 1855–59; San Francisco *Evening Post,* 1878–79, 1884; San Francisco *Examiner,* 1888, 1893; San Francisco *Herald,* 1856–58, 1860; San Francisco *Times,* 1861; San Francisco *Town Talk,* 1856–57; San Francisco *Varieties,* 1856–57; San Francisco *Weekly Star,* 1887; Santa Barbara, Calif., *Gazette,* 1856; Steilacoom, Wash., *Puget Sound Herald,* 1859; Tubac, N.M., *Arizonian,* 1859; Tucson, N.M. and Ariz., *Arizonian,* 1859–60.

Clipping Collections

The scrapbooks of Winfield J. Davis, pioneer California librarian, and evidently much interested in McGowan, are held by the Huntington Library at San Marino, Calif., which, too, holds the quoted bulletin of the Noisy Carrier's Book and Stationery Co.

There are several scrapbooks covering the Vigilance Committee era in the Bancroft Library of the University of California at Berkeley, which also holds a mass of unmarshaled clippings collected by the Rev. William Anderson Scott, at one time Chaplain of California's Senate.

Books and Pamphlets

Anonymous, HISTORY OF SANTA BARBARA AND VENTURA COUNTIES. Berkeley, Calif., 1961.

Arizona Constitutional Convention, THE CONSTITUTION AND THE PROVISIONAL GOVERNMENT OF THE TERRITORY OF ARIZONA. Tucson, Ariz., 1860.

Asbury, Herbert, THE BARBARY COAST. New York, 1933.

Atherton, Gertrude, THE GOLDEN GATE. New York, 1945.

Bancroft, Hubert Howe, CHRONICLES OF THE BUILDERS, 7 Vols. plus one devoted to the index. San Francisco, 1891–92. (A connected prospectus shows that the title originally chosen was CHRONICLES OF THE KINGS.)

——, HISTORY OF ARIZONA AND NEW MEXICO. San Francisco, 1888.

——, HISTORY OF BRITISH COLUMBIA. San Francisco, 1888.

——, HISTORY OF CALIFORNIA, Vols. VI and VII. San Francisco, 1888.

——, THE NATIVE RACES OF THE PACIFIC STATES OF NORTH AMERICA, 5 Vols. San Francisco, 1874–76.

——, POPULAR TRIBUNALS, 2 Vols. San Francisco, 1887.

Barry, T. A. and Patten, B. A., MEN AND MEMORIES. San Francisco, 1873.

Barry, W. Jackson, PAST AND PRESENT MEN OF THE TIMES. Wellington, New Zealand, 1897.

Bates, Mrs. D. B., INCIDENTS ON LAND AND WATER. Boston, 1857.

Beebe, Lucius and Clegg, Charles, SAN FRANCISCO'S GOLDEN ERA. Berkeley, Calif., 1960.

Bell, Horace, REMINISCENCES OF A RANGER. Los Angeles, 1881.

Bosqui, Edward, MEMOIRS OF EDWARD BOSQUI. Oakland, Calif., 1952.

Bruce, John R., GAUDY CENTURY. New York, 1948.

Buchanan, Albert Russell, DAVID S. TERRY, *Dueling Judge*. San Marino, Calif., 1956.

Buchanan, James, THE WORKS OF JAMES BUCHANAN, 12 vols. New York, 1960.

Buel, J. W., METROPOLITAN LIFE UNVEILED. San Francisco, 1882.

Burnett, Peter Hardeman, RECOLLECTIONS AND OPINIONS OF AN OLD PIONEER. New York, 1880.

Camp, William Martin, SAN FRANCISCO, PORT OF GOLD. Garden City, N.Y., 1943.

Cary, Thomas Greaves, THE SAN FRANCISCO VIGILANCE COMMITTEE. Boston, 1877.

Caughey, John Walton, GOLD IS THE CORNER STONE. Berkeley, Calif., 1948.

————, HUBERT HOWE BANCROFT. Berkeley, Calif., 1946.

Cleland, Robert Glass, FROM WILDERNESS TO EMPIRE. New York, 1944.

————, A HISTORY OF CALIFORNIA: *The American Period*. New York, 1922.

Coblentz, Stanton A., VILLAINS AND VIGILANTES. New York, 1957.

Cowan, Robert G., A BIBLIOGRAPHY OF THE HISTORY OF CALIFORNIA AND THE PACIFIC WEST. San Francisco, 1952.

Cozzens, Samuel, THE MARVELOUS COUNTRY. Boston, 1873.

Cremony, John C., LIFE AMONG THE APACHES. New York, 1868.

Davis, Winfield J., HISTORY OF POLITICAL CONVENTIONS IN CALIFORNIA. Sacramento, Calif., 1889.

DeFord, Miriam Allen, THEY WERE SAN FRANCISCANS. Caldwell, Idaho, 1941.

DICTIONARY OF AMERICAN BIOGRAPHY, 20 Vols. New York, 1928–1936.

Dillon, Richard H., THE HATCHET MEN. New York, 1962.

———, SHANGHAIING DAYS. New York, 1961.

Dunaway, Wayland F., A HISTORY OF PENNSYLVANIA. New York, 1948.

Eldredge, Zoeth Skinner (Ed.), HISTORY OF CALIFORNIA, 5 Vols. New York, 1915.

Ellison, William H., A SELF GOVERNING DOMINION: *California from 1849 to 1860*. Berkeley, Calif., 1950.

Estell, James M., SPEECH OF GEN. JAMES M. ESTELL DELIVERED IN THE HALL OF REPRESENTATIVES. Sacramento, Calif., 1857.

Evans, Albert S., A LA CALIFORNIA, *Sketches of Life in the Golden State*. San Francisco, 1873.

Fargo, Frank F., A TRUE AND MINUTE ACCOUNT OF THE ASSASSINATION OF JAMES KING OF WM. San Francisco, 1856.

Farnham, Eliza W., CALIFORNIA, INDOORS AND OUT. New York, 1856.

Farish, Thomas E., THE GOLD HUNTERS OF CALIFORNIA. Chicago, 1904.

———, HISTORY OF ARIZONA, 8 Vols. Phoenix, Ariz., 1915.

Farragut, Loyall, THE LIFE OF DAVID GLASGOW FARRAGUT. New York, 1879.

Field, Stephen J., PERSONAL REMINISCENCES OF EARLY DAYS IN CALIFORNIA. Washington, 1893.

Fitzgerald, O. P., CALIFORNIA SKETCHES (First Series). Nashville, Tenn., 1879.

———, CALIFORNIA SKETCHES (Second Series). Nashville, Tenn., 1882.

Foote, Henry S., THE BENCH AND BAR OF THE SOUTH AND SOUTHWEST. St. Louis, 1876.

———, TEXAS AND THE TEXANS, 2 Vols. Philadelphia, 1841.

Gard, Wayne, FRONTIER JUSTICE. Norman, Okla., 1949.

Garnett, Porter (Ed.), PAPERS OF THE SAN FRANCISCO COMMITTEE OF VIGILANCE OF 1851. Berkeley, Calif., 1910–19.

Gentry, Curt, THE MADAMES OF SAN FRANCISCO. Garden City, N.Y., 1964.

Gray, Henry M., JUDGES AND CRIMINALS. San Francisco, 1858.

HARPER'S ENCYCLOPAEDIA OF UNITED STATES HISTORY, 10 Vols. New York, 1901–1905.

Haskins, C. W., THE ARGONAUTS OF CALIFORNIA. New York, 1890.

Helper, Hinton Rowan, THE LAND OF GOLD. Baltimore, 1855.

Hittell, John S., HISTORY OF THE CITY OF SAN FRANCISCO. San Francisco, 1878.

Hittell, Theodore, HISTORY OF CALIFORNIA, 4 Vols. San Francisco, 1885–1897.

Howay, F. W., THE EARLY HISTORY OF THE FRASER RIVER MINES. Victoria, B.C., 1926.

Jackson, Joseph Henry, BAD COMPANY. New York, 1949.

——— (Ed.), THE WESTERN GATE, *A San Francisco Reader*. New York, 1952.

Johnson, Byron R., VERY FAR WEST INDEED. London, 1872.

Kane, Harry Hubble, OPIUM SMOKING IN AMERICA. New York, 1881.

Kemble, Edward C., A HISTORY OF CALIFORNIA NEWSPAPERS. Los Gatos, Calif., 1962.

Knox, Thomas W., UNDERGROUND OR LIFE BELOW THE SURFACE. Hartford, Conn., 1875.

Lewis, Oscar, THIS WAS SAN FRANCISCO. New York, 1962.

Lloyd, Benjamin Estelle, LIGHTS AND SHADOWS IN SAN FRANCISCO. San Francisco, 1876.

Lynch, Jeremiah, A SENATOR OF THE FIFTIES: *David Broderick*. New York, 1911.

Mayne, Richard Charles, FOUR YEARS IN BRITISH COLUMBIA AND VANCOUVER ISLAND. London, 1862.

McClintock, James H., ARIZONA, THE YOUNGEST STATE, 3 Vols. Chicago, 1916.

McGowan, Edward, MCGOWAN VS. CALIFORNIA VIGILANTES; Foreword by Joseph A. Sullivan. Oakland, Calif., 1946.

McGowan, Edward, THE NARRATIVE OF EDWARD MCGOWAN, IN-CLUDING A FULL ACCOUNT OF THE AUTHOR'S ADVENTURES AND

PERILS WHILE PERSECUTED BY THE SAN FRANCISCO VIGILANCE COMMITTEE IN 1856. San Francisco, 1857.

——, THE STRANGE AND EVENTFUL HISTORY OF PARKER H. FRENCH. Los Angeles, 1958.

McGroarty, John Steven, CALIFORNIA, ITS HISTORY AND ROMANCE. Los Angeles, 1911.

Monaghan, Jay, THE GREAT RASCAL, *The Life and Adventures of Ned Buntline*. Boston, 1952.

Mowry, Sylvester, ARIZONA AND SONORA. New York, 1864.

Myers, John Myers, THE DEATHS OF THE BRAVOS. Boston, 1962.

——, I, JACK SWILLING. New York, 1961.

——, THE LAST CHANCE: *Tombstone's Early Years*. New York, 1950.

NATIONAL ENCYCLOPAEDIA OF AMERICAN BIOGRAPHY, 46 Vols. New York, 1898–1963.

O'Day, Edward F., JAMES WOOD COFFROTH. San Francisco, 1926.

O'Meara, James, BRODERICK AND GWIN. San Francisco, 1881.

——, THE VIGILANCE COMMITTEE OF 1856. San Francisco, 1887.

Palmer, Lyman, HISTORY OF NAPA AND LAKE COUNTIES. San Francisco, 1881.

PAMPHLETS ON SAN FRANCISCO COMMITTEE OF VIGILANCE, 1856. Ten pamphlets bound in one volume, held by Bancroft Library, University of California at Berkeley.

Paterson, Thomas V., THE PRIVATE LIFE, PUBLIC CAREER AND REAL CHARACTER OF THAT ODIOUS RASCAL, NED BUNTLINE. New York, 1849.

Pennsylvania, Commonwealth of, JOURNAL OF THE HOUSE OF REPRESENTATIVES, SESSION OF 1843, 2 Vols. Harrisburg, Pa., 1843.

Peplow, Edward H., HISTORY OF ARIZONA, 3 Vols. New York, 1958.

Riesenberg, Felix, Jr., GOLDEN GATE. New York, 1940.

Roches, James Jeffrey, BYWAYS OF WAR: *The Story of the Filibusters*. New York, 1901.

Rolle, Andrew F., CALIFORNIA: *A History*. New York, 1963.

Rowe, Joseph Andrew, CALIFORNIA'S PIONEER CIRCUS. San Francisco, 1926.

Royce, Josiah, CALIFORNIA FROM THE CONQUEST IN 1846 TO THE SECOND VIGILANCE COMMITTEE OF SAN FRANCISCO: *A Study of American Character.* New York, 1886.

Sacks, Benjamin, BE IT ENACTED. Phoenix, Ariz., 1964.

Scharf, J. Thomas and Wescott, Thompson, HISTORY OF PHILADELPHIA, 3 Vols. Philadelphia, 1884.

Scherer, James A. B., THE LION OF THE VIGILANTES: *William T. Coleman and the Life of Old San Francisco.* Indianapolis, Ind., 1939.

Schmitt, Jo Ann, FIGHTING EDITORS. San Antonio, Tex., 1958.

Sherman, William Tecumseh, MEMOIRS OF GEN. WILLIAM T. SHERMAN, *Written by Himself.* New York, 1875.

Shinn, Charles Howard, MINING CAMPS: *A Study in Frontier Government.* New York, 1948.

Shirley, Glenn, BUCKSKIN AND SPURS. New York, 1958.

Shuck, Oscar Tully, HISTORICAL ABSTRACT OF SAN FRANCISCO. San Francisco, 1897.

————, HISTORY OF THE BENCH AND BAR IN CALIFORNIA. Los Angeles, 1901.

Smith, Frank Meriweather, SAN FRANCISCO VIGILANCE COMMITTEE, 1856. San Francisco, 1883.

Soule, Frank, Gihon, John and Nisbet, James, THE ANNALS OF SAN FRANCISCO. New York, 1855.

Stevenson, Robert Louis, THE SILVERADO SQUATTERS. London, 1883.

Stewart, George A., COMMITTEE OF VIGILANCE. New York, 1964.

Taylor, Alexander Smith, A BIBLIOGRAPHY OF NEWSPAPERS PUBLISHED IN CALIFORNIA IN 1855. Edited by Douglas C. McMurtrie, Evanston, Ill., 1943.

Taylor, Bayard, ELDORADO. New York, 1850.

Tevis, James Henry, ARIZONA IN THE '50S. Albuquerque, N.M., 1954.

United States Navy Department, OFFICIAL RECORDS OF THE UNION AND CONFEDERATE NAVIES IN THE WAR OF THE REBELLION, Series 1, Vol. 20. Washington, 1905.

Valentine, Alan Chester, VIGILANTE JUSTICE. New York, 1956.

Vilas, Martin S., THE BARBARY COAST OF SAN FRANCISCO. San Francisco, 1915.

Wagstaff, A. E., LIFE OF DAVID S. TERRY. San Francisco, 1911.

Wells, Evelyn and Peterson, Harry C., THE '49ERS. Garden City, N.Y., 1949.

Wheat, Carl I. (Ed.), THE SHIRLEY LETTERS FROM THE CALIFORNIA MINES. New York, 1946.

Williams, Mary Floyd, HISTORY OF THE SAN FRANCISCO COMMITTEE OF VIGILANCE OF 1851. Berkeley, Calif., 1921.

Wilson, Neill C., HERE IS THE GOLDEN GATE. New York, 1962.

Woods, S. D., LIGHTS AND SHADOWS ON THE PACIFIC COAST. New York, 1910.

Wyllys, Rufus Kay, ARIZONA: *The History of a Frontier State.* Phoenix, Ariz., 1950.

INDEX